D1477260

World Electric Locomotives

Compiled and edited by

KEN HARRIS

JANE'S

London . New York . Sydney

For Jean

Copyright © Ken Harris 1981

First published in the United Kingdom in 1981 by
Jane's Publishing Company Limited
238 City Road, London EC1V 2PU
ISBN 0 7106 0101 8

Published in the United States of America in 1981 by
Jane's Publishing Incorporated
730 Fifth Avenue
New York
N.Y. 10019

ISBN 0 531 03728 2

Designed by Bernard Crossland Associates

Printed in Great Britain by
Netherwood, Dalton Co. Ltd., Huddersfield.

**Previous page: Chinese SS3 prototype no
SS3001 nears completion in the Zhuzhou
factory in 1979** *(New China Pictures)*

**Right: German Federal Railways class 194 no
194 092** *(Friedrich Franz)*

Introduction

This book is intended to provide a convenient and concise guide to the main locomotive types in service on the world's more important electrified railway systems. Its publication occurs during a period when the economic consequences of diminishing oil reserves have focused fresh attention on the use of electricity as a prime energy source for rail transport.

Advances in traction design since the end of the Second World War have ensured that any argument made now for major new electrification is supported by the outstanding performance and efficiency of the modern electric locomotive. The development of reliable rectifier motive power, leading to the widespread adoption of a single-phase industrial frequency power supply for new schemes, has been particularly significant, as has the more recent application to traction control systems of power electronics. These trends are reflected in the selection of locomotive types included in this book. At the same time, present day traffic demands and investment limits have ensured the survival of a wide variety of older designs on networks which were early to adopt electric traction. Several important types dating from the 1920s and 1930s are included and these provide a striking contrast, both technologically and aesthetically, with today's sophisticated machines.

The contents of the book are arranged alphabetically by country, although in certain cases, for example the French National Railways CC-7100 series, details of derived designs may be found in the parent entry. Readers are recommended to use the index, where all text and picture references are fully listed. As far as possible mechanical, electrical and performance data have been obtained from the railway administrations which operate the classes featured, although manufacturers' specifications have also been consulted. Dimensions and performance figures are presented both in imperial and metric equivalents. Rated power output data are also expressed in *force de cheval:* the subtle distinction between British/US and continental European practice has been necessary to ensure accurate conversion to the kilowatt units now in general use. US users of this book should note that locomotive weights are given in *imperial* tons, and that these figures should be multiplied by a factor of 2240 to give a value in pounds. All types featured in *World Electric Locomotives* were in service in mid-1980.

Electrification plays a major role in the plans of many railway administrations to meet the challenges of the closing decades of this century and beyond. As this introduction is written several national networks, including Danish State Railways and National Railways of Zimbabwe are making firm preparations for their first main line schemes. In other countries, such as Brazil, substantial extensions to existing catenary are planned. These developments will add fresh interest and variety to the field of electric motive power and the compiler looks forward to being able to record them in a future edition of this book.

St Albans
Hertfordshire

September 1980

Abbreviations

The following abbreviations are used in the data tables and descriptions accompanying each class:

ac	alternating current
ch	force de cheval
	(metric horsepower)
dc	direct current
emu	electric multiple-unit
ft	feet
hp	horsepower
h.t.	high tension
Hz	Hertz (cycles per second)
in	inches
km	kilometres
km/h	kilometres per hour
kN	kilonewtons
kV	kilovolts
kW	kilowatts
lbs	pounds
l.t.	low tension
m	metres
mm	millimetres
mph	miles per hour
TEE	Trans-Europe Express
yd	yards

Acknowledgements

The compiler and publishers express their gratitude to the following organisations and individuals for their ready cooperation in providing material for this book or assistance during its preparation:

AEG-Telefunken; Amtrak; ASEA; Australian Railway and Historical Society (New South Wales Division); Austrian Federal Railways (ÖBB); John R Batts; Ing Zdeněk Bauer CSc; Belgian National Railways (SNCB/NMBS); Bernese Alpine Railway, Berne-Loetschberg-Simplon (BLS); Benno Bickel; Brazilian Railway Preservation Association (ABPF), in particular Sérgio Martire; British Rail (BR); British Rail Engineering Ltd (BREL); Canadian National Railways (CNR); Central Electric Railfans' Association (CERA), in particular Donald L MacCorquodale; ConRail; Constructions Ferroviaires et Métalliques "BN" SA; Marc Dahlström; Finnish State Railways (VR), in particular Eero Tuurna; French National Railways (SNCF); Friedrich Franz; Ganz Electric Works; Ganz-MÁVAG; Brian Garvin; GEC Traction Ltd; General Electric do Brazil SA (GEBSA); General Electric Company; General Motors, Electro-Motive Division; German Federal Railways (DB); John Gillham; Ing Villányi György; Günter Haslbeck; Hitachi Ltd; Hugh Hughes; 50Hz Group; David Ibbotson; India House Library, London; Indian Railways (IR); Japan Railfan Club, in particular Ken Matuzawa; David K Johnson; Col F W S Jourdain; P M Kalla-Bishop; Kawasaki Heavy Industries Ltd; Kolmex; Krauss-Maffei AG; Fried Krupp GmbH; VEB Lokomotivbau-Elektrotechnische "Hans Beimler" (LEW); Fred D Lonnes; Luxembourg Railways (CFL); Maurice Lyon; Anne McKrill; William D Middleton; Mitsubishi Heavy Industries Ltd; Netherlands Railways (NS), in particular J B Meijer; New China Pictures; New Zealand Railways (NZR); New Zealand Railway and Locomotive Society, in particular Tom McGavin; Norwegian State Railways (NSB); Portuguese Railways (CP); Pascal Pontremoli; Rhaetian Railways (RhB); Philip Robinson; Gottfried Schilke; Simmering-Graz-Pauker AG (SGP); Škoda; Soviet Railways (SZD); Spanish National Railways (RENFE); South African Railways (SAR); State Railway Authority of New South Wales; Yves Steenebruggen; Frank Stenvall; Swedish State Railways (SJ), in particular Lars Olov Karlsson; Swiss Federal Railways (SBB); Swiss Locomotive and Machine Works (SLM); Taiwan Railway Administration (TRA); Tecnomasio Italiano Brown Boveri (TIBB); Alex Vanags; Victorian Railways (VicRail); Marcel Vleugels; Brian Webb; Zaïre National Railways (SNCZ).

Thanks are also due to the many photographers whose work enriches the pages which follow: they are credited individually in the captions accompanying illustrations.

Finally, I would like to thank my wife, Jean, for her support and help during the compilation of this book.

Algeria

SNTF class 6 CE

Operating system Algerian National Railways (SNTF)
Year introduced 1972
Axle arrangement Co-Co
Gauge 1435 mm *(4 ft 8½ in)*
Power supply system 3 kV dc
One-hour output 2440 kW *(3270 hp, 3315 ch)*
Continuous output 2150 kW *(2880 hp, 2920 ch)*
Maximum speed 80 km/h *(50 mph)*
Maximum tractive effort 393 kN *(88 200 lbs)*
Continuous tractive effort 241 kN *(54 200 lbs)* at 32 km/h *(20 mph)*
Weight in working order 130 tonnes *(128 tons)*
Length over buffers 18 640 mm *(61 ft 2 in)*
Bogie wheelbase 2000 + 2450 mm = 4450 mm *(14 ft 7¼ in)*
Wheel diameter 1350 mm *(4 ft 5⅛ in)*
Traction motors Six dc series-wound, nose-suspended, axle-hung
Control Rheostatic
Electric brake Rheostatic
Builder
  mechanical parts VEB LEW "Hans Beimler"
  electrical equipment VEB LEW "Hans Beimler", Škoda
Number built 32
Number series 6 CE 1 — 6 CE 32

The East German builder LEW supplied these powerful units to SNCFA, later SNTF*, in 1972/3 for operation over the important mountain line from the port of Annaba to Tebessa and Djebel Onk, in eastern Algeria. Iron ore and phosphates form the principal traffic over this difficult route which includes gradients of up to 3% (1 in 33). Introduction of the class led to the retirement of the original motive power for the line, the French built 6 AE series of 1932.

LEW's rugged design incorporates low gearing and a high-adhesion axle-loading of 21·5 tonnes. Electrical equipment was developed by the Czechoslovak organisation Škoda. Resistance control is employed and traction motor groupings are six in series, two parallel groups of three in series and three parallel groups of two in series, each with three field-weakening steps. Rheostatic braking of 2170 kW capacity is provided and multiple-unit operation is possible. Current collection is by Faively-type single-arm pantographs.

Externally the locomotives resemble LEW built designs for German State Railways (DR), especially the class 251 silicon rectifier units. Livery is red with a waist-level cream flash and grey roof.

*The activities of the former Société Nationale des Chemins de Fer Algériens (SNCFA) were taken over in 1976 by a restructured organisation entitled Société Nationale des Transports Ferroviaires (SNTF).

Class 6 CE no 6 CE 2 *(LEW)*

Australia

SRA (New South Wales) class 46

Operating System State Railway Authority of New South Wales (SRA)
Year introduced 1956
Axle arrangement Co+Co
Gauge 1435 mm *(4 ft 8½ in)*
Power supply system 1.5 kV dc
One-hour output 2820 kW *(3780 hp, 3835 ch)*
Continuous output 2535 kW *(3400 hp, 3450 ch)*
Maximum speed 105 km/h *(65 mph)*
Maximum tractive effort 270 kN *(60 500 lbs)*
One-hour tractive effort 182 kN *(40 800 lbs)* at 55 km/h *(34½ mph)*
Weight in working order 114 tonnes *(112 tons)*
Length over coupler centres 16 866 mm *(55 ft 4 in)*
Bogie wheelbase 2286+1982=4268 mm *(14 ft 0in)*
Wheel diameter 1143 mm *(3 ft 9 in)*
Traction motors Six dc series-wound Metropolitan-Vickers type MV272, nose-suspended, axle-hung
Control Rheostatic
Electric brake Regenerative
Builder
  mechanical parts Metropolitan-Vickers/Beyer Peacock
  electrical equipment Metropolitan-Vickers
Number built 40
Number series 4601—4640

Introduction in 1956 of the mixed-traffic class 46 followed the decision by New South Wales Government Railways (NSWGR) to extend its Sydney suburban electrification westwards as a main-line scheme through the Blue Mountains to Wallerawang, source of important coal traffic. This plan was slightly modified as work proceeded, and the catenary was only taken as far as Bowenfels, 13 km short of Wallerawang and 2 km west of Lithgow.

The locomotives were built in England by Metropolitan-Vickers/Beyer Peacock at their Stockton-on-Tees works and were designed to take 400-tonne loads up continuous 3% (1 in 33) gradients at 56 km/h (35 mph). Regenerative braking is provided to hold trains on steep downhill runs and to return current to the supply system. Bogies are of the articulated type, with no traction loads transmitted to the body. This arrangement has not proved entirely satisfactory for passenger operation, resulting in a reduction of the maximum permitted speed from 113 to 105 km/h (70 to 65 mph). Multiple-unit control equipment is fitted, allowing the heaviest trains to be double-headed under the control of one crew. The body is of rivetted construction, with the standard SRA livery of maroon and yellow.

Changing traffic patterns between 1950, when the 40 locomotives were ordered, and the arrival of the last unit in February 1958 had created an electric motive power surplus which hastened extension of the Northern line electrification from Hornsby to Hawkesbury River and Gosford. This scheme was completed in 1960 and today the class handles freight and principal passenger duties on both lines, as well as the important Glenlee coal traffic on the Southern line.

One unit, no 4620, has been withdrawn following accident damage in 1977.

SRA class 46 no 4618 *(SRA)*

Australia

SRA (New South Wales) class 85

Operating system State Railway Authority of New South Wales (SRA)
Year introduced 1979
Axle arrangement Co-Co
Gauge 1435 mm *(4 ft 8½ in)*
Power supply system 1.5 kV dc
One-hour output 2880 kW *(3860 hp, 3915 ch)*
Continuous output 2700 kW *(3620 hp, 3670 ch)*
Maximum speed 130 km/h *(80 mph)*
Maximum tractive effort 362 kN *(81 350 lbs)*
Continuous tractive effort 222 kN *(49 900 lbs)* at 45 km/h *(28 mph)*
Weight in working order 123 tonnes *(121 tons)*
Length over coupler centres 19 000 mm *(62 ft 4 in)*
Bogie wheelbase 2000 + 2000 = 4000 mm *(13 ft 1½ in)*
Wheel diameter 1250 mm *(4 ft 1¼ in)*
Traction motors Six dc series-wound Mitsubishi type MB-485-AVR, nose-suspended, axle-hung
Control Rheostatic
Electric brake Regenerative
Builder
  mechanical parts Comeng
  electrical equipment Mitsubishi
Number built 10
Number series 8501 — 8510

The ten class 85 units are the first electric locomotives to be designed and built by an Australian company. They are intended to supplement the British built class 46 machines (see previous entry) and their introduction also foreshadows extension of the Northern line 1·5 kV dc electrification from Gosford to the important port of Newcastle.

Construction of the class was carried out at the Clyde, New South Wales, plant of Comeng, with electrical apparatus coming from the Japanese company Mitsubishi, who have also supplied traction equipment for several series of diesel-electric locomotives and emu stock operated by the SRA. Mechanical design is similar to that of the Comeng built 1640 kW (2200 hp) class 80 diesel-electric units, which the 85s closely resemble.

The first locomotive entered service in July 1979.

SRA class 85 no 8501 *(SRA)*

7

Australia

VicRail class L

Operating system Victorian Railways (VicRail)
Year introduced 1953
Axle arrangement Co-Co
Gauge 1600 mm *(5 ft 3 in)*
Power supply system 1.5 kV dc
Continuous output 1800 kW *(2400 hp, 2435 ch)*
Maximum speed 120 km/h *(75 mph)*
Maximum tractive effort 209 kN *(47 000 lbs)*
Continuous tractive effort 112 kN *(25 200 lbs)* at 48 km/h *(30 mph)*
Weight in working order 98.5 tonnes *(97 tons)*
Length over coupler centres 17 983 mm *(59 ft 0 in)*
Wheel diameter 1016 mm *(3 ft 4 in)*
Traction motors Six English Electric type EE 519 dc series-wound, nose-suspended, axle-hung
Control Rheostatic
Electric brake Rheostatic
Builder
 mechanical parts English Electric
 electrical equipment English Electric
Number built 25
Number series L1150—L1174

As in New South Wales, the electrified railway network in Victoria originated as a suburban passenger undertaking and later matured to main line status. Extensive electrification of metropolitan routes radiating from Melbourne was carried out by Victorian Railways (VR) from 1919 using a 1·5 kV dc overhead power supply. The subsequent post-war development of brown coal mining in the Gippsland region prompted VR to upgrade and operate with electric traction the line beyond Dadenong, outer limit of the catenary from Melbourne, to Traralagon, 157 km from the state capital. This scheme was completed in March 1956.

The L series was developed by English Electric to handle passenger and freight traffic on the Gippsland line. Assembly was carried out at the former Dick, Kerr works at Preston, and the first examples arrived in Australia in January 1953. All 25 were in service by August of the following year. Features of the design include multiple-unit control facilities and rheostatic braking. Livery is standard VicRail blue and gold. No L 1150 is named *Robert G. Wishart* in honour of the one-time Chairman of Commissioners of VR and pioneer of modernisation of the system after the Second World War.

Gippsland line traffic levels never reached those originally forecast, and today the L series handle a wide range of work on many parts of VicRail's electrified network.

VicRail class L no L 1152 *(ILA Günther Barths)*

Austria

ÖBB class 1042.500

Operating system Austrian Federal Railways (ÖBB)
Year introduced 1967
Axle arrangement Bo-Bo
Gauge 1435 mm *(4 ft 8½ in)*
Power supply system 15 kV ac 16⅔ Hz
One-hour output 4000 kW *(5360 hp, 5435 ch)*
Continuous output 3810 kW *(5100 hp, 5175 ch)*
Maximum speed 150 km/h *(93 mph)*
Maximum tractive effort 248 kN *(55 600 lbs)*
One-hour tractive effort 137 kN *(30 700 lbs)* at
   102 km/h *(63 mph)*
Weight in working order 83.8 tonnes *(82½ tons)*
Length over buffers 16 220 mm *(53 ft 2⅝ in)*
Bogie wheelbase 3400 mm *(11 ft 1⅞ in)*
Wheel diameter 1250 mm *(4 ft 1¼ in)*
Traction motors Four single-phase commutator,
   fully suspended with Siemens rubber spring drive
Control h.t. tap-changer
Electric brake Rheostatic
Builder
   mechanical parts Simmering-Graz-Pauker (SGP)
   electrical equipment Brown Boveri (Austria),
   Elin-Union, Siemens (Austria)
Number built 197
Number series 1042.501 — 1042.520, 1042.531 —
   1042.707

The highly successful 1042.500 series is the most numerous in the ÖBB electric locomotive fleet with 197 examples constructed between 1967 and 1977, when production switched to the thyristor controlled class 1044 (see following entry). Developed as an all-purpose machine to avoid the complex maintenance arrangements associated with a diversity of specialised types, the class is employed on a wide variety of passenger and freight traffic, both on mountain routes and the flatter lines of the ÖBB network. They also penetrate the German Federal Railways' system, notably to Frankfurt and Munich, on international passenger services.

Design of the class is derived from the 60-strong 1042 series of 1963 (these are rated at 3560 kW hourly with a top speed of 130 km/h) and represents the final ÖBB electric locomotive type with ac motors. Construction of the first 30 (nos 1042.501-520, 531-540) was carried out at the Floridsdorf (Vienna) works of SGP. The remainder were built at the company's Graz plant. Supply of electrical equipment was shared amongst three main Austrian contractors (see data). The class was the first in the ÖBB fleet to appear in the present red livery which replaced the earlier green.

Class 1042.500 no 1042.669 *(SGP)*

Austria

ÖBB class 1044

Operating system Austrian Federal Railways (ÖBB)
Year introduced 1974
Axle arrangement Bo-Bo
Gauge 1435 mm *(4 ft 8½ in)*
Power supply system 15 kV ac 16⅔ Hz
One-hour output 5280 kW *(7075 hp, 7175 ch)*
Maximum speed 160 km/h *(100 mph)*
Maximum tractive effort 314 kN *(70 600 lbs)*
One-hour tractive effort 211 kN *(47 400 lbs)* at
  88 km/h *(55 mph)*
Weight in working order 84 tonnes *(83 tons)*
Length over buffers 16 000 mm *(52 ft 6 in)*
Bogie wheelbase 2900 mm *(9 ft 6¼ in)*
Wheel diameter 1300 mm *(4 ft 3⅛ in)*
Traction motors Four ripple current series-wound,
  fully suspended with BBC spring drive
Control Thyristor
Electric brake Rheostatic
Builder
  mechanical parts Simmering-Graz-Pauker (SGP)
  electrical equipment Austrian Brown Boveri,
  Elin-Union, Siemens
Number built 98 (including units on order at
  1 January 1981)
Number series 1044.01 — 1044.98

The thyristor-controlled class 1044 locomotives are the most powerful, and at 160 km/h (100 mph), the fastest in the ÖBB fleet. Construction of the first two as prototypes in 1974 and 1975 followed the favourable performance of ten Swedish built class 1043 units which also employ thyristors for traction motor voltage control. During an early test run, one of the prototypes took a trailing load of 800 tonnes over the severely graded Semmering Pass, and in normal service conditions the class is loaded to 650 tonnes over Alpine routes with gradients of 2·6% (1 in 38), compared with 550 tonnes for a 1042.500. An Austrian railway speed record of 180 km/h (112 mph) has also been established by one member of the class.

Amongst special features to ensure optimum adhesion is a low-level traction system to transmit haulage and braking forces from the body to the bogies, so keeping axle-load changes to a minimum. Bogie wheelsets are axially sprung and have an element of sideplay to ease the negotiation of sharply curving track.

Delivery of an order for 48 series-built machines started in 1978 and during the following year 24 more were ordered by ÖBB. Some 70 units were in traffic by the end of 1980, when an order for a final batch of 24 was announced. Deliveries of the class are due to end in August 1982.

ÖBB class 1044 no 1044.02 *(ÖBB)*

Austria

ÖBB classes 1245 and 1245.00

Operating system Austrian Federal Railways (ÖBB)
Year introduced Class 1245 — 1934;
  class 1245.500 — 1938
Axle arrangement Bo + Bo
Gauge 1435 mm *(4 ft 8½ in)*
Power supply system 15 kV ac 16⅔ Hz
One-hour output 1840 kW *(2465 hp, 2500 ch)*
Maximum speed 80 km/h *(50 mph)*
Maximum tractive effort 196 kN *(44 100 lbs)*
One-hour tractive effort 115 kN *(25 800 lbs)* at
  56 km/h *(35 mph)*
Weight in working order 83 tonnes *(82 tons)*
Length over buffers 12 920 mm *(42 ft 4⅝ in)*
Bogie wheelbase 3100 mm *(12 ft 2 in)*
Wheel diameter 1350 mm *(4 ft 5⅛ in)*
Traction motors Four single-phase commutator,
  fully suspended with Sécheron spring drive
Control Electro-pneumatic l.t. switchgear
Electric brake Class 1245 — none; class 1245.500 —
  Rheostatic
Builder
  mechanical parts Vienna Locomotive Works,
  Floridsdorf
  electrical equipment AEG-Union, BBC, Elin,
  Siemens-Schuckertwerke
Number built Class 1245 — 8; class 1245.500 — 33
Number series Class 1245 — 1245.01 — 1245.08;
  class 1245.500 — 1245.509 — 1245.541

This elderly but useful class is the last of three pre-war four-axle bogie designs constructed for the old Austrian Federal Railways (BBÖ) during a brief period of development which witnessed increases in power and top speed from the 1140 kW (1530 hp)/60 km/h (37 mph) of the 1170 series (ÖBB class 1045) to the 1840 kW (2465 hp) and 80 km/h (50 mph) of these present machines.

Conceived as all-purpose locomotives, the first eight (nos 1245.01-08) were constructed at Floridsdorf in 1934 and received the BBÖ designation 1170.200. They were considered quite modern machines for the period, with electro-pneumatic control and a hollow-axle spring drive, although buffers and drawgear remained incorporated in the bogies. To correspond with the Salzburg-Linz electrification a further 33 (nos 1245.509-541) were delivered between 1938 and 1940. Originally these later units were given a higher power rating than their predecessors and they bear detail differences. Ten of them entered service without electric brakes, and in the ÖBB 1953 renumbering scheme the nine then extant bore the numbers 1245.619-625, 627 and 628 until installation of this equipment saw them absorbed into the main class and numbered accordingly.

Although the Second World War delayed further development of the design, an even more powerful version, class 1040, appeared in 1950.

At the beginning of 1980, 38 members of the class remained in operation handling secondary and shunting duties, although by this time ÖBB authorities were looking towards modern three-phase machines for such tasks.

ÖBB class 1245.500 no 1245.511 shunting at Vordernberg in May 1978 *(E. van Hoeck)*

Austria

ÖBB class 1099

Operating system Austrian Federal Railways (ÖBB)
Year introduced 1910
Axle arrangement C-C
Gauge 760 mm *(2 ft 6 in)*
Power supply system 6.6 kV ac 25 Hz
One-hour output 420 kW *(560 hp, 570 ch)*
Maximum speed 50 km/h *(31 mph)*
Maximum tractive effort 102 kN *(23 000 lbs)*
One-hour tractive effort 45 kN *(10 150 lbs)* at 29 km/h *(18 mph)*
Weight in working order 50 tonnes *(49.5 tons)*
Length over buffers 11 020 mm *(36 ft 1⅞ in)*
Bogie wheelbase 2400 mm *(7 ft 10½ in)*
Wheel diameter 800 mm *(2 ft 7½ in)*
Traction motors Two single-phase commutator, bogie-mounted with jackshaft/coupling rod drive
Control Electro-pneumatic switchgear
Electric brake None
Builder
  mechanical parts Krauss Locomotive Works
  electrical equipment Siemens-Schuckertwerke
Number built 16
Number series 1099.01 — 1099.16

The Mariazellerbahn, a 91 km (56 mile) 760 mm gauge scenic route linking St Pölten and Gusswerk by way of the popular resort of Mariazell, was the subject of Austria's first significant railway electrification in 1911. At first the line was operated by the Niederösterreichische Landesbahn (NÖLB) before being absorbed by the pre-war Austrian Federal (BBÖ) in 1921. Today it survives as the only ÖBB electrified narrow-gauge railway.

The 16 class 1099 locomotives which serve this line are the original units supplied for the inauguration of electric services in 1911. Since then their external appearance has been much changed by refurbishment carried out from 1959 onwards, when the present cream and red body of "modern" profile was added. An overhead line current of 6·6 kV at a frequency of 25 Hz is employed and power is collected by a single pantograph. The locomotive body is carried on two bogies, in each of which is mounted one traction motor with jackshaft drive to the three coupled axles. Buffers and drawgear are incorporated in the bogies. All 16 examples survive and are allocated to St Pölten depot. They handle both passenger and freight traffic.

ÖBB class 1099 no 1099.04 *(ÖBB)*

Belgium

SNCB class 16

Operating system Belgian National Railways
(SNCB/NMBS)
Year introduced 1966
Axle arrangement Bo-Bo
Gauge 1435 mm *(4 ft 8½ in)*
Power supply system (Four-current) 3 kV dc;
1.5 kV dc; 25 kV ac 50 Hz; 15 kV ac 16⅔ Hz
One-hour output 2780 kW *(3730 hp, 3780 ch)*
Continuous output 2620 kW *(3510 hp, 3560 ch)*
Maximum speed 160 km/h *(100 mph)*
Maximum tractive effort 197 kN *(44 100 lbs)*
Weight in working order 82.6 tonnes *(81.5 tons)*
Length over buffers 16 650 mm *(54 ft 7½ in)*
Bogie wheelbase 3150 mm *(10 ft 4 in)*
Wheel diameter 1250 mm *(4 ft 1¼ in)*
Traction motors Four dc series-wound, frame-
suspended with Alsthom flexible drive
Control Rheostatic
Electric brake None
Builder
  mechanical parts La Brugeoise et Nivelles
  electrical equipment ACEC, Siemens
Number built 8
Number series 1601 — 1608

SNCB class 16 no 1602 at Leuven in April
1978 *(Yves Steenebruggen)*

The major railway administrations whose lines connect with the Belgian
network use power supply systems which differ from each other and from the 3
kV dc used by SNCB. To permit through running irrespective of overhead line
voltage, and to avoid time-consuming locomotive changes at frontiers, SNCB
operates three multi-current designs, mainly on expresses linking France and
the Netherlands and on services into West Germany.

The class 16 four-voltage units which first appeared in 1966 are a development of the earlier class 15 three-current series, with the added facility of being
able to operate under the German Federal Railway's 15 kV 16⅔ Hz catenary,
thus permitting running over the Liège-Aachen-Cologne route. Three single-
arm pantographs are provided (except on no 1601, which has four): one for
each ac system and a third for Belgian and Dutch supplies. As with the class 15,
a fixed-ratio transformer/silicon rectifier arrangement with dc control is used
during ac running. Rectifier equipment for nos 1601-4 was supplied by
Siemens, while that for nos 1605-8 is of ACEC design.

The departure from the established SNCB raked cab design in favour of the
distinctive "wedge" styling represents an attempt to reduce the disturbing
effects of upward air currents on pantograph behaviour during high-speed
running.

Until the early 1970s the locomotives were designated class 160 and numbered 160 001-004 (now 1601-4) and 160 021-024 (now 1605-8). Since 1977 a
striking livery of yellow and blue has been applied to the class in place of the
original all-over blue.

Belgium

SNCB class 20

Operating system Belgian National Railways (SNCB/NMBS)
Year introduced 1975
Axle arrangement Co-Co
Gauge 1435 mm *(4 ft 8½ in)*
Power supply system 3 kV dc
One-hour output 5420 kW *(7260 hp, 7360 ch)*
Continuous output 5130 kW *(6875 hp, 6970 ch)*
Maximum speed 160 km/h *(100 mph)*
Maximum tractive effort 314 kN *(70 600 lbs)*
Continuous tractive effort 231 kN *(52 100 lbs)* at 80 km/h *(50 mph)*
Weight in working order 110 tonnes *(108.5 tons)*
Length over buffers 19 504 mm *(63 ft 11⅞ in)*
Bogie wheelbase 2100 + 2100 = 4200 mm *(13 ft 9⅜ in)*
Wheel diameter 1250 mm *(4 ft 1¼ in)*
Traction motors Six ACEC type LE 772 G dc series-wound, frame-suspended with ACEC flexible drive
Control Full chopper
Electric brake Rheostatic
Builder
  mechanical parts La Brugeoise et Nivelles (from January 1977, BN Constructions Ferroviaires et Métalliques)
  electrical equipment ACEC
Number built 25
Number series 2001 — 2025

Introduced in 1975, these sophisticated and powerful machines are the world's first series-built electric locomotives to employ thyristor chopper control of traction motor voltage. Principal contractor for the design of the class was the Belgian electrical company ACEC, who developed the advanced traction control equipment. The six separately-excited traction motors are fully suspended in bogies designed in Switzerland by SLM and built under licence in Belgium by BN. Electronically controlled rheostatic braking is independently excited and is blended with locomotive air brakes. The higher adhesion factors available with chopper control are enhanced by a low-level traction system and this has allowed an axle-load of only 18·5 tonnes.

First examples of the original order for 15 units were put to work on the busy Brussels-Luxembourg main line to reduce double-heading with less powerful locomotives. Their performance led SNCB to order a further batch of ten machines which entered service in 1977/8. The last two of these, nos 2024 and 2025, were delivered in the yellow and blue livery which is to be progressively applied to the rest of the class in place of the original olive green.

ACEC and BN have developed a four-axle chopper-controlled design for SNCB based on experience with class 20. Designated class 27, the first of an order for 30 units is due to be delivered in June 1981.

SNCB class 20 no 2024 at Schaerbeek depot, Brussels, in December 1978 *(Yves Steenebruggen)*

Belgium

SNCB class 23

Operating system Belgian National Railways (SNCB/NMBS)
Year introduced 1955
Axle arrangement Bo-Bo
Gauge 1435 mm *(4 ft 8½ in)*
Power supply system 3 kV dc
One-hour output 1885 kW *(2525 hp, 2560 ch)*
Continuous output 1735 kW *(2330 hp, 2360 ch)*
Maximum speed 130 km/h *(80 mph)*
Maximum tractive effort 197 kN *(44 100 lbs)*
Continuous tractive effort 123 kN *(27 600 lbs)* at 51 km/h *(32 mph)*
Weight in working order 93.3 tonnes *(92 tons)*
Length over buffers 18 000 mm *(59 ft 0⅝ in)*
Bogie wheelbase 3450 mm *(11 ft 3⅞ in)*
Wheel diameter 1262 mm *(4 ft 1⅝ in)*
Traction motors Four dc series-wound, nose-suspended, axle hung
Control Rheostatic
Electric brake Regenerative
Builder
 mechanical parts La Brugeoise et Nivelles
 electrical equipment ACEC, SEM
Number built 83
Number series 2301 — 2383

The 3 kV dc overhead power supply system was adopted as standard by SNCB in 1935, although the Second World War prevented any significant extension of catenary until the 1950s. Progressive electrification of main lines followed and between 1954 and 1961 over 150 domestically constructed four-axle machines of 1885 kW (2525 hp) were placed in service to handle traffic on the newly energised routes. The largest series is the 83-strong class 23, built in 1955 as a direct development of the earlier class 22. Principal modification is the provision of regenerative braking, producing a weight increase of some six tonnes. This contributes to the relatively high axle-loading of 23·5 tonnes. Electrically, the 23s are conventional resistance-controlled machines, equipped for multiple-unit operation. Traction motors of the main series are nose-suspended, although the last of the class was originally constructed with spring-borne traction motors and ACEC flexible drive. This unit, now numbered 2383, was originally designated class 124 (no 124 001) and for a short period during the early 1970s bore the number 2401. Until 1970, the main series was identified as class 123 and numbered 123 001-082.

In 1976, nos 2355, 2376 and 2380 were experimentally painted in various green and yellow liveries before the SNCB administration in 1977 settled on the standard scheme of blue and canary yellow for electric locomotives.

SNCB class 23 no 2336 in green livery
(Yves Steenebruggen)

Brazil

FEPASA class 2100

Operating system São Paulo Railways (FEPASA)
Year introduced 1968
Axle arrangement Bo – Bo
Gauge 1000 mm *(3 ft 3⅜ in)*
Power supply system 3 kV dc
One-hour output 1375 kW *(1840 hp, 1865 ch)*
Maximum speed 90 km/h *(56 mph)*
Maximum tractive effort 179 kN *(40 300 lbs)*
Continuous tractive effort 113 kN *(25 400 lbs)* at
22 km/h *(14 mph)*
Weight in working order 73 tonnes *(72 tons)*
Length over coupler centres 13 942 mm
(45 ft 9 in)
Bogie wheelbase 2742 mm *(9 ft 0 in)*
Wheel diameter 1118 mm *(3 ft 8 in)*
Traction motors Four dc series-wound General
Electric type GE 734, nose-suspended, axle-hung
Control Rheostatic
Electric brake Regenerative
Builder
  mechanical parts General Electric of Brazil
  (GEBSA)
  electrical equipment General Electric of Brazil
  (GEBSA)
Number built 30
Number series 2101 — 2130

Brazil's most extensive electrified railway system comprises certain 3 kV dc metre-gauge lines of the ex-Sorocabana Railway, mostly running west of São Paulo to Itapetininga and Assis, and operated since 1971 by FEPASA. In 1979 657 route-km (408 miles) were energised, the first section having been worked electrically since 1944. Original main line motive power took the form of 46 class 2000/2050 1-Co+Co-1 units built in the USA by General Electric during the 1940s and still extant in 1980. These were joined in 1968 by this series of 30 single-cab four-axle units built domestically at the Campinas works of GEBSA and mainly intended for freight haulage.

In many respects the design of the 2100s follows diesel-electric practice of the parent US General Electric company. Bogies and traction motors are standard GE units and the full width body is built up on a fabricated underframe. The three main body sections are removeable for access to main items of machinery, and as these locomotives normally operate as pairs in multiple, coupled "back-to-back", only one cab is provided.

Current collection is by single-arm pantograph, with locomotive speed controlled conventionally by resistances and motor-groupings. Detection and correction of wheel slip is automatic and regenerative braking is provided.

FEPASA class 2100 no 2120 at Sorocaba in 1975
(Sérgio Martire)

FEPASA class 6350

Operating system São Paulo Railways (FEPASA)
Year introduced 1967
Axle arrangement Co-Co
Gauge 1600 mm *(5 ft 3 in)*
Power supply system 3 kV dc
One-hour output 3825 kW *(5130 hp, 5200 ch)*
Maximum speed 135 km/h *(84 mph)*
Maximum tractive effort 353 kN *(79 400 lbs)*
Continuous tractive effort 224 kN *(50 300 lbs)* at
   20 km/h *(12½ mph)*
Weight in working order 144 tonnes *(142 tons)*
Length over coupler centres 18 340 mm
   (60 ft 2 in)
Bogie wheelbase 4200 mm *(13 ft 9⅜ in)*
Wheel diameter 1168 mm *(3 ft 10 in)*
Traction motors Six dc series-wound General
   Electric type GE 729, nose-suspended, axle-hung
Control Rheostatic
Electric brake Regenerative
Builder
  mechanical parts General Electric of Brazil
   (GEBSA)
  electrical equipment General Electric of Brazil
   (GEBSA)
Number built 10
Number series 6351 — 6360

Built in 1967, FEPASA's class 6350 units were the first electric locomotives constructed at the Campinas plant of GEBSA and, with an hourly rating of 3825 kW, are Brazil's most powerful. The ten machines were ordered by the former Paulista Railway for both passenger and freight duties over its 3 kV dc 1600 mm (5 ft 3 in) gauge system, and were operated by this company until 1971, when control of the 493 electrified route-km (306 miles) passed to the state of São Paulo.

The 6350s have a multiple-unit capability and are equipped with regenerative braking. A feature of the control equipment is automatic detection and regulation of wheelslip, although this is minimised by a 24 tonne axle-load.

Like the same builder's metre-gauge Bo-Bo units supplied to the Sorocabana line (see previous entry) in 1968, the full-width body consists of removeable sections mounted on a fabricated underframe, although in this case two cabs are provided.

FEPASA class 6350 no 6353 at Campinas in January 1978
(Sérgio Martire)

Brazil

FEPASA class 6450

Operating system São Paulo Railways (FEPASA)
Year introduced 1951 (built 1948)
Axle arrangement 2-Do+Do-2
Gauge 1600 mm *(5 ft 3 in)*
Power supply system 3 kV dc
One-hour output 3765 kW *(5050 hp, 5120 ch)*
Continuous output 3470 kW *(4655 hp, 4720 ch)*
Maximum speed 110 km/h *(68 mph)*
Continuous tractive effort 343 kN *(77 200 lbs)* at
   9 km/h *(6 mph)*
Weight in working order 243 tonnes *(239 tons)*
Length over coupler centres 27 076 mm
   (88 ft 10 in)
Wheel diameter Driving—1200 mm *(3 ft 11¼ in)*,
   carrying—950 mm *(3 ft 1⅜ in)*
Traction motors Eight dc series-wound General
   Electric type GE 750, nose-suspended, axle-hung
Control Rheostatic
Electric brake Regenerative
Builder
   mechanical parts General Electric
   electrical equipment General Electric
Number built 5 (see text)
Number series 6451—6455

One of the more curious sagas in the history of electric traction surrounds these massive US built 2-Do+Do-2 locomotives. In 1946 20 such machines were ordered from General Electric (GE) by Soviet Railways for 1524 mm (5 ft 0 in) gauge 3 kV dc operation, but two years later, before construction had been completed, growing tension between the two countries led to prohibition of the sale by the US government. Nonetheless all 20 were built, the last six to 1435 mm (4 ft 8½ in) gauge, and GE found other purchasers. Three units were modified for 1·5kV dc operation and went in 1949 to the interurban Chicago South Shore & South Bend Railroad, becoming nos 801-803; the latter two of these remained in service in 1980. Twelve more went to the Rocky Mountain Division of the Chicago, Milwaukee & St Paul Railway in 1950, and survived until June 1974, when this company's electric operations ceased. The five remaining units were modified for operation on the 1600 mm (5 ft 3 in) gauge Paulista Railway in Brazil, entering service in 1951.

Dubbed "Little Joes" by the US railroad fraternity as a reference to Soviet leader Josef Stalin, these machines were, at the time of their construction, the most powerful single-unit electric locomotives to be built in the USA. Like other high-powered US built designs of the period, they run on a heavy articulated underframe which accounts for much of the 243 tonne service weight. Regenerative braking is fitted, and provision was made originally for multiple-unit operation, although in the case of the Paulista and Chicago South Shore locomotives, this facility was soon removed to avoid overloading the supply system.

Ownership of the Paulista units changed in 1971 when, along with several other lines, this system was placed under the control of São Paulo State as part of FEPASA. The five locomotives are now retained for the heaviest freight traffic on the former Paulista electrified network.

FEPASA class 6450 no 6451 at Campinas in January 1978 *(Sérgio Martire)*

Brazil

RFFSA class 2000

Operating system Brazilian Federal Railways
(RFFSA)
Year introduced 1973 (built 1972) and 1980
Axle arrangement B-B
Gauge 1600 mm *(5 ft 3 in)*
Power supply system 3 kV dc
One-hour output 2820 kW *(3780 hp, 3830 ch)*
Continuous output 2460 kW *(3295 hp, 3345 ch)*
Maximum speed Adhesion — 45 km/h *(28 mph)*;
rack — 30 km/h *(19 mph)*
Maximum tractive effort 378 kN *(84 900 lbs)* in
rack operation
Continuous tractive effort 314 kN *(70 600 lbs)* in
rack operation
Weight in working order 118 tonnes *(116 tons)*
Length over coupler centres 16 760 mm
(55 ft 0 in)
Bogie wheelbase 3950 mm *(12 ft 11½ in)*
Wheel diameter 1120 mm *(3 ft 8 in)*
Traction motors Six dc series-wound Hitachi type
EFFZO — H — 60, comprising two for adhesion
operation and four for rack. Rack motors nose-
suspended, adhesion motors bogie-mounted with
coupling rod/jackshaft drive
Control Rheostatic
Electric brake Rheostatic
Builder
 mechanical parts Hitachi
 electrical equipment Hitachi
Number built 12
Number series 2001 — 2012

**No 2007 leads another member of the class at
Paranapiacaba in November 1978** *(Sérgio
Martire)*

The first eight of these unusual rack-and-adhesion units were purpose-built by
Hitachi in 1972 for operation on the remarkable 8 km (5 mile) Old Serra Incline
which climbs the 773 m (2537 ft) Serra do Mar to link Latin America's largest
city, São Paulo, with the busy port of Santos. Opened in 1867 by the Santos-
Jundiai Railway, the line was originally cable-worked by four British built
stationary winding engines, each handling traffic over a 2 km (1¼ mile)
section. Maximum gradient was 10·7% (1 in 9½), and loads limited to 40 tons
took one hour for the ascent. A second line, the New Serra Incline, was added
in 1901. In 1965 the demand for increased capacity led RFFSA to close the
original incline for upgrading.

Reopened eight years later, the Old Serra Incline is now rack-operated using
a 3-bar Abt system and electrified at 3 kV dc between Rais da Serra, at the foot
of the climb, and Paranapiacaba, previous limit of the electrification from São
Paulo some 53 km (33 miles) distant. On the incline itself, the catenary is
duplicated to maintain current supply and this is backed up by a third rail
contact system. The single-cab 2000 series are provided with six traction
motors, two for adhesion working and four powering retractable pinions. In
normal operations, two units coupled in multiple and marshalled at the lower
end of their train are permitted a maximum load of 500 tonnes. The speed of
descending trains is regulated by rheostatic braking.

Passenger services are worked over the Old Serra Incline with four-car emus
which run conventionally from São Paulo to Paranapiacaba whence they are
taken down the gradient as trailers by a pair of 2000s. This transit now takes 22
minutes. From Rais da Serra to Santos the emu is hauled by a diesel locomotive.

Increased traffic requirements led to the supply of four more locomotives,
nos 2009-2012, in 1979/80. One unit, no 2005, has been scrapped following
accident damage.

Brazil

RFFSA class 2150

Operating system Brazilian Federal Railways (RFFSA)
Year introduced 1963
Axle arrangement Co-Co
Gauge 1600 mm *(5 ft 3 in)*
Power supply system 3 kV dc
One-hour output 3285 kW *(4400 hp, 4460 ch)*
Maximum speed 117 km/h *(73 mph)*
One-hour tractive effort 207 kN *(46 600 lbs)* at 27 km/h *(17 mph)*
Weight in working order 125 tonnes *(123 tons)*
Length over coupler centres 16 857 mm *(55 ft 3¾ in)*
Bogie wheelbase 4164 mm *(13 ft 8 in)*
Wheel diameter 1168 mm *(3 ft 10 in)*
Traction motors Six General Electric type GE-729 dc series-wound, nose-suspended, axle-hung
Control Rheostatic
Electric brake Regenerative
Builder
  mechanical parts General Electric
  electrical equipment General Electric
Number built 6
Number series 2151 — 2156

Electrification of the former Central Railway of Brazil began during the 1930s when various suburban lines in the Rio de Janeiro district were energised using the 3 kV dc system. Catenary eventually covered some 268 route-km (167 miles) and although most traffic was handled by emus, through passenger and freight traffic was later handled by locomotives of both Brazilian and US origin, notably the GE built 2-Co+Co-2 2100 series. The fleet was subsequently augmented by the German built class 2200 (see following entry) and these six freight units, now the most modern and powerful electric locomotives on the RFFSA roster. Constructed at General Electric's Erie plant, the 2150s employ typical US diesel locomotive construction techniques in the adoption of a fabricated underframe on which are mounted narrow hoods housing control and auxiliary equipment. Only one driver's cab is provided. The locomotives are fitted for multiple-unit operation and have regenerative braking. Livery is the standard RFFSA red and yellow.

No 2153 at Barro do Pirai depot, Rio de Janeiro, in April 1980 *(Sérgio Martire)*

Brazil

RFFSA class 2200

Operating system Brazilian Federal Railways (RFFSA)
Year introduced 1959 (built 1958)
Axle arrangement Bo-Bo
Gauge 1600 mm *(5 ft 3 in)*
Power supply system 3 kV dc
One-hour output 2350 kW *(3150 hp, 3195 ch)*
Maximum speed 100 km/h *(62 mph)*
One-hour tractive effort 153 kN *(34 400 lbs)* at 60 km/h *(37 mph)*
Weight in working order 110 tonnes *(108¼ tons)*
Length over coupler centres 16 270 mm *(53 ft 4½ in)*
Bogie wheelbase 3500 mm *(11 ft 5¾ in)*
Wheel diameter 1250 mm *(4 ft 1¼ in)*
Traction motors Four SSW type VB320/22a dc series-wound, nose-suspended, axle-hung
Control Rheostatic
Electric brake Regenerative
Builder
 mechanical parts Henschel
 electrical equipment Siemens
Number built 7
Number series 2201 — 2207

Introduced by the former Central Railway of Brazil in 1959, these seven German built Bo-Bo machines were primarily intended for freight haulage. Design incorporates many features of contemporary European practice, such as an all-welded steel body, roller-bearing axle boxes and monobloc wheels. A diagonal coupling between bogies is intended to minimise track forces on the leading axle, and flange lubrication is also provided. Multiple-unit control facilities allow up to three locomotives to be operated by one crew, and regenerative braking is fitted.

Today the 2200s operate passenger services over RFFSA's important Santos-Jundiai line.

Nos 2202 and 2203 at Barro do Pirai depot in January 1980, before transfer to the Santos-Jundiai line *(Sérgio Martire)*

Bulgaria

BDŽ class 41

Operating system Bulgarian State Railways (BDŽ)
Year introduced 1962
Axle arrangement Bo-Bo
Gauge 1435 mm *(4 ft 8½ in)*
Power supply system 25 kV ac 50 Hz
Continuous output 2800 kW *(3750 hp, 3805 ch)*
Maximum speed 110 km/h *(68 mph)*
Maximum tractive effort 314 kN *(70 600 lbs)*
Continuous tractive effort 196 kN *(44 100 lbs)* at 56 km/h *(35 mph)*
Weight in working order 88 tonnes *(87 tons)*
Length over buffers 16 140 mm *(52 ft 11⅜ in)*
Bogie wheelbase 2800 mm *(9 ft 2¼ in)*
Wheel diameter 1250 mm *(4 ft 1¼ in)*
Traction motors Four dc series-wound, frame-suspended with Škoda flexible drive
Control h.t. tap-changer
Electric brake Rheostatic
Builder
  mechanical parts Škoda
  electrical equipment Škoda
Number built 41
Number series 41-01 — 41-41

The first BDŽ main line to be electrified, on which work started in 1961 using the 25 kV ac single-phase system, was the busy Sofia-Plovdiv route in the south-west of the country. Motive power came from Czechoslovakia in the form of a series of 41 mixed-traffic Bo-Bo units then designated class E41. These were the first series-built rectifier locomotives to be constructed by Škoda, and the design follows closely that of four experimental prototypes supplied by the company to Czechoslovak State Railways (ČSD) in 1961. Two of these were silicon rectifier machines (ČSD class E479.0, later S479.0) and two had ignitron rectifiers (ČSD class E479.1, later S479.1). Trials with these prototypes were conducted in Bulgaria, Romania and the USSR (after re-gauging) as well as in Czechoslovakia, but only the BDŽ order resulted.

As built, the E41 series was equipped with ignitron rectifiers but these were later replaced by Škoda with the dry silicon variety. Body construction and styling are similar to contemporary dc designs from this manufacturer, with a colour scheme of red and cream. Roof is silver, bogies and undergear are black. The original "E" prefix to the class designation is no longer used.

Introduction of the class set the pattern for future BDŽ electric locomotive acquisitions, all of which have been four-axle silicon rectifier machines supplied by Škoda.

BDŽ class 41 no 41-08 at Plovdiv in August 1972 *(Marc Dahlström)*

22

Canada

CNR class Z-1-a

Operating system Canadian National Railways (CNR)
Year introduced 1914
Axle arrangement Bo+Bo
Gauge 1435 mm *(4 ft 8½ in)*
Power supply system 2.4 kV dc
One-hour output 930 kW *(1250 hp, 1270 ch)*
Continuous output 820 kW *(1100 hp, 1115 ch)*
Maximum speed 88 km/h *(55 mph)*
Maximum tractive effort 193 kN *(43 400 lbs)*
Continuous tractive effort 83 kN *(18 600 lbs)* at 36.5 km/h *(22.7 mph)*
Weight in working order 79 tonnes *(78 tons)*
Length over coupler centres 11 380 mm *(37 ft 4 in)*
Bogie wheelbase 2642 mm *(8 ft 8 in)*
Wheel diameter 1168 mm *(3 ft 10 in)*
Traction motors Four General Electric type GE-754C dc series-wound, nose-suspended, axle-hung
Control Rheostatic
Electric brake None
Builder
  mechanical parts Canadian General Electric Company
  electrical equipment Canadian General Electric Company, General Electric Company
Number built 6
Number series 6710 — 6715

Amongst the oldest locomotives featured in this book are six units dating from 1914 which form CNR class Z-1-a. In 1980 these veteran machines were still operating commuter traffic in the Montreal suburban area in a form little altered since their construction.

Ordered by the Canadian Northern Railway, a major constituent of CNR, the Z-1-a units were destined to serve an important scheme to gain improved access to Montreal by way of the 5 km (3·1 mile) Mount Royal Tunnel to a new terminal at Montreal Central. For environmental and operational reasons, electric traction was used from the start using a 2·4 kV overhead supply system, thus becoming one of the earliest schemes using a voltage then considered high. At its greatest extent, total electrified route length was 44 km (27·3 miles) and both suburban and through passenger traffic were worked electrically. The latter necessitated exchanges with steam traction where the catenary began, but this practice ended with the demise of CNR steam, leaving the Z-1-a units to share the Cartierville and Deux-Montagnes commuter traffic with British and US built locomotives of 1925 and 1950 respectively.

The locomotives were assembled at the Peterborough (Ontario) works of the Canadian General Electric Company, and the design is of the early North American "box-cab" type. The body is carried on two articulated bogies which bear all tractive and buffing forces. Multiple-unit control equipment is fitted.

During their long careers, the six locomotives have been renumbered three times. Originally numbered 600-605 by the Canadian Northern Railway, they were allocated nos 9100-9105 by CNR on its formation in 1923. They later became nos 100-105 before receiving the present nos 6710-6715.

Two CNR class Z-1-a units, led by no 6715, at Val Royal, Montreal in July 1971
(William D Middleton)

Chile

FFCCdelE class E30

Operating system Chilean State Railways
(FFCC del E)
Year introduced 1961
Axle arrangement Bo-Bo
Gauge 1676 mm *(5 ft 6 in)*
Power supply system 3 kV dc
One-hour output 2245 kW *(3005 hp, 3050 ch)*
Continuous output 1790 kW *(2400 hp, 2435 ch)*
Maximum speed 130 km/h *(80 mph)*
One-hour tractive effort 229 kN *(51 400 lbs)*
Continuous tractive effort 153 kN *(34 400 lbs)* at
52.5 km/h *(33 mph)*
Weight in working order 98 tonnes *(96½ tons)*
Length over coupler centres 17 770 mm
(58 ft 3⅝ in)
Wheel diameter 1260 mm *(4 ft 1⅝ in)*
Traction motors Four dc series-wound, nose-
suspended with Siemens resilient drive
Control Rheostatic
Electric brake None
Builder
mechanical parts Ferroviaria Breda Pistoiesi (on
behalf of Gruppo Aziende Italiane)
electrical equipment ASGEN, Ercole Marelli (on
behalf of Gruppo Aziende Italiane)
Number built 22
Number series 3001 — 3022

Electrification of Chilean State Railways' Southern (Red Sur) trunk line from Santiago to San Rosendo and Concepción was undertaken in the 1960s by GAI, a consortium of Italian companies who supplied both fixed installations and motive power. The latter comprised eight four-car emus and four- and six-axle electric locomotives of broadly similar design.

Class E30 is the Bo-Bo version, principally used for passenger work, built by Breda in 1961. Traction motors are 1·5 kV machines controlled conventionally by resistances, motor groupings and field-weakening, with electro-pneumatic switchgear. A feature of the control equipment is the provision of automatic wheel-slip protection through partial field-shunting of the slipping axle. Unlike the Co-Co E32 series, multiple-unit operation is possible but the E30 lacks the regenerative braking of the six-axle design. Both classes are provided with driver vigilance devices.

Characteristic styling is reminiscent of US practice of the 1940s and 1950s, largely due to the bonnets forward of each driver's cab which house compressors and battery equipment. Small frontal doors in each nose provide limited access between locomotives coupled in multiple. Livery is red with a broad central maroon band relieved by yellow flashes.

The class shares principal Red Sur duties with the 34-strong class E32 Co-Co units of 3360 kW (4504 hp).

FFCCdelE class E30 no 3012 at San Bernardo with a Santiago-Talca express in February 1979 *(Marc Dahlström)*

China

Class 6G

Operating system Railways of the People's Republic of China
Year introduced 1972
Axle arrangement Co-Co
Gauge 1435 mm *(4 ft 8½ in)*
Power supply system 25 kV ac 50 Hz
Continuous output 5350 kW *(7170 hp, 7270 ch)*
Maximum speed 112 km/h *(70 mph)*
Continuous tractive effort 353 kN *(79 400 lbs)* at 55 km/h *(34 mph)*
Weight in working order 138 tonnes *(136 tons)*
Length over coupler centres 23 060 mm *(75 ft 7⅞ in)*
Bogie wheelbase 2335+2335=4670 mm *(15 ft 3⅞ in)*
Wheel diameter 1250 mm *(4 ft 1¼ in)*
Traction motors Six pulsating current series-wound type TAO 649C, nose-suspended, axle-hung
Control Thyristor
Electric brake 6G-51 — 6G-88 — rheostatic; 6G-89 — 6G-90 — regenerative
Builder
 mechanical parts Alsthom, MTE (for 50 Hz Group)
 electrical equipment Alsthom, MTE (for 50 Hz Group)
Number built 40
Number series 6G-51 — 6G-90

Progress with electrification of the mountainous 679 km (422 mile) Baoji-Chengdu railway outpaced Chinese electric locomotive development, and services on the first 90 km (56 mile) section from Baoji to Fung Shien were inaugurated in 1960 with French built class 6Y2 machines of 4410 kW (5915 hp). Ten years later, with the domestically-built SSI (see next entry) still to prove itself, a further order was placed with French industry via the 50Hz Group for this series of 40 heavy-duty class 6G units. These were intended to meet immediate motive power needs created by continuing electrification and dramatically increased traffic.

Mechanical design is derived from that of the earlier 6Y2, but the adoption of thyristor control enabled the continuous rating to be raised to 5350 kW, placing the 6G amongst the world's most powerful single-unit electric locomotives. Thirty-eight units were supplied with rheostatic brakes; the last two were fitted experimentally with regenerative braking. Despite their great power, all examples are provided with multiple-unit control equipment to allow double-heading of the heaviest trains with one crew. Deliveries started in 1972 and were completed during the following year.

Railways of the People's Republic of China class 6G no 6G-52
(Alsthom)

China

Class SS1 (Shaoshan 1)

Operating system Railways of the People's Republic of China
Year introduced 1969
Axle arrangement Co-Co
Gauge 1435 mm *(4 ft 8½ in)*
Power supply system 25 kV ac 50 Hz
One-hour output 4200 kW *(5630 hp, 5705 ch)*
Continuous output 3780 kW *(5065 hp, 5135 ch)*
Maximum speed 95 km/h *(59 mph)*
Maximum tractive effort 530 kN *(119 100 lbs)*
Weight in working order 138 tonnes *(136 tons)*
Length over coupler centres 20 368 mm *(66 ft 9⅞ in)*
Bogie wheelbase 2300 + 2300 = 4600 mm *(15 ft 1¼ in)*
Wheel diameter 1250 mm *(4 ft 1¼ in)*
Traction motors Six dc series-wound, nose-suspended, axle-hung
Control l.t. tap-changer
Electric brake Rheostatic
Builder
  mechanical parts Zhuzhou Electric Locomotive Factory
  electrical equipment Zhuzhou Electric Locomotive Factory
Number built Not known (see text)
Number series Shaoshan 1001 — ?

Although Chinese industry produced its first electric locomotive in 1958, it was not until 1969 that a domestic design entered series production in the form of the silicon rectifier SS1, or *Shaoshan*. These powerful machines were introduced initially to provide motive power for the 679 km (422 mile) Baoji-Chengdu line through the Qinling mountains which was electrified between 1958 and 1975, and are derived from the earlier French built 6Y2 ignition rectifier units supplied from 1960. Primarily (but not exclusively) intended for freight operation, three SS1s are claimed to be able to take 2400 tonne loads up a continuous 3·3% (1 in 30) gradient at 50 km/h (31 mph). With mountain work in mind, the design includes a powerful rheostatic brake continuously rated at 3600 kW.

Subsequent electrification in 1977 of the 359 km (223 mile) Yangpingguan-Ankang line, which connects with the Baoji-Chengdu railway, has resulted in the reported production of over 200 units by 1980.

A thyristor-controlled version of the SS1 appeared in prototype form, also in 1969. Designated SS2 (or *Shaoshan* 2), it did not enter series production but has provided valuable data for development of the SS3 (see next entry) destined to replace the SS1 on the Zhuzhou production lines.

Railways of the People's Republic of China class SS1 (Shaoshan 1) no SS1139
(New China Pictures)

China

Class SS3 (Shaoshan 3)

Operating system Railways of the People's Republic
of China
Year introduced 1979
Axle arrangement Co-Co
Gauge 1435 mm *(4 ft 8½ in)*
Power supply system 25 kV ac 50 Hz
One-hour output 4800 kW *(6430 hp, 6520 ch)*
Maximum speed 100 km/h *(62 mph)*
Continuous tractive effort 337 kN *(75 900 lbs)* at
50 km/h *(31 mph)*
Wheel diameter 1250 mm *(4 ft 1¼ in)*
Traction motors Six dc series-wound, nose-
suspended, axle-hung
Control l.t. tap-changer
Electric brake Rheostatic
Builder
 mechanical parts Zhuzhou Electric Locomotive
 Factory
 electrical equipment Zhuzhou Electric Locomotive
 Factory
Number built Not known
Number series SS3001 — ?

At the time this book was prepared for press, comparatively few details had emerged from China of the powerful SS3 (*Shaoshan* 3) prototype locomotive which appeared during 1979. The design was developed from the experimental SS2 model and, subject to satisfactory performance in service, is destined to become standard freight motive power for future electrification schemes in China. Like the SS1, the SS3 employs a tap-changer/silicon rectifier arrangement, but thyristors are used to control traction motor excitation.

In 1980, electrification work in hand or planned covered some 2026 route-km (1258 miles) in addition to the 1520 km (944 miles) already energised, and manufacturing capacity at Zhuzhou was being increased to meet the consequent demand for locomotives, which will be mostly of this type.

The same plant was also developing a 120 km/h (75 mph) passenger version of the SS3.

**Railways of the People's Republic of China
class SS3 (Shaoshan 3) no SS3001** (*New
China Pictures*)

Czechoslovakia

ČSD class E458.0

Operating system Czechoslovak State Railways (ČSD)
Year introduced 1971
Axle arrangement Bo-Bo
Gauge 1435 mm *(4 ft 8½ in)*
Power supply system 3 kV dc
Continuous output 800 kW *(1075 hp, 1090 ch)*
Maximum speed 80 km/h *(50 mph)*
Maximum tractive effort 157 kN *(35 300 lbs)*
Continuous tractive effort 87 kN *(19 400 lbs)* at 32 km/h *(20 mph)*
Weight in working order 72 tonnes *(71 tons)*
Length over buffers 14 400 mm *(47 ft 3 in)*
Bogie wheelbase 2800 mm *(9 ft 2¼ in)*
Wheel diameter 1050 mm *(3 ft 5⅜ in)*
Traction motors Four dc series-wound, nose-suspended, axle hung
Control Rheostatic
Electric brake None
Builder
  mechanical parts Škoda
  electrical equipment Škoda
Number built 52
Number series E458.0001 — E458.0052

First examples of this 72 tonne design for heavy shunting and trip work entered ČSD service in 1971 when they replaced diesel traction on stock marshalling duties in Prague's main station (Hlavní Nádraží) area. Their specification includes special slow-speed control apparatus for hump shunting, and electric train heating facilities for pre-heating coaching stock. Traction motors are derived from those of the successful T669 series diesel-electric units. Secondary suspension is of the coil spring type and in high tractive effort conditions, axle-load changes are restricted pneumatically to maintain adhesion. Air cylinders for this purpose are visible behind each buffer-beam. The low bonnets and central cab, which has two identical diagonal control positions, afford excellent vision during shunting movements, and safe retreats for yard staff are provided at each extremity of the locomotive. These Škoda built units are also identified by the manufacturer's designation 33E.

Derivatives of the design in ČSD service are:
  - class E426.0 (also Škoda type 33E) of 64 tonnes and rated at 400 kW (540 hp) for 1·5 kV dc branch line operation. Six examples were built in 1973.
  - class S458.0 (Škoda type 51E) for operation on 25 kV ac 50 Hz lines. These units are thyristor-controlled. Thirty-one were built in 1973.
  - class E457.0 (Škoda type 78E) with chopper control and a continuous rating of 780 kW (1045 hp) for 3 kV dc service. A ČSD order for 80 units is due for delivery in 1981.

Class E458.0 no E458.0001 marshals stock at Prague Hlavní Nádraží in November 1971 *(Ing Zdeněk Bauer)*

No E426.0002 is one of a series of six 400 kW machines based on the E458.0 and delivered in 1973 by Škoda for light duties on lines electrified at 1.5 kV dc (*Ing Zdeněk Bauer*)

Thyristor control is employed in the single-phase S458.0, which appeared in 1973. (*Škoda*)

Czechoslovakia

ČSD class E499.0

Operating system Czechoslovak State Railways (ČSD)
Year introduced 1953
Axle arrangement Bo-Bo
Gauge 1435 mm *(4 ft 8½ in)*
Power supply system 3 kV dc
One-hour output 2344 kW *(3140 hp, 3185 ch)*
Continuous output 2032 kW *(2725 hp, 2760 ch)*
Maximum speed 120 km/h *(75 mph)*
Maximum tractive effort 255 kN *(57 400 lbs)*
Continuous tractive effort 112 kN *(25 200 lbs)* at 63 km/h *(39 mph)*
Weight in working order (E499.001 — 040) 80 tonnes *(79 tons;)* (E499.041 — 0100) 82 tonnes *(81 tons)*
Length over buffers (E499.001 — 017) 15 600 mm *(51 ft 2¼ in)*; (E499.018 — 040) 15 800 mm *(51 ft 10 in)*; (E499.041 — 0100) 15 740 mm *(51 ft 7⅝ in)*
Bogie wheelbase 3330 mm *(10 ft 11⅛ in)*
Wheel diameter 1250 mm *(4 ft 1¼ in)*
Traction motors Four dc series-wound, fully suspended with Sécheron flexible drive
Control Rheostatic
Electric brake None
Builder
  mechanical parts Škoda
  electrical equipment Škoda
Number built 100
Number series E499.001 — E499.0100

Two ČSD class E499.0 units led by no E499.022 operating in tandem at Nový Bohumín in March 1970. The characteristic "porthole" windows to the machinery compartment distinguish this class from other ČSD designs. *(Ing Zdeněk Bauer)*

The E499.0 universal four-axle series was the first ČSD 3 kV dc design, and was intended to meet a wide range of haulage requirements ranging from 720 tonne expresses at 120 km/h (75 mph) to freight trains of 1440 tonnes at 60 km/h (37 mph). Škoda was provided with technical assistance by Swiss companies, and the mechanical specification reflects contemporary all-adhesion developments in that country, with roller-bearing bogies designed by SLM and Sécheron flexible transmission. The first example was completed in 1953, although it was not until the following year that ČSD energised its first 3 kV dc section between Tábor and Bechyně, and early locomotives in the series were tested in neighbouring Poland. Construction of the class continued until 1958.

As the forerunner of all modern Škoda designs, the E499.0 is significant in the development of electric traction in Czechoslovakia, with the following important derivatives:

- ČSD class E499.1, an immediate development of the E499.0 with similar performance; 61 were placed in service between 1957 and 1961.
- a series of ten 3 kV dc machines designated Škoda type 22E supplied in 1958 to the railways of the Korean Democratic People's Republic.
- Soviet Railways (SZD) class ChSl, a 1524 mm gauge version of the E499.1 for express work; two prototypes supplied in 1957 were followed by 100 more in 1959/60.
- Polish State Railways (PKP) class EP05, 30 of which were built in 1961. Originally designated class EU05 and geared for 120 km/h (75 mph), they were later modified for 160 km/h (100 mph) running.
- a large number of four-axle "freight" locomotives of the ČSD E469 family built in several versions since 1960 and used for a wide range of work.

Czechoslovakia

ČSD class E669.3

Operating system Czechoslovak State Railways (ČSD)
Year introduced 1971
Axle arrangement Co-Co
Gauge 1435 mm *(4 ft 8½ in)*
Power supply system 3 kV dc
One-hour output 3000 kW *(4020 hp, 4075 ch)*
Continuous output 2790 kW *(3740 hp, 3790 ch)*
Maximum speed 90 km/h *(56 mph)*
Maximum tractive effort 353 kN *(79 400 lbs)*
Weight in working order 120 tonnes *(118 tons)*
Length of buffers 18 800 mm *(61 ft 8⅛ in)*
Bogie wheelbase 4500 mm *(14 ft 9⅛ in)*
Wheel diameter 1250 mm *(4 ft 1¼ in)*
Traction motors Six dc series-wound, nose-suspended, axle-hung.
Control Rheostatic
Electric brake None
Builder
  mechanical parts Škoda
  electrical equipment Škoda
Number built 43
Number series E669.3001 — E669.3043

The important role of ČSD as a carrier of substantial tonnages of freight, especially transit traffic, is underlined by the presence in its electric locomotive fleet of a large number of powerful six-axle machines of the E669 series built specifically for heavy goods work over 3 kV dc lines.

The E669.3 sub-series of 1971 is the final development of a design introduced in 1958, and with a continuous rating of 2790 kW (3740 hp) is slightly more powerful than the earlier 2640 kW (3540 hp) E669.1 and E669.2 models. The low gearing of these locomotives gives them great haulage capabilities, and two units in tandem (they are not fitted for multiple-unit operation) are claimed to be able to take loads of 2500 tonnes over continuous gradients of 1·8% (1 in 56).

A total of 363 examples of the E669 family have been placed in ČSD service. Building details of the antecedents of the E669.3 are:
- two prototype machines built in 1958 and numbered E669.001 and 002 (Škoda type 23E).
- 150 units of class E669.1 (Škoda type 31E) built as two batches in 1960 and 1961.
- 168 units of class E669.2 (Škoda type 59E) constructed as three batches between 1963 and 1965.

ČSD class E669.3 no E669.3006. This example has leaf spring secondary suspension; later members of the class are equipped with the coil spring type.
(Ing Zdeněk Bauer)

Czechoslovakia

ČSD class ES499.0

Operating system Czechoslovak State Railways (ČSD)
Year introduced 1974
Axle arrangement Bo-Bo
Gauge 1435 mm *(4 ft 8½ in)*
Power supply system (dual-current) 3 kV dc; 25 kV ac 50 Hz
Continuous output 4000 kW *(5360 hp, 5435 ch)*
Maximum speed 160 km/h *(100 mph)*
Maximum tractive effort 255 kN *(57 400 lbs)*
Continuous tractive effort 129 kN *(28 900 lbs)* at 108.5 km/h *(67 mph)*
Weight in working order 87.4 tonnes *(86 tons)*
Length over buffers 16 740 mm *(54 ft 11 in)*
Bogie wheelbase 3200 mm *(10 ft 6 in)*
Wheel diameter 1250 mm *(4 ft 1¼ in)*
Traction motors: Four dc series-wound, fully suspended with Škoda flexible drive
Control Rheostatic
Electric brake Rheostatic
Builder
  mechanical parts Škoda
  electrical equipment Škoda
Number built 20
Number series ES499.0001 — ES499.0020

Since the early 1960s, ČSD has adopted high frequency ac electrification for major new schemes while still retaining a substantial network (some 1700 km by 1979) energised at the former standard 3 kV dc. The 20 class ES499.0 dual-current units were introduced to permit through running of internal express passenger traffic irrespective of power supply, and to facilitate penetration of certain Hungarian State Railways (MÁV) 25 kV ac lines. After extensive trials with two prototype machines delivered in 1974, a further 18 entered service during the following year to form the present class.

Designated type 55E by Škoda, the ES499.0 is the first "second generation" Czechoslovak electric locomotive and incorporates several important developments including high-performance bogie and suspension design. In service the class can operate at up to 160 km/h (100 mph) and is therefore ČSD's fastest form of motive power. However, the design was conceived with 200 km/h running in mind, and one of the two prototype units achieved a speed of 220 km/h (137 mph) during trials. In this high-speed form, the ES499.0 served as a basis for development of the 200 km/h (125 mph) Soviet Railways ChS200 twin-unit express locomotives built by Škoda (see p. 135).

During ac operation, dc control of a rectified fixed-ratio transformer output is used. Rheostatic braking is independent of overhead supply. Electrical equipment is arranged in modular form for easy replacement and maintenance.

ČSD class ES499.0 no ES499.0001 during trials at the Velim test track, near Prague *(Škoda)*

Further construction of the class is unlikely in view of the development of a chopper-controlled dual-voltage design, the ES499.1, prototypes of which were completed by Škoda in 1980.

Apart from the SZD class ChS200 referred to above, the other important derivative of the ES499.0 is a dc version, ČSD class E499.2. Also rated at 4000 kW, 27 units were delivered in 1978.

ČSD also operates a dc-only version of the ES499.0 designated class E499.2. Seen here is no E499.2023 (*Ing Bohumil Skála*)

Czechoslovakia

ČSD class S489.0

Operating system Czechoslovak State Railways (ČSD)
Year introduced 1966
Axle arrangement Bo-Bo
Gauge 1435 mm *(4 ft 8½ in)*
Power supply system 25 kV ac 50 Hz
One-hour output 3200 kW *(4290 hp, 4350 ch)*
Continuous output 3080 kW *(4130 hp, 4185 ch)*
Maximum speed 110 or 120 km/h *(68 or 75 mph)*
Maximum tractive effort 250 kN *(56 300 lbs)*
Continuous tractive effort 170 kN *(38 200 lbs)* at 64 km/h *(40 mph)*
Weight in working order 85 tonnes *(84 tons)*
Length over buffers 16 440 mm *(53 ft 11¼ in)*
Bogie wheelbase 2800 mm *(9 ft 2¼ in)*
Wheel diameter 1250 mm *(4 ft 1¼ in)*
Traction motors Four dc series-wound, fully suspended with Škoda flexible drive
Control h.t. tap-changer
Electric brake Rheostatic (on some units only)
Builder
  mechanical parts Škoda
  electrical equipment Škoda
Number built 110
Number series S489.0001 — S489.0110

Class S489.0 no S489.0094 *(Ing Zdeněk Bauer)*

Below right: Bulgarian State Railways (BDŽ) class E42 is generally similar to the ČSD S489.0 series. No E42-01 is seen new at Škoda's Plzeň works in 1965 *(Škoda)*

Below: Class S499.1 no S499.1022 is one of 25 140 km/h express units developed from the S489.0 design *(Ing Zdeněk Bauer)*

The first ČSD series-built ac design, the mixed-traffic S489.0, was introduced in 1966 for service on newly electrified lines in south-west Czechoslovakia. Developed by Škoda as a domestic version of the E42 (Škoda type 46E) units supplied to Bulgarian State Railways (BDŽ) during the previous year, the locomotives feature a body of glass-fibre laminate. Adoption of this unusual construction technique followed successful results obtained with the 25 kV ac Co-Co prototype no S699.01, built in 1963. The use of this material in place of sheet steel was claimed to simplify manufacture and maintenance, reduce weight and afford greater protection in the event of a collision.

Electrically, the design draws on experience gained with the four prototype S479.0 and S479.1 machines (see p 22), with traction motor voltage control by means of a high-tension tap-changer/silicon rectifier arrangement.

The same basic model has been built in the following versions:
- Bulgarian State Railways (BDŽ) class 42 (originally class E42), of which 90 were supplied between 1965 and 1970, geared for 110 km/h (68 mph) and equipped for operation as pairs in multiple.
- ČSD classes S499.0 (120 units) and S499.1 (25 units) with design speeds of 120 km/h (75 mph) and 140 km/h (87 mph) respectively. The latter series has rheostatic brakes. Both are designated Škoda type 47E.

Finland

VR class Sr1

Operating system Finnish State Railways
Year introduced 1973
Axle arrangement Bo-Bo
Gauge 1524 mm *(5 ft 0 in)*
Power supply system 25 kV ac 50 Hz
One-hour output 3280 kW *(4395 hp, 4455 ch)*
Continuous output 3100 kW *(4155 hp, 4215 ch)*
Maximum speed 140 km/h *(87 mph)*
Maximum tractive effort 255 kN *(57 400 lbs)*
Continuous tractive effort 177 kN *(39 700 lbs)* at
  70 km/h *(44 mph)*
Weight in working order 84 tonnes *(83 tons)*
Length over buffers 18 960 mm *(62 ft 2½ in)*
Bogie wheelbase 2700 mm *(8 ft 10¼ in)*
Wheel diameter 1250 mm *(4 ft 1¼ in)*
Traction motors Four dc series-wound Novocherkassk
  type HБ 501, fully suspended with Škoda flexible drive
Control Thyristor
Electric brake Rheostatic
Builder
  mechanical parts Novocherkassk Electric
  Locomotive Works
  electrical equipment Oy Strömberg Ab,
  Novocherkassk Electric Locomotive Works
Number built 87
Number series 3001 — 3087

VR's only series-built electric locomotives are the thyristor-controlled Soviet built Sr1 class. The first order, placed with Energomachexport in late 1970, was for 27 units to handle passenger and freight traffic on main line routes then being electrified at 25 kV ac 50 Hz. Design and development was undertaken by the Soviet All-Union Electric Locomotive Research and Design Institute (VELNII) in close cooperation with the Finnish company Strömberg, who supplied the power control equipment. Various other European manufacturers participated in the project, especially in those areas where Soviet domestic components would have been too heavy or unsuitable for VR conditions. Design of flexible axle drives was a case in point; these were developed by Škoda in Czechoslovakia from those fitted to their ChS4 express locomotives supplied to Soviet Railways (SZD).

The first two machines arrived in Finland in late 1973, and one soon distinguished itself by establishing a new VR speed record of 164·8 km/h (102·3 mph), a creditable achievement for a railway not associated with speeds of this order. However, with present operations limited to 120 km/h (75 mph), it will not be until the mid-1980s that infrastructure improvements allow the full speed capabilities of the Sr1 to be used in normal service.

As VR electrification has progressed, further batches of the design have been ordered. Eighty-seven of the class were due to have been delivered by the end of 1980.

VR class Srl no 3041 *(VR)*

France

SNCF class CC-6500

Operating system French National Railways (SNCF)
Year introduced 1969
Axle arrangement C-C
Gauge 1435 mm *(4 ft 8½ in)*
Power supply system 1.5 kV dc
Continuous output 5900 kW *(7905 hp, 8015 ch)*
Maximum speed (high gear) 220 km/h *(135 mph)*;
   (low gear) 100 km/h *(62 mph)*
Maximum tractive effort (high gear) 131 kN
   (29 500 lbs); (low gear) 288 kN *(64 700 lbs)*
Continuous tractive effort (high gear) 119 kN
   (26 700 lbs) at 136 km/h *(84½ mph)*; (low gear)
   269 kN *(60 400 lbs)* at 62 km/h *(38½ mph)*
Weight in working order
   (CC-6501-6538) 116.7 tonnes *(115 tons)*;
   (CC-6539-6559) 119.9 tonnes *(118 tons)*;
   (CC-6560-6574) 119.7 tonnes *(118 tons)*
Length over buffers 20 190 mm *(66 ft 2⅞ in)*
Bogie wheelbase 3216 mm *(10 ft 6⅝ in)*
Wheel diameter 1140 mm *(3 ft 8⅞ in)*
Traction motors Two double-armature dc series-
   wound Alsthom type TTB 665 A1, fully suspended with
   cardan shaft drive
Control Rheostatic
Electric brake Rheostatic
Builder
   mechanical parts Alsthom, MTE
   electrical equipment Alsthom, MTE
Number built 74
Number series CC-6501 — CC-6574

No CC-6515, one of the first series of 38
delivered between 1969 and 1972,
photographed at Savigny sur Orge with a
Paris-Toulouse express. The locomotive is
named *Blois (Marc Dahlström)*

The elegant CC-6500 series was developed to increase train speeds and load-ings over the important Toulouse and Bordeaux main lines of the Sud-Est and Sud-Ouest regions of SNCF, where the haulage of principal express traffic called for daily scheduled speeds of up to 200 km/h (125 mph). With a continuous output of 5900 kW, they are the most powerful SNCF electric locomotives. The general mechanical design shares features common to the CC-72000 diesel-electrics introduced in 1968, notably the adoption of three-axle single-motor bogies. In each of these is mounted a twin-armature traction motor, the output of which is transmitted to the axles by intermediate gearing. A change of gear ratio, which can only be effected while the locomotive is stationary, provides considerable operational flexibility, and the CC-6500 can be equally used as a high speed passenger unit or, with the lower gear engaged, as a powerful express freight machine.

The class of 74 includes a sub-series of 21 units (nos CC-6539 to CC-6559) formerly used on the steeply graded Chambéry-Modane "Maurienne" line in the Savoy region. These locomotives were originally equipped for third rail current collection until an overhead power supply was adopted on the line in 1976, and are distinguishable from their sisters by a simple green and white livery. The remainder of the class bears a striking colour scheme of grey, silver, red and orange which harmonises with *Grand Confort* coaching stock. There are visual differences in the ventilation grilles on the sides of the body between the "Maurienne" units and both preceding and following series. Many of the class have received names and coats of arms of French towns and cities since SNCF's decision in 1972 to introduce this practice.

A series of four dual-current (1·5 kV dc/25 kV ac 50 Hz) locomotives of class CC-21000 are mechanically similar but feature thyristor control during ac operation. One of these, no CC-21003, was shipped to the USA in 1977 for trials on Amtrak's Northeast Corridor. Temporarily renumbered X996, the locomotive proved unsatisfactory for US permanent way conditions.

Derivatives of the CC-6500 for 3 kV dc operation have been exported from France to Morocco (ONCFM class E-900) and Yugoslavia (JŽ class 363).

Right: Twenty-one CC-6500s are finished in a spartan green and white livery and were originally equipped with collector shoes for third rail operation. No CC-6546 is seen at Dijon in April 1979 *(Marcel Vleugels)*

Centre right: SNCF also operates a dual-current (1·5 kV/25 kV ac 50 Hz) version of the CC-6500 designated class CC-21000. These are mainly used on Sud-Est region international traffic, such as the Paris-Milan-Venice *Cisalpin* TEE seen here at Paris (Gare de Lyon) headed by no CC-21004 *(Marc Dahlström)*

Bottom: The mechanical design of the CC-6500 formed the basis of a 3 kV dc export model, which at 2750 kW is considerably less powerful than the SNCF units. The largest series, 39 examples, was supplied to Yugoslav Railways (JŽ), but seven went to Moroccan Railways (ONCFM), including no E-906, seen at Marrakesh in April 1979 *(Marcel Vleugels)*

Below: The final batch (nos CC-6560-74) feature the revised ventilation grille layout evident here on no CC-6561 at Paris (Gare de Lyon) in September 1977 *(Marc Dahlström)*

France

SNCF class CC-7100

Operating system French National Railways (SNCF)
Year introduced 1952
Axle arrangement Co-Co
Gauge 1435 mm *(4 ft 8½ in)*
Power supply system 1.5 kV dc
Continuous output
(CC-7101 — 7143) 3490 kW *(4675 hp, 4740 ch)*;
(CC-7144 — 7158) 3240 kW *(4340 hp, 4400 ch)*
Maximum speed 150 km/h *(93 mph)*
Maximum tractive effort 226 kN *(50 800 lbs)*
Continuous tractive effort 153 kN *(34 600 lbs)* at
79.5 km/h *(49½ mph)*
Weight in working order
(CC-7101 — 7143) 107 tonnes *(106 tons)*;
(CC-7144 — 7158) 106 tonnes *(105 tons)*
Length over buffers 18 922 mm *(62 ft 1 in)*
Bogie wheelbase 2335 + 2510 = 4845 mm
(15 ft 10¾ in)
Wheel diameter 1250 mm *(4 ft 1¼ in)*
Traction motors Six dc series-wound Alsthom type
TA 621-B or TA 628-C, fully suspended with Alsthom
quill drive
Control Rheostatic
Electric brake None
Builder
 mechanical parts Alsthom, Fives-Lille
 electrical equipment Alsthom, CEM
Number built 58
Number series CC-7101 — CC-7158

SNCF class CC-7100 no CC-7140. The
fairings below the bodysides and
buffer-beams have been progressively
removed from the class during overhaul.
(SNCF)

The development in Switzerland of all-adhesion express designs during the 1940s led SNCF soon after the Second World War to order two prototype 2770 kW (3710 hp) six-axle machines of this type for evaluation on the 1·5 kV dc main lines of the former PO and PLM systems. Delivered in 1949 and numbered CC-7001 and 7002, these two locomotives were the first SNCF bogie express design and incorporated many innovative features, including a revolutionary method of mounting the body on the bogies by means of two oscillating pivots in each bogie—a development intended to yield stability at speed and optimum use of tractive effort. The excellent performance of these prototypes, which were still in service in December 1980, terminated further evolution of rigid-frame designs like the contemporary 2D2-9100, and opened a new era in French electric locomotive practice. Deliveries of the more powerful series-built CC-7100 version followed, with 58 examples constructed between 1952 and 1955. One member of the class, no CC-7107, earned a place in the record books on 28 March 1955 when it established a world speed record on rails of 331 km/h (205·6 mph) during trials in the Landes. This record was equalled the following day by four-axle prototype no BB-9004 and in 1980 remained unbeaten for conventional rail vehicles.

The second series, nos CC-7144 to CC-7158, have slightly less powerful traction motors (see data) and modified transmission. Until 1976, six were fitted with collector shoes for third rail operations over the "Maurienne" line.

In 1980, the entire class was allocated to SNCF's Sud-Est region, except no CC-7133 which suffered irreparable accident damage in 1977.

Other versions of the design are in service in Algeria (SNTF class 6 BE), Morocco (ONCFM class CC.800), the Netherlands (NS class 1300) and Spain (RENFE classes 276/286—see p 109). Only the Dutch locomotives are for 1·5 kV dc operation. The remainder are 3 kV machines.

Above: No 1314 is one of 16 machines generally similar to the SNCF CC-7100 series supplied to Netherlands Railways (NS) by Alsthom between 1952 and 1956
(*Marcel Vleugels*)

Right: Both Algerian National Railways (SNTF) and Moroccan Railways (ONCFM) operate 3kV dc freight locomotives derived from the CC-7100 design. Bogies are similar to the SNCF CC-14000 series, with nose-suspended traction motors. Seven units were supplied to ONCFM including no CC.803 seen here at Meknès in April 1979
(*Marcel Vleugels*)

France

SNCF class 2D2-9100

Operating system French National Railways (SNCF)
Year introduced 1950
Axle arrangement 2-Do-2
Gauge 1435 mm *(4 ft 8½ in)*
Power supply system 1.5 kV dc
One-hour output 3970 kW *(5325 hp, 5400 ch)*
Continuous output 3590 kW *(4810 hp, 4880 ch)*
Maximum speed 140 km/h *(87 mph)*
Maximum tractive effort 226 kN *(50 800 lbs)*
Continuous tractive effort 183 kN *(41 200 lbs)* at 70.5 km/h *(44 mph)*
Weight in working order 144 tonnes *(142 tons)* total ; 88 tonnes *(87 tons)* adhesive
Length over buffers 18 080 mm *(59 ft 3¾ in)*
Bogie wheelbase 2400 mm *(7 ft 10½ in)*
Rigid wheelbase 2050 + 2050 + 2050 = 6150 mm *(20 ft 2⅛ in)*
Wheel diameter (driving wheels) 1750 mm *(5 ft 8⅞ in)*; (carrying wheels) 1000 mm *(3ft 3⅜ in)*
Traction motors Four dc series-wound CEM type GLM 1033, frame-suspended with Büchli flexible drive
Control Rheostatic
Electric brake None
Builder
  mechanical parts Fives-Lille
  electrical equipment CEM
Number built 35
Number series 2D2-9101 — 2D2-9135

Already outmoded by rapid progress with all-adhesion techniques when they entered service in 1950, the 2D2-9100 is the final example of French rigid-frame express locomotive design. The class was constructed to haul heavy passenger trains of 850 tonnes at speeds up to 140 km/h (87 mph) on the ex-PLM Paris-Lyons main line, on which full electric services were inaugurated in June 1952. The design is a more powerful development of the successful classes 2D2-5400 and 2D2-5500 supplied to the former Ouest and Sud-Ouest companies between 1926 and 1943. The Swiss Brown Boveri company was responsible for the general concept of these earlier series which retained steam locomotive features such as a fixed driving frame with bogies to perform guiding and carrying functions. These principles were retained for the 2D2-9100 series, but post-war track improvements enabled the axle load to be increased from the 20 tonnes of the 2D2-5500 to 22 tonnes to gain maximum adhesive benefit from increased motor output.

The four traction motors are mounted in the locomotive chassis and lateral and vertical movement of the four driven axles is afforded by Büchli flexible transmission. The two centre axles have up to 25 mm sideplay, and each of the two-axle carrying bogies up to 163 mm sideplay, enabling curves of 80 m radius to be negotiated.

In mid-1980, all 35 members of the class remained in service on SNCF's Sud-Est region, where their high power is found useful for a wide range of passenger and express freight duties.

No 2D2-9102 at Dijon in April 1979. A dual-voltage BB-22200 waits in the background *(Marcel Vleugels)*

France

SNCF class BB-9200

Operating system	French National Railways (SNCF)
Year introduced	1957
Axle arrangement	Bo-Bo
Gauge	1435 mm *(4 ft 8½ in)*
Power supply system	1.5 kV dc

Continuous output
(BB-9201-90) 3825 kW *(5130 hp, 5200 ch)* ;
(BB-9291 & 92) 4240 kW *(5680 hp, 5760 ch)*
Maximum speed (BB-9201-90) 160 km/h
(100 mph) ; (BB-9291 & 92) 250 km/h *(155 mph)*
Maximum tractive effort (BB-9201-90) 260 kN
(58 500 lbs) ; (BB-9291 & 92) 160 kN *(36 000 lbs)*
Continuous tractive effort (BB-9201-90) 145 kN
(32 600 lbs) at 93 km/h *(58 mph)* ; (BB-9291 & 92)
95 kN *(21 400 lbs)* at 150 km/h *(93 mph)*
Weight in working order (BB-9201-90) 82 tonnes
(81 tons) ; (BB-9291 & 92) 80 tonnes *(79 tons)*
Length over buffers 16 200 mm *(53 ft 1¾ in)*
Bogie wheelbase 3200 mm *(10 ft 6 in)*
Wheel diameter 1250 mm *(4 ft 1¼ in)*
Traction motors Four dc series-wound CEM type
GLM 931B, fully suspended with cardan shaft drive
Control Rheostatic
Electric brake (BB-9201-90) none ; (BB-9291 & 92)
rheostatic
Builder
mechanical parts Schneider-Jeumont, MTE
electrical equipment Jeumont, CEM, MTE
Number built 92
Number series BB-9201 — BB-9292

**Sixty-two examples of an ac version of the
BB-9200 were built from 1958. Designated
class BB-16000, these rectifier machines have
the same basic body and bogie design as the
dc locomotives. All are based at La Chapelle
depot, Paris, from where they operate Nord
and Ouest region expresses. Pictured here is
no BB-16009.** *(SNCF)*

The BB-9200 was the first French series-built four-axle express design, and represented a remarkable advance in power-to-weight ratio over the 144 tonne 3970 kW (5320 hp) 2D2-9100 introduced just six years previously. Construction of the class was based on experience gained with four highly successful 1·5 kV dc prototypes supplied by French and Swiss builders between 1952 and 1954 and numbered BB-9001-9004. The last of these, no BB-9004, jointly with no CC-7107 (see p. 38) attained a world record speed of 331 km/h (205·6 mph) during the Morcenx trials in March 1955, and has been retained for display at the French Railway Museum at Mulhouse.

The production locomotives incorporate the control equipment and mechanical features of the second two prototypes, with traction motors derived from the Brown Boveri machines fitted to nos BB-9001 and 9002, which were found to yield tractive effort characteristics more favourable for the sustained high speed running required on the Toulouse and Bordeaux main lines. Mechanically, the design incorporated features later to be adopted for other classes, such as Jacquemin bogies, and characteristics of the BB-9200 are to be found in the single-phase BB-12000 and BB-16000 series, the dual-frequency class BB-20100 units and the dual-voltage BB-25100/25150/25200 family. Forty examples of an improved version of the class for 1·5 kV dc operation, class BB-9300, entered service between 1968 and 1970.

From 1966, six units, nos BB-9278/81/82/88/91/92, were specially modified for operation at speeds up to 200 km/h (125 mph), notably with the *Capitole* express, and repainted in a red and grey livery. The last two of these were experimentally re-geared for a maximum speed of 250 km/h (155 mph). In 1978/79 the last five of these units, along with no BB-9280, were re-equipped for push-pull operation and repainted in *Corail* colour scheme for Paris-Orléans-Tours-Poitiers services. No BB-9278 was the first of the class to emerge from overhaul in 1979 finished in a fresh green, white and yellow livery devoid of the original rust-attracting metallic embellishments.

In March 1980 the entire class was operating in the Sud-Ouest region from Paris Sud-Ouest and Bordeaux depots.

**Dual-current (1·5 kV dc/25 kV ac 50 Hz)
express and mixed-traffic derivatives of the
BB-9200 have been evolved by combining in
one design separate control systems for each
supply voltage. No BB-25111, photographed
at Chalindrey in September 1976, belongs to
a series of 25 130 km/h BB-25100 mixed-traffic**
units allocated to the Est region. The
45-strong BB-25150 class is generally similar,
as are the 51 machines forming class
BB-25200. The latter units are geared for 160
km/h running. *(Yves Steenebruggen)*

**No BB-9269 at Marseilles with a Toulouse
express in December 1976** *(Marc Dahlström)*

France

SNCF class BB-12000

Operating system French National Railways (SNCF)
Year introduced 1954
Axle arrangement Bo-Bo
Gauge 1435 mm *(4 ft 8½ in)*
Power supply system 25 kV ac 50 Hz
One-hour output 2650 kW *(3550 hp, 3600 ch)*
Continuous output 2470 kW *(3315 hp, 3360 ch)*
Maximum speed 120 km/h *(75 mph)*
Maximum tractive effort 255 kN *(57 400 lbs)*
Continuous tractive effort 186 kN *(41 900 lbs)* at
47.5 km/h *(29½ mph)*
Weight in working order (BB-12001-5) 86 tonnes
(85 tons); (BB-12006-14) 85 tonnes *(84 tons)*;
(BB-12015-148) 84 tonnes *(83 tons)*
Length over buffers 15 200 mm *(49 ft 10⅜ in)*
Bogie wheelbase 3200 mm *(10 ft 6 in)*
Wheel diameter 1250 mm *(4 ft 1¼ in)*
Traction motors Four dc series-wound type SW-435,
fully suspended with cardan drive
Control h.t. tap-changer
Electric brake None
Builder
 mechanical parts Alsthom, MTE
 electrical equipment MTE, SW
Number built 148
Number series BB-12001 — BB-12148

These mixed traffic rectifier machines were constructed from 1954 to 1961 for the pioneer Valenciennes-Thionville 50 Hz electrification and its subsequent extensions. Body construction features a single, central driver's cab flanked by bonnets housing control apparatus and auxiliary machinery. Access to this equipment is by means of removeable panels which are locked automatically while the pantograph is raised. The main transformer is located beneath the cab and the two pantographs are mounted on a framework extending forward and aft of the cab roof. The Jacquemin bogies have flexible cardan drives and are derived from those of dc prototypes BB-9003 and BB-9004.

The four SW-435 traction motors are 675 V machines permanently connected in parallel. They are fed rectified current via mercury arc (ignitron) or silicon semi-conductor equipment. Auxiliaries are powered by an Arno asynchronous three-phase convertor group.

Livery is green with high visibility yellow warning panels on the nose ends.

SNCF also operates the mechanically similar BB-13000 series. These units have ac motors and with a continuous rating of 2000 kW (2680 hp) are less powerful than their rectifier counterparts. Fifty-three examples were built. Luxembourg Railways (CFL) also have in service a version of the BB-12000. Designated class 3600, 20 were supplied by Alsthom, MTE and SW in 1958-9.

SNCF class BB-12000 no BB-12037 at Velosnes in July 1977 *(Yves Steenebruggen)*

Above: The BB-13000 series, 53 of which were constructed between 1954 and 1961, is mechanically similar to the BB-12000 but has single-phase commutator traction motors. No BB-13005 is the subject of this early view. (*MTE*)

Below: Luxembourg Railways (CFL) class 3600 is based on the SNCF BB-12000 design. Wearing the smart CFL maroon and yellow livery, no 3608 was photographed at Luxembourg in April 1975 (*ILA Günther Barths*)

France

SNCF class CC-14100

Operating system French National Railways (SNCF)
Year introduced 1954
Axle arrangement Co-Co
Gauge 1435 mm *(4 ft 8½ in)*
Power supply system 25 kV ac 50 Hz
Continuous output 1860 kW *(2495 hp, 2525 ch)*
Max speed 60 km/h *(37 mph)*
Maximum tractive effort 412 kN *(92 600 lbs)*
Continuous tractive effort 228 kN *(51 200 lbs)* at 28.5 km/h *(18 mph)*
Weight in working order 127 tonnes *(125 tons)*
Length over buffers 18 890 mm *(61 ft 11¾ in)*
Bogie wheelbase 2335+2335=4670 mm *(15 ft 3⅞ in)*
Wheel diameter 1100 mm *(3 ft 7¼ in)*
Traction motors Six dc series-wound Alsthom type TA 636, axle-suspended with resilient drive
Control Field regulation of main generator excitation
Electric brake Regenerative
Builder
 mechanical parts Alsthom, Fives-Lille
 electrical equipment Alsthom, CEM
Number built 102
Number series CC-14101 — CC-14202

The Valenciennes-Thionville electrification of the 1950s in north-east France was one of the first major schemes to employ successfully industrial frequency power supply, and the results obtained contributed to the subsequent adoption of this system as a world standard. Heavy coal and mineral traffic demanded freight locomotives whose tractive effort was more important than speed, and two six-axle designs were developed. The more numerous and successful were the class CC-14100 synchronous/dc convertor machines, in which a synchronous motor drives two separately excited dc generators each feeding current to three traction motors connected in parallel. The constant power characteristics of this system have proved especially suitable for hauling loads of up to 1800 tonnes at speeds limited to 60 km/h (37 mph). Wheel-slip is limited by the electrical coupling of the traction motors, and the locomotives have earned the reputation of being simple to drive. Regenerative braking is provided. The characteristic body configuration ensures ease of access for maintenance of the convertor group and other electrical equipment located in the bonnet housings fore and aft of the central driving cab.

Although rather handicapped in present-day terms by their limited speed, most of the class remain in service in north-east France, along with a few survivors of the 20-strong CC-14000 class rotary phase-convertor units with three-phase traction motors.

Final Example of SNCF class CC-14100, no C-14202 at Longuyon in July 1977
(Yves Steenebruggen)

France

SNCF class BB-15000

Operating system French National Railways (SNCF)
Year introduced 1971
Axle arrangement B-B
Gauge 1435 mm *(4 ft 8½ in)*
Power supply system 25 kV ac 50 Hz
One-hour output 4400 kW *(5900 hp, 5980 ch)*
Continuous output 4300 kW *(5760 hp, 5845 ch)*
Maximum speed 160 km/h *(100 mph)*
Maximum tractive effort 294 kN *(66 100 lbs)*
Continuous tractive effort 135 kN *(30 400 lbs)* at 106.5 km/h *(66 mph)*
Weight in working order 90 tonnes *(89 tons)*
Length over buffers 17 480 mm *(57 ft 4⅛ in)*
Bogie wheelbase 2800 mm *(9 ft 2¼ in)*
Wheel diameter 1250 mm *(4 ft 1¼ in)*
Traction motors Two dc series-wound Alsthom type TAB 674, fully suspended with cardan shaft drive
Control Thyristor
Electric brake Regenerative
Builder
  mechanical parts Alsthom, MTE
  electrical equipment Alsthom, MTE
Number built 65
Number series BB-15001 — BB-15065

The most modern electric locomotives in the SNCF fleet are a family of advanced designs built in ac, dc and dual-voltage versions but sharing a common mechanical concept. The thyristor controlled BB-15000 for 25 kV ac operation was the first to appear, in 1971, and incorporated MTE-designed single-motor bogies derived from those of the BB-67400 diesel-electrics, with a body structure based on the earlier CC-6500 and CC-72000 machines. Since their introduction on the Paris-Strasbourg route, where they supplanted the BB-16000 series, the class has earned a reputation for outstanding reliability and low maintenance requirements.

Unlike several other modern SNCF designs, there is no facility for changing gear ratio, although the BB-15000s are considered mixed-traffic machines. The control equipment enables speed to be maintained at a level determined by the driver, irrespective of line conditions and trailing load. Similarly, traction motor current can be held at a pre-set level. Normal service braking is regenerative, but rheostatic emergency braking is also provided. Although nominally restricted to 160 km/h (100 mph), the design is capable of 200 km/h (125 mph), although cab signalling would be necessary for speeds of this order.

The first five members of the class were turned out by Alsthom in a metallic green livery. Subsequent examples are finished in a silver, red, orange and grey intended to match *Grand Confort* rolling stock. No BB-15006 *Metz* was the first locomotive to benefit from SNCF's naming policy in June 1973, and other units have been similarly treated. No BB-15007, renumbered BB-7003, has served as a test-bed for the development of chopper control equipment for the 1·5 kV dc BB-7200 version, and was scheduled to be further rebuilt in 1981 as a 25 kV prototype with three-phase motors. No BB-15063 has undergone suspension modifications in an attempt to improve the export potential of the design to railways with more critical permanent way. The other two versions of the class in SNCF service are:
 – the BB-7200 chopper controlled design for 1·5 kV dc operation, 210 examples of which were in service or on order by late 1980. In addition, 48 similar machines were ordered in 1979 by Netherlands Railways (NS class 1600) for delivery from January 1981, following NS trials with no BB-7003.
 – the dual-voltage (1·5 kV dc/25 kV ac 50 Hz) class BB-22200, also chopper controlled, with 150 on order or in service in 1980.

No BB-15021 *Château-Thierry* **at La Ferté-sous-Jouarre with a Colmar-Paris express in March 1978** *(Marc Dahlström)*

The first five BB-15000s are finished in a simple livery of metallic green and white. No BB-15001 is seen at Charleville in April 1976 (*Yves Steenebruggen*)

Chopper control is used in the 1·5 kV dc BB-7200, introduced in 1976. No BB-7219 prepares to leave Paris (Gare de Lyon) (*J L Paris/MTE*)

The dual-current derivative of the BB-15000 is classified BB-22200 and appeared in 1977. In December of that year no BB-22216 waits at Nice with the Milan-Avignon *Ligure* TEE (*Marc Dahlström*)

France

SNCF class BB-165000

Operating system French National Railways (SNCF)
Year introduced 1958
Axle arrangement B-B
Gauge 1435 mm *(4 ft 8½ in)*
Power supply system 25 kV ac 50 Hz
One-hour output 2650 kW *(3550 hp, 3600 ch)*
Continuous output 2580 kW *(3455 hp, 3505 ch)*
Maximum speed 150/90 km/h *(93/56 mph)*
Maximum tractive effort (low gear) 324 kN *(72 800 lbs)* ; (high gear) 192 kN *(43 000 lbs)*
Continuous tractive effort (low gear) 188 kN *(42 300 lbs)* at 48 km/h *(30 mph)* ; (high gear) 111 kN *(24 900 lbs)* at 82 km/h *(51 mph)*
Weight in working order 71-74 tonnes *(70-73 tons)*
Length over buffers 14 400 mm *(47 ft 3 in)*
Bogie wheelbase 1608 mm *(5 ft 3¼ in)*
Wheel diameter 1100 mm *(3 ft 7½ in)*
Traction motors Two dc series-wound Alsthom type TOA-646-A1, fully suspended with Alsthom flexible drive
Control h.t. tap-changer
Electric brake Regenerative on Nos. BB-16656-84 & 16686-16750 only
Builder
  mechanical parts Alsthom
  electrical equipment Alsthom
Number built 294
Number series BB-16501 — BB-16794

Two important features of contemporary French motive power practice first appeared in the BB-16500 lightweight mixed-traffic series, introduced in 1958 for service on 25 kV ac lines of SNCF's Est and Nord regions. The first was the employment of single-motor bogies in a modern design, offering excellent adhesion, low power-to-weight ratio and reduced motor maintenance. The second was the provision of double-reduction gearing which enabled the character of the locomotive to be changed in a few minutes from a 150 km/h express unit to a powerful 90 km/h freight machine. A measure of the satisfactory performance of the design is that no less than 294 were constructed between 1958 and 1964, making the class the largest in the SNCF electric locomotive fleet. Furthermore, the 458 examples of the BB-25500 family (see following entry) are a direct development of the BB-16500.

The main locomotive superstructure comprises three separate sections plus cabs. Each section is removeable, allowing free access to equipment. On nos BB-16501-655, body suspension is by means of oscillating pivots derived from the CC-7100 series (see p 38). The rest of the class have a pendular suspension employing articulated links at each corner of the bogies. The original mercury arc rectifiers of nos BB-16501-534, and 537-539 have been progressively replaced by the silicon diode variety. Later units have either excitron or silicon rectifiers. The class is equipped for multiple-unit/push-pull operation and 94 units have regenerative braking.

No BB-16700 has been modified to accept automatic couplers, somewhat changing its front-end appearance, although it is not intended to treat other class members in this way.

SNCF class BB-16500 no BB-16692 *(SNCF)*

France

SNCF class BB-25500

Operating system French National Railways (SNCF)
Year introduced 1964
Axle arrangement B-B
Gauge 1435 mm $(4 ft 8\frac{1}{2})$ in
Power supply system (dual-current) 1.5 kV dc;
25 kV ac 50 Hz
Continuous output
(BB-25501-30) 2610 kW *(3500 hp, 3545 ch)*;
(BB-25531-694) 2940 kW *(3940 hp, 3995 ch)*
Maximum speed 150/90 km/h *(93/56 mph)*
Maximum tractive effort (low gear) 329 kN
(73 850 lbs); (high gear) 200 kN *(45 000 lbs)*
Continuous tractive effort (low gear) 186 kN
(41 900 lbs) at 48 km/h *(30 mph)*; (high gear)
112 kN *(25 100 lbs)* at 82 km/h *(51 mph)*
(tractive effort figures apply to nos. BB-25531-694
operating under 25 kV ac 50 Hz)
Weight in working order 77-80 tonnes
(76-79 tons)
Length over buffers (BB-25501-44) 14 700 mm
(48 ft $2\frac{3}{4}$ in); (BB-25545-87) 14 940 mm *(49 ft
$0\frac{1}{8}$ in)*; (BB-25588-694) 15 570 mm *(51 ft 1 in)*
Bogie wheelbase 1608 mm *(5 ft $3\frac{1}{4}$ in)*
Wheel diameter 1100 mm *(3 ft $7\frac{1}{4}$ in)*
Traction motors Two dc series-wound Alsthom type
TAB-660-A1 (1305 kW) or TAB-660-B (1470 kW),
fully suspended with Alsthom flexible drive
Control (ac operation) h.t. tap-changer; (dc operation)
rheostatic
Electric brake Rheostatic
Builder
 mechanical parts Alsthom
 electrical equipment Alsthom
Number built 194
Number series BB-25501 — BB-25694

Development of the dual-voltage BB-25500 multi-purpose series followed a traffic requirement for a locomotive capable of unhindered operation in those districts where single-phase ac electrification met earlier 1·5 kV dc schemes. This resulted in a highly successful design, later to form the basis of a large and important motive power family in the SNCF fleet. Prototype for the class was class BB-16500 no BB-16540, experimentally converted for dual-voltage operation and numbered BB-20004. This machine incorporated separate current collection and power control equipment for each system in the form of transformer/tap-changer/rectifier for 25 kV ac 50 Hz and traditional resistance control for 1·5 kV dc. These features are retained in the BB-25500, along with the single-motor bogie and dual gear ratio of the earlier design. The sectional body construction of the BB-16500 was eschewed in favour of a stronger monocoque bodyshell. Conversion of single-phase voltage to dc is by means of silicon diode rectifiers, and the presence of resistances for dc control allows provision of rheostatic braking. The locomotives are equipped for multiple-unit/push-pull operation.

The provision of separate control equipment for ac and dc systems simplified subsequent adaptation of the basic design to a straight dc or single-phase machine by incorporating only the apparatus appropriate to the type of power supply. This led to the introduction of these derivatives:
- SNCF class BB-8500 for 1·5 kV dc, of which 146 have been built.
- SNCF class BB-17000 for 25 kV ac 50 Hz operation. Apart from the 105 units constructed for SNCF, 15 similar machines have been supplied to Turkish State Railways (TCDD class E40—see p 132).
- the dual-frequency (25 kV ac 50 Hz/15 kV ac 16⅔ Hz) SNCF class BB-20200, 13 of which operate border traffic into West Germany and Switzerland.

From no BB-25588 the layout of the bodyside ventilation louvres was revised, as seen here on no BB-25674 at Nice in December 1976 with a local for Cannes (*Marc Dahlström*)

The 1·5 kV dc BB-8500 design was created simply by omitting ac power equipment from the dual-current BB-25500 model. Two of the final batch of this series, nos BB-8589 and BB-8611, were photographed operating in multiple at Savigny sur Orge in June 1975 (*Marc Dahlström*)

Left: No BB-25506 is one of the first 30 units, which are rated continuously at 2610 kW: subsequent examples have an output of 2940 kW. The wrap-around windscreens were fitted to nos BB-25501-14 only (*SNCF*)

Class BB-17000 is the ac-only version of the BB-25500. These units are used extensively on Paris commuter traffic, as illustrated here by no BB-17056 at Paris (Gare St Lazare) with a push-pull train formed of modern double-deck stock (*Ken Harris*)

France

SNCF class CC-40100

Operating system French National Railways (SNCF)
Year introduced 1964
Axle arrangement C-C
Gauge 1435 mm *(4 ft 8½ in)*
Power supply system (four-current) 1.5 kV dc;
3 kV dc; 15 kV ac 16⅔ Hz; 25 kV ac 50 Hz
Continuous output (CC-40101-40103) 3670 kW
(4920 hp, 4985 ch); (CC-40104-40110) 4480 kW
(6005 hp, 6085 ch)
Maximum speed
(CC-40101-40104) 240/160 km/h *(150/100 mph)*;
(CC-40105-40110) 220/180 km/h *(137/112 mph)*
Maximum tractive effort (low gear) 200 kN
(45 000 lbs); (high gear) 150 kN *(33 800 lbs)*
Continuous tractive effort (low gear) 118 kN
(26 500 lbs) at 110 km/h *(68 mph)*; (high gear)
84 kN *(19 000 lbs)* at 153.5 km/h *(95½ mph)*
(tractive effort figures apply to nos. CC-40105-40110)
Weight in working order 108 tonnes *(107 tons)*
Length over buffers 22 030 mm *(72 ft 3⅜ in)*
Bogie wheelbase 1608+1608=3216 mm
(10 ft 5⅝ in)
Wheel diameter 1100 mm *(3 ft 7¼ in)*
Traction motors Two double-armature dc series-
wound Alsthom type TDQ657A1/TDQ662A1/
TDQ662B1, fully suspended with Alsthom flexible
drive
Control Rheostatic
Electric brake Rheostatic
Builder
 mechanical parts Alsthom
 electrical equipment Alsthom, Jeumont
Number built 10
Number series CC-40101 — CC-40110

The four-current CC-40100 series was the first locomotive design to function at full power on all four major European electrification systems, and at the time of their introduction in 1964 embodied many innovative features. The class was developed to meet demands for increased capacity and reduced journey times on *TEE* and other international services, notably on the Paris-Brussels-Amsterdam route, but also into West Germany.

The Alsthom lightweight steel body, strikingly styled by the French industrial artist Paul Arzens, meets all European loading gauge requirements and was conceived to harmonise with new TEE stainless steel rolling stock. The aerodynamic reverse-raked frontal treatment was conceived to protect the crew from glare and to enhance visibility. The body is carried on two three-axle bogies each powered by one spring-borne twin-armature traction motor via intermediate gearing. The alternative gear ratios of nos CC-40101—40104 (see data) are designed to be engaged while the locomotive is in motion. Gearing of the remainder of the class can only be changed in workshops. Separate pantographs are provided for each power supply system, with protective devices to guard electrical equipment against incorrect pantograph selection. In ac working, a fixed-ratio transformer output is converted by a silicon bridge rectifier to dc for control by resistances and motor groupings. The six units forming the second batch nos CC-40105—40110, were delivered in 1969-70 and are equipped with more powerful (see data) Alsthom TDQ662B1 traction motors following the successful application of similar motors to no CC-40104. These later machines incorporate other detail differences.

All ten units, now named after French towns and cities, are based at La Chapelle depot, Paris, from where they operate a variety of international and Nord region internal services.

In 1973 six machines similar to nos CC-40105—40110 were placed in service by Belgian National Railways (SNCB class 1800).

Belgian National Railways (SNCB/NMBS) operates a series of six four-current locomotives similar to later machines of the SNCF series. Class 1800 no 1801 was photographed at Liège in March 1980 *(Marcel Vleugels)*

SNCF class CC-40100 no CC-40109 *Cannes* taking current from the Belgian 3 kV dc network at Marche les Dames in January 1979 *(Yves Steenebruggen)*

Germany (Democratic Republic)

Operating system German State Railways (DR)
Year introduced 1962
Axle arrangement Bo-Bo
Gauge 1435 mm *(4 ft 8½ in)*
Power supply system 15 kV ac 16⅔ Hz
One-hour output
(242 001 & 002) 2760 kW *(3700 hp, 3750 ch)*;
(242 003-292) 2920 kW *(3915 hp, 3970 ch)*
Continuous output
(242 001 & 002) 2600 kW *(3485 hp, 3535 ch)*;
(242 003-292) 2740 kW *(3670 hp, 3725 ch)*
Maximum speed 100 km/h *(62 mph)*
Maximum tractive effort 246 kN *(55 200 lbs)*
One-hour tractive effort (242 003-292) 141 kN
(31 800 lbs) at 72 km/h *(45 mph)*
Weight in working order 82.5 tonnes *(81.5 tons)*
Length over buffers 16 260 mm *(53 ft 4⅛ in)*
Bogie wheelbase 3500 mm *(11 ft 5¾ in)*
Wheel diameter 1350 mm *(4ft 5⅛ in)*
Traction motors Four single-phase series-wound,
axle-suspended with resilient axle drive
Control l.t. switchgear with precision control
Electric brake None
Builder
 mechanical parts VEB LEW ''Hans Beimler''
 electrical equipment VEB LEW ''Hans Beimler''
Number built 292
Number series 242 001 — 242 292

No 242 222 at **Altenburg** *(E. Barnes)*

**The 242 series is derived from the less
numerous class 211 passenger design and
differs mainly in gear ratio. No 211 041 is
seen here beneath the impressive roof at
Leipzig Hbf** *(John Chalcraft)*

DR class 242

DR's class 242 mixed-traffic design was developed from the 120 km/h (75 mph) class 211 passenger series, prototypes of which appeared in 1961. The two classes are regarded as one basic design, principally differing in gear ratio and brake equipment, and represent the first new electric locomotive construction for DR following the post-war partition of Germany. Assembly of both types was carried out at the former AEG works at Hennigsdorf, with deliveries proceeding simultaneously as DR electrification spread. Class 211 is considerably less numerous, with a total of 90 units built. The lower gearing of the 242 series has proved more flexible operationally, and on a system virtually devoid of electric multiple-units, they handle a wide variety of passenger traffic as well as freight.

The first series-built machines appeared in 1963 with a slight power increase over the two prototypes supplied by LEW during the previous year. Units up to no 242 022 are equipped for push-pull working. Later class members lack this facility but incorporate electrical improvements based on earlier service experience. They also bear minor visual differences, including the provision of six ventilation louvres on each side of the body rather than four. The protective fairings below the bufferbeams of the first 22 were subsequently removed.

Earlier deliveries were painted olive green and black, with terra-cotta bogies. This has been replaced by the present standard DR livery for main line locomotives of red with a broad white band. Before DR's adoption of a computer-based numbering system, the class was designated E42 and numbered in a series starting with E42 001.

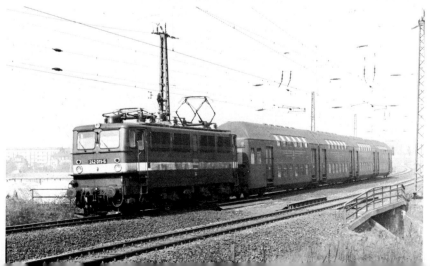

**Nos 242 001-022 are push-pull fitted to
operate with double-deck suburban stock of
the type seen here at Radebeul headed by no
242 011** *(John Chalcraft)*

Germany (Democratic Republic)

Operating system German State Railways (DR)
Year introduced 1974
Axle arrangement Co-Co
Gauge 1435 mm *(4 ft 8½ in)*
Power supply system 15 kV ac 16⅔ Hz
One-hour output 5400 kW *(7235 hp, 7340 ch)*
Continuous output 5140 kW *(6890 hp, 6985 ch)*
Maximum speed 125 km/h *(78 mph)*
Maximum tractive effort 380 kN *(85 500 lbs)*
One-hour tractive effort 192 kN *(43 200 lbs)* at
  100 km/h *(62 mph)*
Weight in working order 120 tonnes *(118 tons)*
Length over buffers 19 600 mm *(64 ft 3⅝ in)*
Bogie wheelbase 2000 + 2500 = 4500 mm
  (14 ft 9⅛ in)
Wheel diameter 1250 mm *(4 ft 1¼ in)*
Traction motors Six single-phase series-wound, with
  LEW conical ring spring drive
Control h.t. tap-changer with thyristor transition
  control
Electric brake Rheostatic
Builder
  mechanical parts VEB LEW ''Hans Beimler''
  electrical equipment VEB LEW ''Hans Beimler''
Number built 113
Number series 250 001 — 250 113

DR class 250

An operational requirement during the 1970s to increase train speeds and weights beyond the capacity of the four-axle 211 and 242 units resulted in the joint development by DR and LEW of the powerful class 250 design. An intensive test programme with the first three machines, which served as prototypes, preceded series production in 1977. The class is intended for heavy or express goods traffic and for more exacting passenger train requirements, especially over graded routes. Both mechanical and electrical design has been conceived to offer minimum maintenance needs. A form of electronic control employing thyristors between main running notches provides near-stepless regulation of the six 900 kW traction motors, and improves tractive characteristics. Main locomotive braking is rheostatic, separately excited and blended automatically with the friction brake, with a capacity of 2500 kW. Cab design shows considerable improvements over earlier LEW locomotives, with good visibility, sound insulation and access via the machinery compartment to avoid draughts.

Series construction ended in 1979, when it was reported that one unit, no 250 002, was engaged in 160 km/h (100 mph) trials expected to lead to development of a high speed design derived from this class.

DR class 250 no 250 001, first of the three prototype machines. These bear minor external detail differences to the main series, including location of the central headlight above the cab windows rather than below. Production locomotives are also equipped with a bogie-mounted snowplough/pilot. (DR)

Germany (Federal Republic)

Operating system German Federal Railways (DB)
Year introduced Prototype — 1965; main series — 1970
Axle arrangement Co-Co
Gauge 1435 mm *(4 ft 8½ in)*
Power supply system 15 kV ac 16⅔ Hz
One-hour output (103 001-004) 6420 kW *(8600 hp, 8725 ch)*; (remainder) 7780 kW *(10 425 hp, 10 570 ch)*
Continuous output (103 001-004) 5950 kW *(7975 hp, 8085 ch)*; (remainder) 7440 kW *(9970 hp, 10 110 ch)*
Maximum speed 200 km/h *(125 mph)* except 103 118 which is geared for 250 km/h *(155 mph)*
Maximum tractive effort 314 kN *(70 500 lbs)*
Continuous tractive effort (103 001-004) 107 kN *(24 000 lbs)* at 200 km/h *(125 mph)*; (remainder) 140 kN *(31 500 lbs)* at 191 km/h *(119 mph)*
Weight in working order (103 001-004) 110 tonnes *(108 tons)*; (remainder) 116 tonnes *(114 tons)*
Length over buffers (103 001-004, 101-215) 19 500 mm *(63 ft 11¾ in)*; (103 216-245) 20 200 mm *(66 ft 3¼ in)*
Bogie wheelbase 2250 + 2250 = 4500 mm *(14 ft 9⅛ in)*
Wheel diameter 1250 mm *(4 ft 1¼ in)*
Traction motors Six single-phase commutator, frame-suspended with SSW flexible cardan drive (103 001 & 003 have Henschel spring drive)
Control h.t. tap-changer
Electric brake Rheostatic
Builder
  mechanical parts Henschel, Krauss-Maffei, Krupp
  electrical equipment SSW, AEG-Telefunken, BBC
Number built 149
Number series 103 001 — 103 004; 103 101 — 103 245

DB class 103

Developed for high speed operation of principal domestic and international passenger services, including TEE traffic, the class 103 locomotives are the fastest and most powerful in the DB fleet. Rheinstahl-Henschel and Siemens cooperated with DB's Central Design Office in Munich to produce a pilot series of four machines (nos 103 001-004) in 1965 in time for the Munich International Transport Exhibition. On this occasion, regular runs were staged at 200 km/h (125 mph) between Munich and Augsburg with the *Blauer Enzian* to form Europe's first advertised service at this speed.

For the first time in a DB design, automatic speed control was adopted, allowing a pre-determined speed to be maintained electronically irrespective of line conditions. Cab signalling was also fitted. Three-axle bogies were used to keep axle-loads within tolerable limits, with an alternative Henschel spring drive on two of the four prototypes for comparative evaluation. Body construction consists of a fabricated under-frame, with a superstructure of three removeable lightweight steel sections between cab ends. The striking air-smoothed body form was evolved after wind-tunnel tests. Both prototype and series built machines are finished in a red and cream livery derived from that of TEE stock.

After a long test programme and DB misgivings about track wear with regular high-speed running, series deliveries started in 1970. These locomotives, numbered from 103 101, are considerably more powerful than the prototypes (see data), with a remarkable ten minute rating of 10 400 kW (13 950 hp). One of the series, no 103 118, was delivered with modifications suitable for operation at 250 km/h (155 mph) and in 1972 achieved a speed of 265 km/h (164·5 mph) during trials. Locomotives numbered from 103 216 have larger cabs, slightly increasing overall length (see data).

Heavy track wear led DB to abandon 200 km/h running in 1967 but this decision was reversed in 1977 when certain stretches of line, including Munich-Augsburg, were approved for speeds of this order, permitting the 103s again to operate to their design capability.

An early view of the first of the four prototype 103s, bearing its original number E03 001

One of the series machines, no 103 144, at Augsburg Central in July 1979 with an IC service. A different arrangement of the ventilation louvres distinguishes production locomotives from the prototypes *(Benno Bickel)*

Germany (Federal Republic)

Operating system German Federal Railways (DB)
Year introduced 110.1—1956; 110.3—1963
Axle arrangement Bo-Bo
Gauge 1435 mm *(4 ft 8½ in)*
Power supply system 15 kV ac 16⅔ Hz
One-hour output 3700 kW *(4960 hp, 5030 ch)*
Continuous output 3620 kW *(4850 hp, 4920 ch)*
Maximum speed 150 km/h *(93 mph)*
Maximum tractive effort 275 kN *(61 800 lbs)*
Continuous tractive effort 107 kN *(24 000 lbs)* at 123 km/h *(76 mph)*
Weight in working order (class 110.1) 86.4 tonnes *(85 tons)*; (class 110.3) 86 tonnes *(84¾ tons)*
Length over buffers
  (class 110.1) 16 490 mm *(54 ft 1¼ in)*;
  (class 110.3) 16 440 mm *(53 ft 11¼ in)*
Bogie wheelbase 3400 mm *(11 ft 1⅞ in)*
Wheel diameter 1250 mm *(4 ft 1¼ in)*
Traction motors Four single-phase commutator, fully suspended with rubber spring drive
Control h.t. tap-changer
Electric brake Rheostatic
Builder
  mechanical parts Henschel, Krauss-Maffei, Krupp
  electrical equipment AEG, BBC, SSW
Number built (class 110.1) 164; (class 110.3) 198
Number series (class 110.1) 110 101 — 110 264;
  (class 110.3) 110 288 — 110 307, 110 313 —
  110 484, 110 505 — 110 510

Right: Class 110.1 no 110 103 near Kircheon in October 1978 *(Friedrich Franz)*

Below left: Class 110.3 no 110 365 at Munich's Freimann works in March 1976. The unflattering embellishment to the cab front was applied experimentally to increase the perception of track staff to the approach of the locomotive *(Friedrich Franz)*

Below right: DB's 112 series was developed directly from the 110.1 design for operation on prestige TEE services. Six were introduced in 1962 as class E10¹² and featured 160 km/h gearing, aerodynamic body profile and TEE red and beige livery. Twenty-five similar units followed, including no 112 309, seen here at Aachen. By the time this photo was taken, DB had removed wind-resistant fairings below the bufferbeams which extended just beyond the cab door *(John Chalcraft)*

DB classes 110.1 and 110.3

Introduced in 1956 as class E10, the 110.1 series was the first modern post-war design introduced by DB and was intended for principal passenger services. Development of the class followed the introduction in 1952/3 of five prototype locomotives (nos E10 001-005) incorporating various forms of control equipment and transmission. Extensive trials with these machines led to the appointment of Krauss-Maffei and SSW as principal contractors for the main series. Construction was shared by Henschel and Krupp, with electrical equipment also provided by AEG and BBC.

In 1963, the E10³ (now 110.3) variant appeared and the original series was reclassified E10¹. Performance and equipment of this later series is similar to the 110.1 but the body design has a cleaner and more aero-dynamic treatment. Two of these units, nos E10 299 and E10 300 (now 110 299 & 300) were regeared experimentally for 200 km/h (125 mph) running in 1963. During the previous year, six locomotives were modified before delivery for 160 km/h (100 mph) running on TEE services and were appropriately painted red and beige. Designated E10¹² and numbered E10 1265-1270, these were joined eventually by 25 similarly adapted units to form DB's present class 112. Gaps occurring in the class 110.3 number series are those originally allocated to the 112s.

The important class 139/140 development (see p 58) of this design appeared in 1956.

Germany (Federal Republic)

Operating system German Federal Railways (DB)
Year introduced 1974
Axle arrangement Bo-Bo
Gauge 1435 mm *(4 ft 8½ in)*
Power supply system 15 kV ac 16⅔ Hz
One-hour output 3700 kW *(4960 hp, 5030 ch)*
Continuous output 3620 kW *(4850 hp, 4920 ch)*
Maximum speed 160 km/h *(100 mph)*
Maximum tractive effort 280 kN *(63 000 lbs)*
One-hour tractive effort 129 kN *(29 100 lbs)* at 120 km/h *(75 mph)*
Weight in working order 83 tonnes *(82 tons)*
Length over buffers 16 750 mm *(54 ft 11½ in)*
Bogie wheelbase 3400 mm *(11 ft 1⅞ in)*
Wheel diameter *1250 mm (4 ft 1¼ in)*
Traction motors Four single-phase commutator SSW type WB 372-22, frame-suspended with rubber spring drive
Control h.t. tapchanger
Electric brake Rheostatic
Builder
  mechanical parts Krauss-Maffei, Henschel, Krupp
  electrical equipment Siemens, AEG-Telefunken, BBC
Number built 210 (including units on order in January 1981)
Number series 111 001 — 111 210

DB class 111

DB's 111 series is a modern passenger design based on the well tried classes 110.1 and 110.3, retaining such features as traction motors, transmission and tap-changers, but incorporating improvements based on experience and technical advances. Siemens and Krauss-Maffei were responsible respectively for development of electrical and mechanical parts of the design. The first unit was delivered in December 1974.

Electrical features include automatic regulation of running speed and braking power. The separately-excited rheostatic brake has a continuous rating of 2000 kW and is blended automatically with the friction brake. Provision is made for push-pull operation and for the control of two units in multiple. Bogie design is completely new, with secondary suspension of the coil spring type. Ergonomic considerations influenced layout of the cab equipment. Central access is provided from the cabs to the machinery compartment to avoid the cramped side layout of the class 110 family, which has side corridors.

Originally designed for a maximum speed of 150 km/h (93 mph), the entire class was approved for 160 km/h (100 mph) running in 1979 to provide adequate motive power for recently introduced and improved IC (inter-city) services. This followed service trials with the forty locomotives of the second batch, nos 110 071-110.

Units numbered from 111 111 to 111 188, distinguishable by an orange and beige livery rather than blue and cream, are equipped with a modified form of push-pull apparatus (type ZWS). They are intended for Rhine-Ruhr *S-Bahn* suburban operation with lightweight three-car train-sets, the driving trailer of which has a cab with similar controls to those of the locomotive. Unit no 111 084 in 1980 was equipped with tap-changer equipment of modified design.

During the closing months of 1979 the number of units ordered by DB was increased from 178 to 210, and by the autumn of 1980 some 150 were in operation. Deliveries to DB are scheduled to end in December 1983.

DB class 111 no 111 038 at Munich Hbf with an IC working in July 1979 *(Benno Bickel)*

Class 111s from no 111 111 to 111 188 bear a special orange and beige livery to harmonise with *S-Bahn* stock and are fitted with a specially adapted form of multiple-unit control. No 111 138 is seen at Rheydt in April 1980 *(ILA Günther Barths)*

Germany (Federal Republic)

Operating system German Federal Railways (DB)
Year introduced 1935
Axle arrangement 1-Do-1
Gauge 1435 mm *(4 ft 8½ in)*
Power supply system 15 kV ac 16⅔ Hz
One-hour output 3180 kW *(4260 hp, 4320 ch)*
Continuous output 2930 kW *(3925 hp, 3980 ch)*
Maximum speed 150 km/h *(93 mph)*
Maximum tractive effort 206 kN *(46 300 lbs)*
Continuous tractive effort 84 kN *(18 800 lbs)* at 122 km/h *(76 mph)*
Weight in working order 109 tonnes *(107.5 tons)* total; 80 tonnes *(79 tons)* adhesive
Length over buffers 16 920 mm *(55 ft 6⅛ in)*
Rigid wheelbase 2100+3000+2100=7200 mm *(23 ft 7½ in)*
Wheel diameter (driving wheels) 1600 mm *(5ft 3 in)*; (carrying wheels) 1000 mm *(3 ft 3⅜ in)*
Traction motors Four single-phase commutator, frame-suspended with AEG-Kleinow quill drive
Control l.t. switchgear with precision control
Electric brake None
Builder
  mechanical parts AEG
  electrical equipment AEG
Number built 55 (see text)
Number series 118 001 — 118 055

No 118 028, one of three examples finished in blue and cream livery, at Munich Hbf depot in March 1977 *(Friedrich Franz)*

DB class 118

Introduced in 1935 as class E18 by the Deutsche Reichsbahn, the DB series 118 express passenger machines are widely regarded as one of the classic electric locomotive designs. Development of the class by AEG followed the satisfactory performance of the earlier 1-Do-1 E17 (DB class 117) series of 1928 and the 2-Co-1 type E04 (DB class 104) of 1933. For the the first time in an electric locomotive the main frames were all-welded. In them are mounted the four traction motors, torque being transmitted to the powered axles by AEG-Kleinow quill drives. Each carrying axle and adjacent pair of driving wheels are linked in an AEG-Krauss-Helmholz frame, an arrangement which was to prove unstable at speed. Subsequent modifications were made to restrict pneumatically lateral movement of the trailing axle.

A total of 55 E18s were built, including two just after the Second World War. Six did not survive the conflict, six more were retained by the East Germans to form their now withdrawn class 218, and two went to Austria to become ÖBB nos 1018.101 and 1118.01. These ÖBB units were joined in 1939 by eight locally constructed machines of similar design. In July 1980, 37 of the 41 taken into DB stock remained in service, handling various passenger duties in southern Germany.

While most members of the class are now finished in a plain blue livery, three have emerged from overhaul in the blue and cream colour scheme applied to more modern DB classes. These are nos 118 013/028 and 048.

The E18 was used as a basis for two celebrated experimental high speed designs, Deutsche Reichsbahn classes E19 and E19[1], introduced in 1939 and 1940 respectively. The two examples of each series were capable of 180 km/h (112 mph). All survived until the early 1970s and an example of each class is preserved.

Above: Austrian Federal Railways (ÖBB) no 1118.01 is one of two German built E18s to remain with that administration after the Second World War: others were constructed locally. The modernised cab was added during the 1960s *(Herbert G Korntheuer)*

Right: The more conventional DB blue livery is seen here on no 118 044 at Bamberg in May 1980 *(Yves Steenbruggen)*

Germany (Federal Republic

Operating system German Federal Railways (DB)
Year introduced 1979
Axle arrangement Bo-Bo
Gauge 1435 mm *(4 ft 8½ in)*
Power supply system 15 kV ac 16⅔ Hz
Continuous output 5600 kW *(7500 hp, 7610 ch)*
Maximum speed (120 001-004) 160 km/h
  (100 mph); (120 005) 200 km/h *(125 mph)*
Maximum tractive effort 340 kN *(76 500 lbs)*
Continuous tractive effort (120 001-004 only)
  200 kN *(45 000 lbs)* at 100 km/h *(62 mph)*
Weight in working order 84 tonnes *(83 tons)*
Length over buffers 19 200 mm *(63 ft 0 in)*
Bogie wheelbase 2800 mm *(9 ft 2¼ in)*
Wheel diameter 1250 mm *(4 ft 1¼ in)*
Traction motors Four three-phase squirrel-cage BBC
  type BQg 4843, fully suspended with flexible cardan
  drive
Control Four-quadrant controller/inverter
Electric brake Rheostatic and regenerative
Builder
  mechanical parts Krauss-Maffei, Krupp, Thyssen-
  Henschel
  electrical equipment BBC
Number built 5
Number series 120 001 — 120 005

DB class 120 no 120 001 on display at the
Munich Exhibition commemorating 100
years of electric railways in May 1979
(Friedrich Franz)

DB class 120

The first of the revolutionary DB class 120 electric locomotives appeared in May 1979, two weeks before the Munich Exhibition celebrating the centenary of electric railway traction. The design marks an important step in electric locomotive development, and incorporates for the first time in a modern high performance machine three-phase asynchronous traction motors. With a continuous output of 5600 kW (7500 hp), the 120 is the world's most powerful four-axle electric locomotive.

DB's order for five prototype machines was placed in 1976 and followed the construction in 1971 by BBC and Henschel of three experimental diesel-electric locomotives with three-phase motors, as well as small series of similarly equipped electric, electro-diesel and diesel-electric shunting units to various operators. The specification of the 120 called for a machine equally capable of hauling on level track 700 tonne expresses at 160 km/h (100 mph) or freight trains of 2700 tonnes at 80 km/h (50 mph), and subject to satisfactory performance of the prototypes, the design will be suitable for most DB traction requirements. Series production is forecast for late 1983.

The principal feature of the electrical design is sophisticated power conditioning equipment developed by BBC which converts the 15 kV single-phase overhead supply into variable voltage three-phase current. This technology has made possible the use of three-phase traction motors, long recognised for their comparative lightness, low maintenance requirements and excellent tractive characteristics. The five locomotives are equipped for both multiple-unit and push-pull operation. Continuous capacity of rheostatic and regenerative braking is 3150 and 3300 kW respectively. The fifth unit, no 120 005, is designed for running at 200 km/h (125 mph), while on 13 August 1980, no 120 002 attained a world speed record for three-phase traction of 231 km/h (143·45 mph).

DB classes 139 and 140

Germany (Federal Republic)

Operating system German Federal Railways (DB)
Year introduced 1957
Axle arrangement Bo-Bo
Gauge 1435 mm $(4 ft 8\frac{1}{2} in)$
Power supply system 15 kV ac $16\frac{2}{3}$ Hz
One-hour output 3700 kW $(4960 hp, 5030 ch)$
Continuous output 3620 kW $(4850 hp, 4920 ch)$
Maximum speed 110 km/h $(68 mph)$
Maximum tractive effort 275 kN $(62 000 lbs)$
Continuous tractive effort 139 kN $(31 200 lbs)$ at 90 km/h $(56 mph)$
Weight in working order (class 139) 86 tonnes $(85 tons)$; (class 140) 83 tonnes $(82 tons)$
Length over buffers 16 440 mm $(53 ft 11\frac{1}{4} in)$
Bogie wheelbase 3400 mm $(11 ft 1\frac{7}{8} in)$
Wheel diameter 1250 mm $(4 ft 1\frac{1}{4} in)$
Traction motors Four single-phase commutator, fully suspended with rubber spring drive
Control h.t. tapchanger
Electric brake (class 139 only) rheostatic
Builder
  mechanical parts Krauss-Maffei, Henschel, Krupp
  electrical equipment SSW, AEG, BBC
Number built (class 139) 31; (class 140) 848
Number series
  (class 139) 139 131 — 139 137;
  139 163 — 139 166; 139 309 — 139 316;
  139 552 — 139 563
  (class 140) 140 001 — 140 130; 140 138 — 140 162;
  140 167 — 140 308; 140 317 — 140 551;
  140 564 — 140 879

With no less than 879 examples constructed between 1957 and 1973, DB classes 139 and 140 formed, when this book went to press in 1980, the largest single series of electric locomotives outside the Soviet Union and represent nearly one third of the DB fleet.

The design is directly based on that of the earlier class 110.1 (formerly E10[1]) express passenger series (see p 54). mainly differing in the provision of a lower gear ratio more suitable for freight and general-purpose duties. The class 140 also lacks the rheostatic braking of the 110.1, although this equipment is retained in the 139 series which is intended for operation on more graded routes. Principal manufacturers cooperating with DB in the development of this important class were Krauss-Maffei for the mechanical portion and SSW for the electrical equipment.

Minor variants within class 140 are:
- nos 140 622-634 and 140 666-879, which incorporate modified control equipment with thyristor load-diverter
- nos 140 001-128 and 140 151-162, which have vertical rather than horizontal grilles in the bodyside ventilation louvres

Until DB's adoption in 1968 of a computer-based numbering system, class 140 was designated E40; locomotives now forming class 139 were classified E40[11].

As major overhauls take place, these locomotives are receiving a blue and cream livery in place of the original green and black.

No 140 697 at Stolberg depot in April 1976
(Marcel Vleugels)

Germany
(Federal Republic)

Operating system German Federal Railways (DB)
Year introduced 1973
Axle arrangement Co-Co
Gauge 1435 mm *(4 ft 8½ in)*
Power supply system 15 kV ac 16⅔ Hz
One-hour output 6300 kW *(8440 hp, 8560 ch)*
Continuous output 6000 kW *(8040 hp, 8155 ch)*
Maximum speed 120 km/h *(75 mph)*
Maximum tractive effort 388 kN *(87 000 lbs)*
Continuous tractive effort 228 kN *(51 200 lbs)* at
    95 km/h *(59 mph)*
Weight in working order 118 tonnes *(116 tons)*
Length over buffers 19 490 mm *(63 ft 11⅜ in)*
Bogie wheelbase 2450 + 2000 = 4450 mm
    (14 ft 7¼ in)
Wheel diameter 1250 mm *(4 ft 1¼ in)*
Traction motors Six single-phase commutator, fully
    suspended with rubber spring drive
Control h.t. tap-changer
Electric brake Rheostatic
Builder
  mechanical parts Krupp, Henschel, Krauss-Maffei
  electrical equipment AEG-Telefunken, BBC,
    Siemens
Number built 170
Number series 151 001 — 151 170

DB class 151

DB's fastest and most powerful electric freight locomotives are the modern class 151 units developed by Krupp and AEG as an improvement of the 150 series of 1957 which had been proving inadequate for traffic needs. High performance characteristics of the design include the capability to maintain their maximum speed of 120 km/h (75 mph) with a trailing load of 1100 tonnes on a ruling gradient of 0·3% (1 in 330). The advance series of twelve machines introduced in 1973 was followed by the first production units in 1975.

Traction motors are similar to those of classes 110, 112 and 140, a factor which simplifies maintenance and training. Bogie design is based on that of the class 103 express passenger units, but with rubber spring transmission more suited to freight operation. Separately-excited rheostatic braking is thyristor-controlled with a continuous capacity of 3000 kW, and a short time rating of 6000 kW. The locomotives are equipped for multiple-unit working, a facility used in a formidable 12 000 kW combination to double-head 5400 tonne iron ore trains between Duisburg and Saar.

A feature common with several other modern DB electric locomotive designs is the employment of lightweight removeable body sections to permit access to, and removal of, principal items of machinery. Construction of the frames foreshadows the eventual adoption of automatic centre-couplers. Earlier units were finished in the former standard livery of green and black; later deliveries are painted blue and cream.

DB class 151 no 151 029 *(Krauss-Maffei)*

Germany (Federal Republic)

Operating system German Federal Railways (DB)
Year introduced 1974
Axle arrangement Bo-Bo
Gauge 1435 mm *(4 ft 8½ in)*
Power supply system (dual frequency) 15 kV ac 16⅔ Hz; 25 kV ac 50 Hz
Continuous output 3100 kW *(4155 hp, 4210 ch)*
Maximum speed 160 km/h *(100 mph)*
Maximum tractive effort 270 kN *(60 700 lbs)*
Continuous tractive effort 124 kN *(27 800 lbs)* at 92 km/h *(57 mph)*
Weight in working order 83 tonnes *(82 tons)*
Length over buffers 17 940 mm *(58 ft 10¼ in)*
Bogie wheelbase 3000 mm *(9 ft 10⅛ in)*
Wheel diameter 1250 mm *(4 ft 1¼ in)*
Traction motors Four ripple current series-wound, fully suspended with flexible cardan drive
Control Thyristor
Electric brake Rheostatic
Builder
  mechanical parts Krupp
  electrical equipment AEG
Number built 25
Number series 181 201 — 181 225

DB class 181.2

This series of modern dual-frequency locomotives was constructed to handle international freight and passenger traffic between the German Federal 15kV ac low-frequency system and the electrified lines of France and Luxembourg, where both SNCF and CFL catenary are energised at 25 kV ac 50 Hz. Based at Saarbrücken, the 25 units are particularly used on the Moselle Valley line between Koblenz and Metz, but they also range as far afield as Stuttgart and Cologne.

The design is derived from that of four prototype machines originally classified E310 and now numbered 181 001/002 and 181 103/104. In their turn, these are dual-frequency variants of a series of five four-current class 184 units built in 1965 by AEG, BBC and Krupp. Thyristor control equipment for the 181.2 series was developed by AEG, and the specification of the locomotives includes rheostatic braking continuously rated at 2500 kW. Provision is made for multiple-unit and push-pull operation.

Body construction follows contemporary German practice, with removeable lightweight body sections mounted on a fabricated frame. Secondary suspension is of the Flexicoil type. A few examples remain in a plain blue livery; the remainder are painted blue and cream. Three members of the class are the only DB locomotives to bear names; these are 181 211 *Lorraine*, 181 212 *Louxembourg* and 181 213 *Saar*.

DB's class 181.2 units occasionally work mundane "filling-in" turns, as in the case of no 181 205 photographed at Mannheim Friedrichsfeld Süd with a local train for Heidelberg in August 1979 *(Berndt Eisenschink)*

Germany (Federal Republic)

Operating system German Federal Railways (DB)
Year introduced 1940
Axle arrangement Co-Co
Gauge 1435 mm *(4 ft 8½ in)*
Power supply system 15 kV ac 16⅔ Hz
One-hour output
(194 012 — 196) 3240 kW *(4340 hp, 4405 ch)*;
(194 541 — 585) 4680 kW *(6270 hp, 6360 ch)*
Continuous output
(194 012 — 196) 3090 kW *(4140 hp, 4200 ch)*;
(194 541 — 585) 4440 kW *(5950 hp, 6035 ch)*
Maximum speed (194 012 — 196) 90 km/h
(56 mph); (194 541 — 585) 100 km/h *(62 mph)*
Maximum tractive effort
(194 012 — 196, 541 & 542) 402 kN *(90 400 lbs)*;
(194 562 — 585) 393 kN *(88 200 lbs)*
(tractive effort figures apply to 200 km/h version)
138 km/h *(86 mph)*
Continuous tractive effort (194 012 — 196 only)
152 kN *(34 200 lbs)* at 77 km/h *(48 mph)*
Weight in working order 118.5 — 123 tonnes
(117 — 121 tons)
Length over buffers 18 600 mm *(61 ft 0¼ in)*
Bogie wheelbase 2450 + 2150 = 4600 mm
(15 ft 1⅛ in)
Wheel diameter 1250 mm *(4 ft 1¼ in)*
Traction motors Six single-phase commutator, axle-suspended
Control l.t. switchgear with precision control, except
194 541, 542, 570 & 571 which are equipped with
h.t. tap-changer
Electric brake Rheostatic, except 194 541, 542, 570
& 571 which have none
Builder
 mechanical parts AEG, Henschel, Krauss-Maffei,
 Krupp, LOFAG
 electrical equipment AEG, BBC, ELIN, SSW
Number built 202 (see text)
Number series 194 012 — 194 196 (with gaps);
194 541, 194 542, 194 562 — 194 585

DB class 194

This historic wartime heavy goods design was developed by AEG for the former Deutsche Reichsbahn as a faster and more powerful version of the earlier E93 (DB class 193) series. Members of the class still play an important role in DB freight service and examples of the design are also to be found in Austria and the German Democratic Republic.

As with the E93, the housing forward of each cab is mounted on the bogie, which is pivoted beneath the cab to form an articulated body. The central part of the superstructure mainly houses the transformer and tap-changer equipment while the two bonnets accommodate the compressor, air reservoirs and blowers for the two outer motors of each bogie. Traction motors are axle-suspended with resilient drives. Buffing and drawgear are mounted on the bogies.

Originally designated class E94, a total of 202 locomotives were constructed, including some 140 built during the war years both in Austria and Germany. After the Second World War Austrian Federal Railways received 44 of these (ÖBB class 1020), to which were added three more in 1954, newly constructed at the Floridsdorf works in Vienna. A further 24 examples passed to German State Railways (DR) where most survive as class 254, while two were damaged beyond repair during the war.

Construction for DB continued until 1956 and included the following variants:-

- 194 541, 542, 570 and 571, with high-tension control, more powerful WBM 487 motors and no rheostatic brake.
- 194 562-569, 572-585. These also have WBM 487 traction motors but retain low-tension tap-changing and an electric brake. All locomotives in the 194 500 number series have a maximum speed of 100 km/h (62 mph) compared with the 90 km/h (56 mph) of the rest of the class.

At the beginning of 1980, 122 examples remained in DB service. Standard colour scheme for the class is green, except for no 194 178 which curiously has been painted blue and beige.

In the German Democratic Republic the design is classified 254. DR no 254 020 was photographed at Neumark in September 1979 *(Gottfried Schilke)*

Left: After the end of the Second World War, E94s were acquired by the Austrian Federal and East German systems. Resplendent in red livery, ÖBB class 1020 no 1020.20 is seen at Rosenbach in October 1978 *(Herbert E Stemmler)*

Below: DB class 194 no 194 107 at Freilassing depot in October 1975 *(Friedrich Franz)*

Hungary

MÁV class V42

Operating system Hungarian State Railways (MÁV)
Year introduced 1962
Axle arrangement Bo-Bo
Gauge 1435 mm *(4 ft 8½ in)*
Power supply system 25/16 kV ac 50 Hz
Continuous output 1215 kW *(1625 hp, 1650 ch)*
Maximum speed 80 km/h *(50 mph)*
Continuous tractive effort 152 kN *(34 200 lbs)* at 70 km/h *(43 mph)*
Weight in working order 74 tonnes *(73 tons)*
Length over buffer 12 290 mm *(40 ft 3¾ in)*
Bogie wheelbase 2200 mm *(7 ft 2⅝ in)*
Wheel diameter 1040 mm *(3 ft 5 in)*
Traction motors Four dc series-wound, nose-suspended, axle-hung
Electric brake None
Builder
  mechanical parts Ganz-MÁVAG
  electrical equipment Ganz Electric Works
Number built 42
Number series V42.501 — V42.542

Class V42 is a more powerful development of MÁV's first 25 kV design, the 845 kW (1135 hp) V41. The design is unusual in the adoption of the Ward-Leonard system, in which the overhead line voltage is transformed down to 1 kV to power a synchronous single-phase motor. This drives two dc generators, each of which supplies direct current to the two traction motors of one bogie. Original specification of the V42 (and of the V41) included provision for operating on sections of line energised at 16 kV ac 50 Hz, the voltage employed for the pioneer MÁV single-phase electrification schemes of the 1930s. Only one driver's cab is provided. This is flanked by two bonnets, the larger of which houses the main generator group. The two pantographs and circuit-breakers are accommodated on platforms extending to the fore and rear of the cab roof.

By mid-1979 six of the 42 examples built had been withdrawn. The survivors handle a variety of lighter tasks, including shunting, stock marshalling and push-pull suburban traffic.

The number V42.001 rather confusingly is borne by former V41 no V41.501, which has been equipped with thyristor control as part of the V63 (see p 64) development programme.

No V42.523 at Budapest East station in August 1968
(Herbert E Stemmler)

Hungary

MÁV class V43

Operating system Hungarian State Railways (MÁV)
Year introduced 1963
Axle arrangement B-B
Gauge 1435 mm *(4 ft 8½ in)*
Power supply system 25 kV ac 50 Hz
One-hour output 2290 kW *(3070 hp, 3110 ch)*
Continuous output 2140 kW *(2870 hp, 2910 ch)*
Maximum speed 130 km/h *(80 mph)*
Maximum tractive effort 265 kN *(59 600 lbs)*
Continuous tractive effort 147 kN *(33 100 lbs)* at 52.5 km/h *(33 mph)*
Weight in working order 80 tonnes *(79 tons)*
Length over buffers 15 700 mm *(51 ft 6⅛ in)*
Bogie wheelbase 2300 mm *(7 ft 6½ in)*
Wheel diameter 1180 mm *(3 ft 10½ in)*
Traction motors Two dc series-wound type SW 7309, fully suspended with hollow-axle cardan drive
Control h.t. tap-changer
Electric brake None
Builder
  mechanical parts (V43.1001-7) Krupp, Schneider (for 50 Hz Group); (remainder) Ganz-MÁVAG
  electrical equipment (V43.1001-7) ACEC, AEG-Telefunken, Alsthom, BBC, Brown Boveri, Oerlikon, MTE, SSW (for 50 Hz Group); (remainder) Ganz Electric Works
Number built 398 (including units on order April 1980)
Number series V43.1001 — V43.1398

Standard motive power for passenger and freight work on Hungary's 25 kV ac 50 Hz network is the versatile V43 series, developed for MÁV by the 50 Hz Group, a consortium of West European manufacturers specialising in the design and supply of equipment for industrial frequency railway electrification. Since their introduction in 1963, these locomotives have proved sufficiently successful to remain in production in 1980, by which time over 300 examples had been delivered.

A feature of the design is the employment of single-motor bogies of French origin, with fully-suspended traction motors and hollow-axle cardan shaft transmission. Body construction consists of a welded underframe supporting a superstructure of three lightweight removeable sections between each cab, reflecting West German practice. Silicon rectifier equipment designed by SSW is used to convert ac to dc. All units are fitted for operation in multiple and for push-pull working.

Construction of the first seven locomotives, nos V43.1001-1007, was carried out in West Germany by Krupp, with bogies supplied by SFAC and electrical equipment by various members of the 50 Hz Group. The first Hungarian built machine, no V43.1008, appeared in 1964 and all subsequent units have been built under licence by Ganz-MÁVAG and the Ganz Electric Works. Production is scheduled to end in 1983, by which time nearly 400 examples will have been supplied to MÁV.

MÁV class V43 no V43 1192 at Budapest West in July 1979
(Frank Stenvall)

Hungary

MÁV class V63

Operating system Hungarian State Railways (MÁV)
Year introduced 1975
Axle arrangement Co-Co
Gauge 1435 mm *(4 ft 8½ in)*
Power supply system 25 kV ac 50 Hz
One-hour output 3680 kW *(4930 hp, 5000 ch)*
Maximum speed 140 km/h *(87 mph)*
Maximum tractive effort 442 kN *(99 200 lbs)*
Continuous tractive effort 257 kN *(57 800 lbs)* at 46 km/h *(29 mph)*
Weight in working order 116 tonnes *(114.5 tons)*
Length over buffers 19 540 mm *(64 ft 1¼ in)*
Bogie wheelbase 2100+2100=4200 mm *(13 ft 9⅜ in)*
Wheel diameter 1250 mm *(4 ft 1¼ in)*
Traction motors Six separately-excited ripple-current series-wound, nose-suspended, axle-hung
Control Thyristor
Electric brake Rheostatic
Builder
  mechanical parts Ganz-MÁVAG
  electrical equipment Ganz Electric Works
Number built 2
Number series V63.001 and V63.002

After several years' development, these two prototype thyristor-controlled V63 locomotives were delivered to MÁV in 1975. Haulage capabilities on level track range from 3000 tonne freight trains at 85 km/h (53 mph) to 700 tonne expresses at the maximum speed of 140 km/h (87 mph). The design can potentially be uprated to 5150 kW (6900 hp) and regearing could increase maximum speed to 160 km/h (100 mph).

Thyristor-controlled rectifier equipment was developed by the Ganz Electric Works and provides automatic speed regulation and wheel-slip protection. Rheostatic braking effort is also thyristor-controlled, with a continuous capacity of 2575 kW. Design of bogies and secondary "pendulum" suspension is derived from that of the 2320 kW (3105 hp) class M63 diesel-electric locomotives built for MÁV in 1970. The six 900V traction motors are nose-suspended, although a rubber spring quill drive has been developed should spring-borne motors be adopted for future construction.

Extensive trials with the two prototypes resulted in a further MÁV order for five pre-production machines for delivery in 1980. Numbered V63.1001-1005, these units were also to be geared for 140 km/h. Series construction of the design is due to start in 1984.

MÁV class V63 thyristor-controlled prototype no V63.001
(Ganz Electric Works)

India

IR class WAG4

Operating system Indian Railways (IR)
Year introduced 1967
Axle arrangement B-B
Gauge 1676 mm *(5 ft 6 in)*
Power supply system 25 kV ac 50 Hz
Continuous output 2370 kW *(3175 hp, 3220 ch)*
Maximum speed 80 km/h *(50 mph)*
Maximum tractive effort 294 kN *(66 200 lbs)*
Continuous tractive effort 228 kN *(51 200 lbs)*
Weight in working order 88 tonnes *(87 tons)*
Length over buffers 17 216 mm *(56 ft 5¾ in)*
Wheel diameter 1140 mm *(3 ft 8⅞ in)*
Traction motors Two dc series-wound, fully
 suspended with cardan shaft drive
Control h.t. tap-changer
Electric brake Rheostatic
Builder
 mechanical parts CLW
 electrical equipment Various members of 50 Hz
  Group ; CLW
Number built 186
Number series 20900 — 21085

Indian Railways were comparatively early to adopt industrial frequency single-phase electrification for new projects, embarking on its first schemes in 1958. Initially motive power came from the European 50 Hz Group (class WAM1) and Mitsubishi (classes WAM2 and WAM3), but in 1963 domestic construction of single-motor bogie class WAG1 freight units began at CLW. One hundred examples were built before the first of the broadly similar but more powerful WAG4 series appeared in 1967. The decision to switch to the improved design followed successful trials with ten class WAG3 units supplied direct by the 50 Hz Group in 1965. Again, the WAG4 was intended for freight work and is geared accordingly. Like the WAG1, each bogie contains a single traction motor, fully suspended with a flexible drive. Silicon diode rectifiers are employed, rather than the excitron type of the earlier class, and electric braking is rheostatic instead of regenerative. The locomotives are equipped for multiple-unit working, and are widely used in freight service on the Central, Eastern, Northern, South-Eastern and Western Railways.

After 186 units had been built, further production was abandoned in 1970. By this time IR had determined that the design was not entirely suitable for the wider range of traffic requirements, especially on graded routes, and that the use of spring-borne traction motors was not appropriate for Indian conditions.

IR class WAG4 no 21015 *(CLW)*

IR class WAM4

Operating system Indian Railways (IR)
Year introduced 1971
Axle arrangement Co-Co
Gauge 1676 mm *(5 ft 6 in)*
Power supply system 25 kV ac 50 Hz
Continuous output 2680 kW *(3590 hp, 3640 ch)*
Maximum speed 120 km/h *(75 mph)*
Maximum tractive effort 332 kN *(74 600 lbs)*
Continuous tractive effort 173 kN *(38 800 lbs)* at 56 km/h *(35 mph)*
Weight in working order 113 tonnes *(111 tons)*
Length over buffers 18 974 mm *(62 ft 3 in)*
Bogie wheelbase 1981 mm *(12 ft 6 in)*
Wheel diameter 1092 mm *(3 ft 7 in)*
Traction motors Six dc series-wound type TAO 659, nose-suspended, axle-hung
Control h.t. tap-changer
Electric brake Rheostatic
Builder
  mechanical parts CLW
  electrical equipment CLW and BHEL
Number built 270
Number series 20400—20669

IR class WAM4 no 20504 near Santragachi in February 1975 with the *Bombay-Howrah Mail* *(Marc Dahlström)*

IR's requirement for a standard rugged multi-purpose machine for its growing single-phase network led to the development by the Research, Designs and Standards Organisation (RDSO) of the important WAM4 series. First examples appeared from CLW in 1971. High tension control is employed and rectifiers are of the silicon diode type. A new type of traction motor was developed jointly by RDSO and French industry, and for the first 30 locomotives these were imported; subsequent units have CLW built motors. Nose-suspension was adopted to avoid the heavy transmission maintenance experienced with spring-borne motors of earlier designs. Axle-load is just under 19 tonnes. Multiple-unit control equipment and rheostatic braking are standard. The class shares many components common to the 1·5 kV dc WCG2 freight units of 1971 and the later dual-current WCAM1 (see following entry).

By 1979, development by RDSO and CLW of three significant derivatives of the class was well advanced:-

- class WAM4B is intended for heavy iron ore haulage on the South Eastern Railway's Kirandul-Waltair line. Five prototypes rated at 2910 kW (3900 hp) and with a top speed of 50 km/h (31 mph) were completed in 1979.
- class WAM4C also of 2910 kW (3900 hp) has been designed primarily for freight haulage, although no construction had taken place by 1979.
- class WAM4R, five prototypes of which were reported to be under construction in 1979, has been developed for express work between Calcutta and Delhi. This design has an air-smoothed front end and a 160 km/h (100 mph) capability.

India

IR class WCAM1

Operating system Indian Railways (IR)
Year introduced 1975
Axle arrangement Co-Co
Gauge 1676 mm *(5 ft 6 in)*
Power supply system (dual-current) 1.5 kV dc;
  25 kV ac 50 Hz
Continuous output (dc) 2155 kW *(2890 hp,
  2930 ch)*; (ac) 2680 kW *(3590 hp, 3640 ch)*
Maximum speed 120 km/h *(75 mph)*
Maximum tractive effort (dc) 277 kN *(62 200 lbs)*;
  ac 332 kN *(74 600 lbs)*
Continuous tractive effort (dc) 222 kN *(49 900 lbs)*
  at 35 km/h *(22 mph)*; *(*ac) 157 kN *(35 300 lbs)* at
  60 km/h *(37 mph)*
Weight in working order 113 tonnes *(111 tons)*
Length over buffers 20 950 mm *(68 ft 8¾ in)*
Bogie wheelbase 1981 mm *(12 ft 6 in)*
Wheel diameter 1092 mm *(3 ft 7 in)*
Traction motors Six dc series-wound type TAO 659,
  nose-suspended, axle-hung
Control ac operation — h.t. tap-changer; dc operation
  — rheostatic
Electric brake None
Builder
  mechanical parts CLW
  electrical equipment CLW and BHEL
Number built 53
Number series 21800 — 21852

IR's dual-current WCAM1 series was designed by the Research, Designs and Standards Organisation (RDSO) for operation on the Western Railway's Bombay Central-Ahmedabad line, where the Bombay-Virar 1·5 kV dc electrification of 1936 meets single-phase catenary erected during the 1970s. Developed to avoid a traction changeover at Virar, the class is intended both for express passenger and heavy freight work. Design is based closely on the WAM4 (see previous entry) and incorporates the same bogies and traction motors. Separate control equipments are provided for ac and dc operation. The class has no electric braking or multiple-unit capability.

No 21800 was handed over on 1 January 1975 for service evaluation, and was subsequently named *Vallabh* in honour of Indian public figure and patriot Sardar Vallabhai Patel. Deliveries of the order for 53 units continued in 1979.

IR class WCAM1 no 21802 *(IR)*

India

IR class WCG1

Operating system Indian Railways (IR)
Year introduced 1928
Axle arrangement C-C
Gauge 1676 mm *(5 ft 6 in)*
Power supply system 1.5 kV dc
One-hour output 1940 kW *(2600 hp, 2635 ch)*
Continuous output 1665 kW *(2230 hp, 2260 ch)*
Maximum speed 80 km/h *(50 mph)*
Weight in working order 125 tonnes *(123 tons)*
Length over buffers 20 142 mm *(66 ft 1 in)*
Bogie wheelbase 4597 mm *(15 ft 1 in)*
Wheel diameter 1219 mm *(4 ft 0 in)*
Traction motors Four dc series-wound, bogie-
mounted with jackshaft/coupling rod transmission
Control Rheostatic
Electric brake Regenerative
Builder
 mechanical parts (20025-34) SLM; (20035-65)
  Vulcan Foundry
 electrical equipment Metropolitan-Vickers
Number built 41
Number series 20025 — 20065

IR class WCG1 no 20048 at Bombay's
Victoria Terminus in March 1975 (*Marc
Dahlström*)

India's first railway electrification was commissioned in 1925, when certain Bombay area suburban lines were energised at 1·5 kV dc. This was extended by the former Great Indian Peninsular Railway (GIPR) in 1929 as a main line scheme across the Western Ghats to Poona and to Igatpuri, eventually totalling some 291 route-km (181 miles). These lines now form part of IR's Central Railway. Originally numbered 4500-4540, the WCG1 series are the original goods locomotives supplied to the GIPR by Metropolitan-Vickers in 1928/29, and they shared main line duties with 22 2-Co-1 passenger units (later IR class WCP1) from the same builder. Mechanical parts for 31 of the class were assembled at Vulcan Foundry, but the first ten were built in Switzerland by SLM. Their construction is unique in British practice and reflects Swiss developments of the period (see p 124) in the provision of an articulated body. The two traction motors of each bogie drive the three coupled axles via intermediate gearing and a common output jackshaft. Driver's cabs and control equipment are housed in the central portion of the body. Speed was originally controlled by motor groupings of series, series-parallel and parallel, each with two stages of field weakening, although the parallel connection is thought to be no longer used now that the surviving locomotives are restricted to shunting work. In main line service the WCG1s were capable of taking 1270 tonnes (1250 tons) over the GIPR's 2·7% (1 in 37) gradients but from 1971 they were replaced on heavy freight work by the Chittaranjan built WCG2 series.

Nineteen examples remained active at various points on the Central network in February 1980.

India

IR class WCM5

Operating system Indian Railways (IR)
Year introduced 1961
Axle arrangement Co-Co
Gauge 1676 mm *(5 ft 6 in)*
Power supply system 1.5 kV dc
Continuous output 2365 kW *(3170 hp, 3215 ch)*
Maximum speed 120 km/h *(75 mph)*
Maximum tractive effort 304 kN *(68 400 lbs)*
Continuous tractive effort 174 kN *(39 000 lbs)* at 48 km/h *(30 mph)*
Weight in working order 125 tonnes *(124 tons)*
Length over buffers 20 168 mm *(66 ft 2 in)*
Wheel diameter 1220 mm *(4 ft 0 in)*
Traction motors Six dc series-wound, nose-suspended, axle-hung
Control Rheostatic
Electric brake None
Builder
  mechanical parts CLW
  electrical equipment English Electric
Number built 21
Number series 20083 — 20103

Deliveries of domestically produced electric locomotives in India began in October 1961, when the first of this series of 21 mixed-traffic machines was completed at the Chittaranjan Locomotive Works (CLW). Intended for service on the 1·5 kV dc Central Railway routes out of Bombay, an initial series of ten incorporating equipment by English Electric was ordered in August 1959. The specification of the class matches closely that of seven series WCM1 machines supplied in 1955 by Vulcan/English Electric, who also provided technical assistance during design and construction of the WCM5 units.

Production of steam locomotives at Chittaranjan had only commenced in November 1950, and the local construction of electric motive power eleven years later was a significant achievement for Indian industry. In terms of value, the import content of the WCM5 was 58%, thus conserving valuable foreign exchange, and the national importance attached to delivery of no 20083 brought Prime Minister Nehru to officiate at the handing over ceremony. No 20083 was later named *Lokamanya*.

IR class WCM5 no 20103 arriving at Bombay's Victoria Terminus with the *Deccan Queen* **express from Pune (Poona) in March 1975** *(Marc Dahlström)*

India

IR class YAM1

Operating system Indian Railways (IR)
Year introduced 1965
Axle arrangement B-B
Gauge 1000 mm *(3 ft 3⅜ in)*
Power supply system 25 kV ac 50 Hz
Continuous output 1200 kW *(1610 hp, 1630 ch)*
Maximum speed 80 km/h *(50 mph)*
Maximum tractive effort 191 kN *(43 000 lbs)*
Continuous tractive effort 121 kN *(27 100 lbs)* at 34.5 km/h *(21½ mph)*
Weight in working order 52 tonnes *(52 tons)*
Length over buffers 13 150 mm *(43 ft 1¾ in)*
Bogie wheelbase 2206 mm *(7 ft 2¾ in)*
Wheel diameter 865 mm *(2 ft 10 in)*
Traction motors Two dc series-wound, fully suspended with WN cardan drive
Control l.t. tap-changer
Electric brake None
Builder
  mechanical parts Mitsubishi
  electrical equipment Mitsubishi, Hitachi, Toshiba
Number built 20
Number series 21904 — 21923

The Japanese built YAM1 series are IR's only metre gauge electric locomotives. Twenty examples were delivered in 1965-66 to the Southern Railway for operation on lines south of Madras. These include the former South India Railway line from Madras Beach to Tambaram which was originally electrified in 1931 at 1·5 kV dc and converted during the 1960s to 25 kV ac. Present limit of the catenary is Villapuram, some 150 km (90 miles) south of Madras.

Motive power for this scheme was originally to have come from CLW, and an order for 18 units was actually placed but later cancelled. Mitsubishi's design is a neat 1200 kW machine running on two single-motor bogies, and is used for passenger and freight work.

IR class YAM1 no 21919 ready to leave Madras Egmore in February 1975 with the *Trivandrum Express*
(Marc Dahlström)

Indonesia

PJKA class WH

Operating system Indonesian State Railways (PJKA)
Year introduced 1924
Axle arrangement 1-Bo+Bo-1
Gauge 1067 mm *(3 ft 6 in)*
Power supply system 1.5 kV dc
One-hour output 765 kW *(1025 hp, 1040 ch)*
Continuous output 590 kW *(790 hp, 800 ch)*
Maximum speed 80 km/h *(50 mph)*
Maximum tractive effort 182 kN *(40 800 lbs)*
Weight in working order 72.6 tonnes *(71.5 tons)*
  total ; 52.4 tonnes *(52 tons)* adhesive
Length over buffers 15 050 mm *(49 ft 4½ in)*
Bogie wheelbase 2500 mm *(8 ft 2½ in)*
Wheel diameter (driving wheels) 1350 mm
  (4 ft 5⅛ in); (carrying wheels) 825 mm *(2 ft 8½ in)*
Traction motors Four dc series-wound, axle-
  suspended
Control Rheostatic
Electric brake None
Builder
  mechanical parts Werkspoor (under Westinghouse
  licence)
  electrical equipment Heemaf, Westinghouse
Number built 6
Number series 201 — 206

**PJKA class WH no 205 at Bogor in
September 1978** *(Günter Haslbeck)*

One of the world's less familiar electrified railways is the 1·5 kV dc, 1067 mm (3 ft 6 in) gauge system operated by Indonesian State Railways (PJKA) on the island of Java, where 77 route-km (48 miles) are energised, including the 60 km (37 mile) line linking Jakarta and Bogor. The scheme was completed during the 1920s by the then Dutch Indies State Railways and employed locally generated hydro-electric power, avoiding the importation of coal for steam traction from Borneo or Sumatra.

Of the three locomotive classes introduced for this electrification, the WH mixed-traffic series was numerically the largest, and design of the class reflects contemporary American practice. The two driven axles of each bogie are mounted rigidly in the bogie frame, within which the carrying axle forms a Bissel truck. The bogies are coupled, and traction and buffing forces are not transmitted to the body. Electro-pneumatic control is employed, with series and parallel motor groupings. One weak-field step is available in each grouping to give four economic running notches.

Construction of the six locomotives was carried out in the Netherlands by Werkspoor, while another Dutch manufacturer, Heemaf, acted as principal contractor and supplied the electrical equipment. Some components were assembled under licence by Heemaf, but other items, such as traction motors and control apparatus, came direct from Westinghouse in the United States. The locomotives were originally numbered 3201-3206.

Five units remained in service in 1979.

Italy

FS class E428

Operating system Italian State Railways (FS)
Year introduced 1934
Axle arrangement 2-Bo+Bo-2
Gauge 1435 mm *(4 ft 8½ in)*
Power supply system 3 kV dc
One-hour output 2800 kW *(3750 hp, 3805 ch)*
Continuous output 2520 kW *(3375 hp, 3425 ch)*
Maximum speed 100 km/h *(62 mph)*
Maximum tractive effort (29/103 gear ratio)
216 kN *(48 500 lbs)*; (31/101 gear ratio) 196 kN
(44 100 lbs); (34/98 gear ratio) 177 kN *(39 700 lbs)*
Continuous tractive effort (29/103 gear ratio)
113 kN *(25 400 lbs)* at 72 km/h *(45 mph)*; (31/101
gear ratio) 103 kN *(23 100 lbs)* at 78 km/h *(48 mph)*;
(34/98 gear ratio) 93 kN *(20 900 lbs)* at 88 km/h
(55 mph)
Weight in working order (E428 001-096) 131
tonnes *(129 tons)*; (E428 097-241) 135 tonnes
(133 tons)

Design of the FS class E428 heavy express locomotives was derived from that of 12 class E326 2-Co-2 machines built by Breda between 1930 and 1933 for light fast passenger work. The rigid body rests on an articulated underframe, each half of which incorporates two driven axles and a four-wheel bogie performing guiding and carrying functions. Each motor axle is driven by two frame-suspended traction motors via a hollow-axle quill drive. Buffers and drawgear are mounted on the underframe. Some members of the class were originally geared for 150 km/h (93 mph) operation, but now all units are restricted to 100 km/h (62 mph). Tractive effort capabilities differ according to which of three gear ratios is fitted (see data).

The class is divided into three sub-series, all of common electrical design but each differing aesthetically (see photo captions).

In January 1979, 240 of these versatile mixed-traffic machines remained in FS service.

This boxy front-end treatment was applied to nos E428 001-122, built between 1934 and 1938. No E428 112 is seen at Mestre depot in April 1980
(Friedrich Franz)

Length over buffers 19 000 mm *(62 ft 4 in)*
Bogie wheelbase 2200 mm *(7 ft 2⅝ in)*
Rigid wheelbase 2350 mm *(7 ft 8½ in)*
Wheel diameter (carrying) 1110 mm *(3 ft 7¾ in)*; (driving) 1880 mm *(6 ft 2 in)*
Traction motors Eight dc series-wound type 42-200 FS, frame-suspended with hollow-axle spring drive
Control Rheostatic
Electrical brake None
Builder
 mechanical parts Ansaldo, Breda, TIBB, FIAT, Reggiane
 electrical equipment Ansaldo, Breda, TIBB, Ercole Marelli
Number built 241
Number series E428 001 — E428 241

Further styling changes were made to nos E428 162 and 204-242, constructed from 1940 to 1943; a hint of streamlining is evident on E428 162, photographed at La Spezia in September 1978 *(Yves Steenebruggen)*

Below: Cabs of more modern design were fitted to nos E428 123-161, 163-203. No E428 147 awaits work at Livorno in September 1978 *(Yves Steenebruggen)*

Italy

FS class E444

Operating system Italian State Railways (FS)
Year introduced 1970
Axle arrangement Bo-Bo
Gauge 1435 mm *(4 ft 8½ in)*
Power supply system 3 kV dc
One-hour output 4440 kW *(5950 hp, 6035 ch)**
Continuous output 4020 kW *(5385 hp, 5465 ch)**
Maximum speed 200 km/h *(125 mph)*
Maximum tractive effort (main series) 232 kN
(52 100 lbs)
Continuous tractive effort (main series) 126 kN
(28 200 lbs) at 104 km/h *(65 mph)*
Weight in working order 81 Tonnes *(80 tons)**
Length over buffers 16 840 mm *(55 ft 3 in)*
Bogie wheelbase 2600 mm *(8 ft 6⅜ in)*
Wheel diameter 1250 mm *(4 ft 1¼ in)*
Traction motors Four dc series-wound type T750,
fully suspended with hollow-axle ''dancing ring''
drive
Control Rheostatic (except E444 005 with full chopper
control, and E444 056 & 057 with shunt chopper
control)
Electric brake Rheostatic
Builder
 mechanical parts Casaralta, FIAT, Reggiane, Sofer,
 Savigliano, TIBB
 electrical equipment ALCE, Asgen, Ercole Marelli,
 Italtrafo, Ocren, TIBB
Number built 113
Number series E444 005 — E444 117
*E444005 has one-hour output of approx. 5040 kW
(6755 hp, 6850 ch), continuous output of approx.
4500 kW *(6030 hp, 6115 ch)* and weighs 84 tonnes
(83 tons)

Series construction of the E444 express design followed the introduction in 1967/68 of four prototype machines built by Savigliano of Turin. Numbered E444 001-004, these locomotives have a one-hour rating of 3660 kW (4905 hp) and a top speed of 180 km/h (112 mph), and formed the basis of this more powerful and faster production series supplied by various Italian manufacturers between 1970 and 1974. Like the prototypes, these units employ resistance control, with motor groupings of series and parallel. Five field-weakening steps in each give a total of 12 economic running notches. Traction motors are fully suspended with a hollow-axle ''dancing ring'' drive derived from that used on the E646 Bo-Bo-Bo series. Rheostatic braking operates in the 200-70 km/h (125-44 mph) speed range. Livery is blue, grey and red. With a little latin humour FS authorities have bestowed on the class the official nickname *Super Tartaruga* (Super Tortoise), and each locomotive bears an appropriate cartoon on the cabside. This acknowledges that the E444s are the fastest units in the FS fleet.

No E444 005 was delivered in 1975 with full chopper control equipment developed by TIBB. Considerably more powerful than the rest of the class, this machine has served as a test-bed for a new generation of electronically controlled FS motive power, of which the E633 (see p 76) is the first example. Two further members of the class nos E444 056 and 057, were introduced in 1974 with experimental shunt chopper equipment designed by Ercole Marelli.

A Co-Co version of the E444, designated class E666 and intended for high speed *Direttissima* operation, has been mooted since the late 1960s but never built. Some years later, Polish State Railways (PKP) investigated the possibility of domestic licence construction but this scheme also failed to materialise.

FS class E444 no E444 016 at Livorno in September 1978
(Yves Steenebruggen)

Italy

FS class E626

Operating system Italian State Railways (FS)
Year introduced 1928
Axle arrangement Bo-Bo-Bo
Gauge 1435 mm *(4 ft 8½ in)*
Power supply system 3 kV dc
One-hour output 2100 kW *(2815 hp, 2855 ch)*
Continuous output 1890 kW *(2535 hp, 2570 ch)*
Maximum speed 95 km/h *(59 mph)*
Maximum tractive effort (21/76 gear ratio) 257 kN
(57 800 lbs); (24/73 gear ratio) 224 kN *(50 300 lbs)*
Continuous tractive effort (21/76 gear ratio)
134 kN *(30 200 lbs)* at 45 km/h *(28 mph)*; (24/73
gear ratio) 116 kN *(26 000 lbs)* at 53 km/h *(33 mph)*
Weight in working order 93 tonnes *(92 tons)*
Length over buffers 14 950 mm *(49 ft 0½ in)*
Bogie/rigid wheelbase 2450 mm *(8 ft 0½ in)*
Wheel diameter 1250 mm *(4 ft 1¼ in)*
Traction motors Six dc series-wound type 32-200
FS, nose-suspended, axle-hung
Control Rheostatic
Electric brake None
Builder
  mechanical parts Ansaldo, Breda, Cemsa, FIAT,
  OM, Reggiane, Savigliano, TIBB
  electrical equipment Ansaldo, Breda, Cemsa, CGE,
  Marelli, Savigliano, TIBB
Number built 448
Number series E626 001 — E626 448

The veteran E626 series was developed from four 1800 kW (2410 hp) proto-types numbered E625 001-004, introduced in 1927 for the electrification of the line from Benevento to Foggia, the first FS scheme at the now standard 3 kV dc. These successful machines were later absorbed into the main class, and by 1939 448 examples had been built.

Unlike later FS Bo-Bo-Bo designs, the E626 does not have an articulated body. The two centre axles are rigidly mounted in the mainframes, to which are articulated the bogie frames of the two outer pairs of axles. These bogies support the outer ends of the body by means of a sliding sprung pivot. The six nose-suspended traction motors are 1·5 kV machines connected permanently in pairs in series. Pairs of motors may be grouped in series, series-parallel and parallel, with one field weakening stage in each. Some locomotives have a 21/76 gear ratio, others 24/73, and although this does not alter their permitted maximum speeds, the lower geared machines have higher tractive effort capabilities. Standard livery for the class is the *Isabella* (khaki) and dark brown common to all FS pre-war designs.

At the beginning of 1979, 405 remained in FS service, performing a variety of secondary duties. A further 17 had passed into Yugoslav hands, following territorial changes after the Second World War, to form the now withdrawn JŽ class 361, and three locomotives found their way to Czechoslovakia where, after being modified to operate under 1·5 kV dc, they survived as ČSD class E666.0 until the mid-1960s.

FS class E626 no E626 118, built by Breda in 1935, at Livorno in September 1978
(Yves Steenebruggen)

Italy

FS classes E632 and E633

Operating system Italian State Railways (FS)
Year introduced 1979
Axle arrangement B-B-B
Gauge 1435 mm *(4 ft 8½ in)*
Power supply system 3 kV dc
One-hour output 5100 kW *(6835 hp, 6930 ch)*
Maximum speed (class E632) 160 km/h *(100 mph)*;
  (class E633) 130 km/h *(80 mph)*
Maximum tractive effort
  (class E632) 227 kN *(51 000 lbs)*;
  (class E633) 278 kN *(62 500 lbs)*
One-hour tractive effort
  (class E632) 185 kN *(41 600 lbs)* at 92 km/h
  (57 mph); (class E633) 227 kN *(51 000 lbs)* at
  75 km/h *(47 mph)*
Weight in working order 102 tonnes *(100½ tons)*
Length over buffers 17 800 mm *(58 ft 4¾ in)*
Bogie wheelbase 2150 mm *(7 ft 0⅝ in)*
Wheel diameter 1040 mm *(3 ft 5 in)*
Traction motors Three separately-excited TIBB type
  T850, fully suspended with "dancing ring" drive
Control Full chopper
Electric brake Rheostatic
Builder
  mechanical parts FIAT-Savigliano
  electrical equipment TIBB
Number built 20 (including units under construction
  or on order at 30 October 1980)
Number series (class E632) E632 001 — E632 016;
  (class E633) E633 001 — E633 004

FS class E633 no E633 002 *(TIBB)*

A new generation of Italian electric traction is represented by the E632 and E633 series, the first FS 3 kV dc design with single-motor bogies and, apart from experimental Bo-Bo no E444 005, the first to employ full chopper control. Output of the class virtually matches that of the earlier E656, but with only three traction motors and a weight saving of nearly 20%. Bogie design is similar to that used successfully in the D343/345/443/445 family of diesel-electrics, but with an enlarged wheelbase to accommodate the single TIBB type T850 traction motor. Unlike previous FS six-axle units, the E632/E633 has a rigid body. Lateral displacement of 140 mm (5½ in) and 60 mm (2⅜ in) in either direction for centre and outer bogies respectively, together with coil spring secondary suspension, provide the flexibility necessary for sharply curved routes. Axle-load is only 17 tonnes.

Electronic power control equipment has been developed by TIBB from prototype no E444 005 (see p 76) and feeds each of the three separately-excited traction motors with continuously-variable voltage up to 2 kV, irrespective of fluctuations in supply voltage. Speed and acceleration are automatically controlled. Resistances for electric braking are mounted visibly on the roof. Ac auxiliary machines are fed by a static inverter.

Originally all locomotives of this design were to be classified E633, although the first example, no E633 001, had gearing for 160 rather than 130 km/h. It was decided by FS in 1980 to form high speed units into a separate series, class E632, with no E633 001 becoming E632 001. Fifteen of the first 20 also feature 160 km/h gearing and were expected to become E632 002-016 when built. No E633 005 was likely to be renumbered E633 001 and deliveries beyond the first 20 would fall into the number series governed by their gear ratio.

Nicknamed the *Tigre* (Tiger) series, construction of 80 units was foreseen in early 1980. In the same year development was reported of a 6000 kW (8040 hp) locomotive based on the E632/E633 to be designated FS classes E642 (160 km/h) and E643 (130 km/h). A B-B-B-B freight version, type E844, has also been mooted.

Italy

FS class E636

Operating system Italian State Railways (FS)
Year introduced 1940
Axle arrangement Bo-Bo-Bo
Gauge 1435 mm *(4 ft 8½ in)*
Power supply system 3 kV dc
One-hour output 2100 kW *(2815 hp, 2855 ch)*
Continuous output 1890 kW *(2535 hp, 2570 ch)*
Maximum speed (21/65 & 24/74 gear ratios)
  105 km/h *(65 mph)*; (28/65 gear ratio) 120 km/h
  (75 mph)
Maximum tractive effort (21/65 & 24/74 gear
  ratios) 216 kN *(48 500 lbs)*; (28/65 gear ratio)
  162 kN *(36 400 lbs)*
Continuous tractive effort (21/65 & 24/74 gear
  ratios) 113 kN *(25 400 lbs)* at 54 km/h *(34 mph)*;
  (28/65 gear ratio) 84 kN *(19 000 lbs)* at 72 km/h
  (45 mph)
Weight in working order 101 tonnes *(99.5 tons)*
Length over buffers 18 250 mm *(59 ft 10½ in)*
Bogie wheelbase 3150 mm *(10 ft 4 in)*
Wheel diameter 1250 mm *(4 ft 1¼ in)*
Traction motors Six dc series-wound type 32R-
  200FS, axle-suspended on some units, frame-
  suspended with flexible quill drive on others
Control Rheostatic
Electric brake None
Builder
 mechanical parts Ansaldo, Breda, TIBB, OM,
  Pistoiesi, Reggiane, Savigliano
 electrical equipment Ansaldo, Breda, TIBB, CGE,
  Savigliano, Marelli
Number built 469
Number series E636 001 — E636 469

A modernised development of the E626 series, the mixed-traffic E636 retains the electrical equipment and power output of the earlier design but differs mechanically. The locomotive body consists of two symmetrical halves, articulated at the centre and carried on three two-axle welded steel bogies. This arrangement provided the flexibility necessary for the many sharply curved routes on the FS network and was repeated in the subsequent E645, E646 and E656 designs. Speed is controlled by motor groupings and field-weakening. The majority of the class has frame-suspended motors and is geared for a maximum speed of 120 km/h (75 mph) but 49 units have nose-suspended motors, with lower gearing for a top speed of 105 km/h (65 mph).

The first 108 units were built between 1940 and 1942. Further construction was halted by the Second World War but resumed in 1952. By 1962 no less than 469 examples had been delivered.

A Bo-Bo version of the E636 is also in FS service. Designated class E424, these locomotives are in effect two-thirds of the parent design. A total of 158 of these machines were delivered between 1943 and 1950.

An unidentified FS class E636 at La Spezia in September 1978
(Yves Steenebruggen)

FS class E656

Operating system Italian State Railways (FS)
Year introduced 1976
Axle arrangement Bo-Bo-Bo
Gauge 1435 mm *(4 ft 8½ in)*
Power supply system 3 kV dc
One-hour output 4800 kW *(6435 hp, 6525 ch)*
Continuous output 4200 kW *(5630 hp, 5705 ch)*
Maximum speed 160 km/h *(100 mph)*
Maximum tractive effort 236 kN *(53 000 lbs)*
Continuous tractive effort 131 kN *(29 500 lbs)* at
   103 km/h *(64 mph)*
Weight in working order 120 tonnes *(118 tons)*
Length over buffers 18 290 mm *(60 ft 0⅛ in)*
Bogie wheelbase 2850 mm *(9 ft 4¼ in)*
Wheel diameter 1250 mm *(4 ft 1¼ in)*
Traction motors Six dc series-wound type 82-400FS
   twin motors, fully suspended with hollow axle
   ''dancing ring'' drive
Controj Rheostatic
Electric brake None
Builder
  mechanical parts Casaralta, Casertane, Reggiane,
   Sofer, TIBB
  electrical equipment Ansaldo, Asgen, Ercole
   Marelli, Italtrafo, TIBB
Number built 211
Number series E656 001 — E656 104, E656 201 —
   E656 307

Development of FS six-axle articulated body designs culminated with the introduction in 1976 of the E656 series, intended for express passenger and heavy freight work. These 4800 kW machines are based on the E645/E646 locomotives built from 1958 to 1967, but have more powerful motors and increased maximum speed. Each axle is driven by a twin-armature traction motor, the output pinions of which engage a common gearwheel. Transmission is by means of a floating lever ''dancing ring'' assembly similar to that used on the E444 express design. The retention of double motors allows the provision of 20 economic running notches. Motor groupings are all 12 in series, series-parallel (6+6), parallel (4+4+4) and super-parallel (3+3+3+3), with five stages of field-weakening in the first two and three in the latter two. Additional features of the design are automatic wheel-slip control, cab-signalling and provision of telephone contact with train control staff.

Locomotives numbered from E656 201 form a sub-series in being equipped with static inverters for supplying auxiliaries in place of the motor-alternator sets of nos E656 001-104.

Standard livery is grey, blue and red, and as with the E444 series, FS has given the class an official nickname, in this case *Caïmano* (Alligator).

Deliveries of these locomotives continued during 1979, permitting progressive retirement of pre-war designs.

FS class E656 no E656 046 at Milan Central in August 1978
(Günther Barths)

Japan

JNR class EF58

Operating system Japanese National Railways (JNR)
Year introduced 1947
Axle arrangement 2-Co + Co-2
Gauge 1067 mm *(3 ft 6 in)*
Power supply system 1.5 kV dc
One-hour output 1900 kW *(2545 hp, 2580 ch)*
Maximum speed 120 km/h *(75 mph)*
One-hour tractive effort 80 kN *(18 100 lbs)* at 86 km/h *(53 mph)*
Weight in working order 115 tonnes *(113 tons)* total ; 86.4 tonnes *(85 tons)* adhesive
Length over coupler centres 19 900 mm *(65 ft 3½ in)*
Bogie wheelbase 4220 mm *(13 ft 10⅛ in)*
Driving wheel diameter 1250 mm *(4 ft 1¼ in)*
Traction motors Six dc series-wound type MT41, MT41A or MT42, nose-suspended, axle-hung
Control Rheostatic
Electric brake Rheostatic
Builder
  mechanical parts Fuji, Hitachi, Kawasaki, KSK, Nippon Sharyo, Mitsubishi, Toshiba
  electrical equipment Hitachi, Kawasaki, Mitsubishi, Nippon Sharyo, Toshiba, Toyo
Number built 175
Number series EF58 1 — EF58 175

The last of a long line of Japanese articulated bogie locomotives, the handsome EF58 was introduced in 1947 for express service on the old Tokaido line and other easily graded 1·5 kV dc routes of the JNR system. Although rather heavy, and soon outmoded by the development of all-adhesion machines, the design incorporated such modern features as an all-welded body and roller-bearing axle-boxes. No less than 175 examples had been supplied by various Japanese builders up to 1958, and some 150 of these remained in JNR passenger service at the beginning of 1980.

Originally equipped with steam generators for train heating, certain members of the class have since been modified for electric heating, notably units based at Utsunomiya and Takasaki. First deliveries were painted maroon while later examples appeared new in light green and yellow. Present standard livery is blue and white.

JNR class EF58 no EF58 121. The shades above the cab-front windows are a later addition *(Masahide Meguriya)*

Japan

JNR class EF65

Operating system Japanese National Railways (JNR)
Year introduced 1964
Axle arrangement Bo-Bo-Bo
Gauge 1067 mm *(3 ft 6 in)*
Power supply system 1.5 kV dc
One-hour output 2550 kW *(3415 hp, 3465 ch)*
Maximum speed 115 km/h *(71 mph)*
One-hour tractive effort 200 kN *(44 900 lbs)* at 45 km/h *(28 mph)*
Weight in working order 96 tonnes *(94½ tons)*
Length over coupler centres 16 500 mm *(54 ft 1⅝ in)*
Bogie wheelbase 2800 mm *(9 ft 2¼ in)*
Wheel diameter 1120 mm *(3 ft 8 in)*
Traction motors Six dc series-wound type MT52A nose-suspended, axle-hung
Control Rheostatic
Electric brake None
Builder
 mechanical parts Kawasaki, Toshiba, Nippon Sharyo Seizo
 electrical equipment Kawasaki, Toshiba, Toyo
Number built 274
Number series EF65 1 — EF65 135 (with gaps — see text); EF65 501 — EF65 542; EF65 1001 — EF65 1139

JNR class EF65 no EF65 1062 is one of a sub-series with **increased braking capacity for express passenger work** *(Kawasaki)*

The successful EF65 is JNR's most numerous dc locomotive series, with 274 examples in service. Intended for operation on routes with gradients not exceeding 1% (1 in 100), the class is divided into three sub-series (see below) to meet specific service requirements. As with most other modern high-powered JNR electric locomotive designs, the flexible Bo-Bo-Bo axle arrangement is used, and features of the electrical equipment include vernier fine control to prevent power surges, automatic wheel-slip control, axle-load compensation and, on the E65 & E65 1000 series, provision for multiple-unit working. Livery is the standard blue and white adopted for all modern JNR dc locomotives.

Three similarly rated JNR dc designs share many common features including traction motors, but the specification of each class varies according to the gradients over which they operate. Class EF62 is a Co-Co machine with rheostatic brakes for steeply graded lines, while the EF63 and EF64 models are of the Bo-Bo-Bo type, again intended for hill work. Both the EF62 and EF63 were designed for service on the Shin-etsu line with adhesion-worked grades of 6·67% (1 in 15).

The three sub-series of class EF65 are:
– nos EF65 1-135, representing the original design for freight work. Forty-two of these units have been modified to form the EF65 500 series and consequently gaps occur in the numbering sequence.
– series EF65 500, with increased brake capacity for express passenger operation. These were converted from the main series.
– series EF65 1000 is a later development used in a mixed-traffic role, but retaining the braking characteristics of the EF65 500.

JNR Class EF66

Operating system Japanese National Railways (JNR)
Year introduced 1966
Axle arrangement Bo-Bo-Bo
Gauge 1067 mm *(3 ft 6 in)*
Power supply system 1.5 kV dc
One-hour output 3900 kW *(5225 hp, 5300ch)*
Maximum speed 120 km/h *(75 mph)*
One-hour tractive effort 192 kN *(43 200 lbs)* at 72 km/h *(45 mph)*
Weight in working order 101 tonnes *(100 tons)*
Length over coupler centres 18 200 mm *(59 ft 8½ in)*
Bogie wheelbase 2800 mm *(9 ft 2¼ in)*
Wheel diameter 1120 mm *(3 ft 8 in)*
Traction motors Six dc series-wound type MT56, fully suspended with hollow-shaft drive
Control Rheostatic
Electric brake Rheostatic
Builder
  mechanical parts Kawasaki, KSK
  electrical equipment Kawasaki, Tôyôdenki
Number built 56
Number series EF66 1 — EF66 55, EF66 901

With an hourly rating of 3900 kW, the impressive EF66 is by far JNR's most powerful electric locomotive, and its fastest. Until the introduction of South African Railways' (SAR) 9E series in 1978 (see p 107) the EF66 could also claim to be the world's most powerful narrow-gauge design in terms of output.

The class was developed by Kawasaki specifically for express freight haulage on the old Tokaido and Sanyo lines, and appeared in 1966 in the form of prototype no EF90 1. A Bo-Bo-Bo axle configuration was adopted, with a system of air suspension and swing-levers to permit lateral displacement of the middle bogie when negotiating curves. The six traction motors are 750V machines rated at 650 kW—half as powerful again as those of other modern JNR dc designs—and are fully suspended. Speed is regulated by motor connection and field control, with fine vernier control and axle-load compensation for optimum adhesion.

Series construction began in 1968, and the entire class is now based in the Hiroshima Area at Hiroshima and Shimonoseki depots. Prototype no EF90 1 survives as no EF66 901 and only differs in minor details.

JNR class EF66 no EF66 26 *(Kawasaki)*

JNR class ED75

Operating system Japanese National Railways (JNR)
Year introduced 1963
Axle arrangement Bo-Bo
Gauge 1067 mm *(3 ft 6 in)*
Power supply system 20 kV ac 50 Hz (except ED75 300 — 20 kV ac 60 Hz)
One-hour output 1900 kW *(2545 hp, 2580 ch)*
Maximum speed 100 km/h *(62 mph)*
One-hour tractive effort 139 kN *(31 100 lbs)* at 49 km/h *(30½ mph)*
Weight in working order 67.2 tonnes *(66¼ tons)*
Length over coupler centres 14 300 mm *(46 ft 11 in)*
Bogie wheelbase 2500 mm *(8 ft 2⅜ in)*
Wheel diameter 1120 mm *(3 ft 8 in)*
Traction motors Four pulsating current series-wound type MT52A, nose-suspended, axle-hung
Control l.t. tap-changer (except ED75 501 — thyristor)
Electric brake None
Builder
  mechanical parts Hitachi, Mitsubishi, Toshiba
  electrical equipment Hitachi, Mitsubishi, Toshiba
Number built 302
Number series ED75 1 — ED75 160; ED75 301 — ED75 311; ED75 501; ED75 701 — ED75 791; ED75 1001 — ED75 1039

JNR class ED75 no ED75 744 in March 1975. This locomotive is one of a series specially snow-proofed for operation in northern Honshu *(Masahide Meguriya)*

The switch by JNR from dc to industrial frequency ac for major new electrification schemes occurred in 1957 when the Hokuriku line was energised at 20 kV. Various locomotive designs, both with ac motors and with mercury arc rectifiers, appeared for earlier single-phase schemes, but after a comparatively brief evolutionary period, the silicon rectifier ED75 emerged in 1963 as standard general purpose motive power for ac lines.

With 302 examples in service, the class is the largest in JNR's electric locomotive fleet, and comprises the following sub-series:

– nos ED75 1-160, forming the standard design.
– series ED75 300, intended for operation at 60 Hz, the local industrial frequency on Kyushu island. These units are all based at Moji.
– no ED75 501, experimentally equipped with thyristor control and specially adapted to prevent the ingress of snow into the machinery compartment and electrical equipment.
– series ED75 700, also snow-proofed for operation in the northern part of Honshu.
– series ED75 1000, with increased brake capacity to permit shorter stopping distances in express passenger operation.

All are equipped for multiple-unit working.

Features such as bogies and traction motors of the ED75 family are common to various JNR dc designs. Ac derivatives include class ED76, a Bo-2-Bo machine for secondary line duty with a novel provision for pneumatically varying driving-axle load, and the similarly equipped ED77 of 75 tonnes for branch line work. Like all JNR ac designs, the ED75s are finished in a red livery.

Japan

JNR class EF81

Operating system Japanese National Railways (JNR)
Year introduced 1968
Axle arrangement Bo-Bo-Bo
Gauge 1067 mm *(3 ft 6 in)*
Power supply system (dual-current) 1.5 kV dc; 20 kV ac 50 or 60 Hz
One-hour output *(dc)* 2550 kW *(3415 hp, 3465 ch)*; *(ac)* 2370 kW *(3175 hp, 3220 ch)*
Maximum speed 115 km/h *(72 mph)*
One-hour tractive effort (dc) 195 kN *(43 800 lbs)* at 45 km/h *(28 mph)*; (ac) 179 kN *(40 200 lbs)* at 45 km/h *(28 mph)*
Weight in working order 100.8 tonnes *(99¼ tons)*
Length over coupler centres 18 600 mm *(61 ft 0¼ in)*
Bogie wheelbase 2600 mm *(8 ft 6⅜ in)*
Wheel diameter 1120 mm *(3 ft 8 in)*
Traction motors Six dc series-wound type MT52A, nose-suspended, axle-hung
Control Rheostatic
Electric brake None
Builder
  mechanical parts Hitachi, Mitsubishi
  electrical equipment Hitachi, Mitsubishi, Toshiba
Number built 156
Number series EF81 1 — EF81 152; EF81 1301 — EF81 1304

The development by JNR of an extensive ac network connecting with parts of the system electrified earlier at 1·5 kV dc has called for considerable numbers of dual-current locomotives. The six-axle EF81 series is the newest and most powerful of three such designs, and is equipped to operate under 1·5 kV dc or 20 kV ac at 50 or 60 Hz. In ac working, a fixed ratio transformer/silicon diode rectifier group is employed to provide dc for control by resistances, motor grouping and field control. Traction motors are type MT52A, as fitted to classes EF65, ED75 and several other JNR electric locomotive classes of the 1960s. Bogie design is also derived from earlier models, and incorporates coil spring secondary suspension. Lateral displacement of the centre bogie assists the negotiation of curves. Electric train heating facilities are provided.

The 156 units in JNR service include four, nos EF81 1301-1304, used for operations through the undersea Kanmon Tunnel linking Honshu and Kyushu. Based at Uchigo and Moji, these locomotives have bodies of stainless steel to resist the corrosive effects of the salt-laden atmosphere.

JNR class EF81 no EF81 1

Korea (South)

KNR class WAG1

Operating system Korean National Railroad (KNR)
Year introduced 1972
Axle arrangement Bo-Bo-Bo
Gauge 1435 mm *(4 ft 8½ in)*
Power supply system 25 kV ac 60 Hz
One-hour output 3990 kW *(5350 hp, 5420 ch)*
Continuous output 3930 kW *(5270 hp, 5340 ch)*
Maximum speed 85 km/h *(53 mph)*
Maximum tractive effort 426 kN *(95 800 lbs)*
Continuous tractive effort 322 kN *(72 400 lbs)* at
43 km/h *(27 mph)*
Weight in working order 128 tonnes *(126 tons)*
Length over coupler centres 20 730 mm
(68 ft 0⅛ in)
Bogie wheelbase 2900 mm *(9 ft 6⅛ in)*
Wheel diameter 1250 mm *(4 ft 1¼ in)*
Traction motors Six pulsating current series-wound,
nose-suspended, axle-hung
Control Thyristor
Electric brake Rheostatic
Builder
mechanical parts Alsthom, La Brugeoise et Nivelles,
MTE (for 50 Hz Group)
electrical equipment ACEC, AEG-Telefunken,
Alsthom, BBC, MTE, Siemens (for 50 Hz Group)
Number built 90
Number series 8001 — 8090

Spectacular growth in the economy of South Korea since 1960 is mirrored by the rapid development and modernisation of its railway system. In 1975, a major scheme was completed to electrify the difficult route through the Taebaeg mountains from Seoul to Bugpyeong, a total route length (with branches) of 449 km (279 miles). Contracts for both fixed electrical installations and motive power were awarded to the 50 Hz Group, a consortium of leading West European companies specialising in various aspects of railway electrification at industrial frequency.

The thyristor-controlled WAG1 was designed by the Group to meet exacting haulage requirements which included a capability to lift 870 tonne loads up 2·5% (1 in 40) gradients with radii down to 250 m (12½ chains). The necessary combination of flexibility and power was achieved by adopting a Bo-Bo-Bo axle arrangement with a rigid body. The centre bogie employs a novel form of secondary suspension which permits lateral movement of up to 230 mm (9 in) in either direction when sharp curves are negotiated. As well as controlling traction motor voltage, the thyristor rectifier equipment regulates wheel-slip and electric braking effort. Traction motors are 820V machines, with nose suspension. The Alsthom designed body is based on contemporary SNCF practice, and is finished in a livery of blue and cream with grey roof and bogies.

Assembly of the locomotives was shared by Alsthom, who built 43 of the original batch of 66 and all 24 of a follow-up order, and La Brugeoise et Nivelles in Belgium. Bogie design and construction was by MTE. ACEC, a member of the Westinghouse group, acted as project managers for the 50 Hz Group.

KNR class WAG1 no 8001 *(ACEC)*

Morocco

ONCFM class E-1000

Operating system Moroccan Railways (ONCFM)
Year introduced 1975
Axle arrangement Co-Co
Gauge 1435 mm *(4 ft 8½ in)*
Power supply system 3 kV dc
One-hour output 3120 kW *(4180 hp, 4240 ch)*
Continuous output 3000 kW *(4020 hp, 4075 ch)*
Maximum speed 125 km/h *(78 mph)*
Maximum tractive effort 412 kN *(92 600 lbs)*
Continuous tractive effort 212 kN *(47 600 lbs)* at
  50 km/h *(31 mph)*
Weight in working order 120 tonnes *(118.5 tons)*
Length over buffers 19 240 mm *(63 ft 1½ in)*
Bogie wheelbase 1900+1900=3800 mm
  (12 ft 5⅝ in)
Wheel diameter 1250 mm *(4 ft 1¼ in)*
Traction motors Four dc series-wound type EE5416,
  fully suspended with flexible quill drive
Control Rheostatic
Electric brake None
Builder
  mechanical parts Pafawag
  electrical equipment Dolmel
Number built 23
Number series E-1001 — E-1023

The first railway electrification in Morocco, commissioned in February 1924, was the 140 km (87 mile) line from Casablanca to Khourigba which had only been opened to traffic five months earlier. The system adopted was the present standard overhead 3kV dc using hydro-electric power generated by rivers flowing down from the Atlas Mountains. By 1980, 708 route-km (440 miles) had been energised, accounting for nearly 40% of the ONCFM network.

A break with the long tradition of operating French designed electric locomotives came in 1975 with delivery of the E-1000 series of Polish construction. These all-purpose 3120 kW machines are a modified version of the Pafawag model 201E built in large numbers for Polish State Railways (PKP class ET22—see p 98), and form Poland's first export order for main line electric locomotives.

Principal departures from the standard PKP design include the provision of Faively-type single-arm pantographs in place of the diamond pattern type, substantially larger bodyside ventilation louvres to suit Moroccan climatic conditions, and an absence of train heating/air conditioning facilities. Although the class is particularly used for front line passenger work, ONCFM operates separate generator vehicles to provide auxiliary power for train-board services.

ONCFM class E-1000 no E-1009 at Meknès in April 1979 *(Marcel Vleugels)*

Morocco

ONCFM class E-1100

Operating system Moroccan Railways (ONCFM)
Year introduced 1977
Axle arrangement Co-Co
Gauge 1435 mm *(4 ft 8½ in)*
Power supply system 3kV dc
One-hour output 3000 kW *(4020 hp, 4075 ch)*
Continuous output 2850 kW *(3820 hp, 3870 ch)*
Maximum speed 100 km/h *(62 mph)*
Maximum tractive effort 314 kN *(70 500 lbs)*
Weight in working order 120 tonnes *(118 tons)*
Length over buffers 19 700 mm *(64 ft 7½ in)*
Bogie wheelbase 4300 mm *(14 ft 1¼ in)*
Wheel diameter 1250 mm *(4 ft 1¼ in)*
Traction motors Six dc series-wound, nose-suspended, axle-hung
Control Rheostatic
Electric brake Rheostatic
Builder
  mechanical parts Hitachi
  electrical equipment Hitachi
Number built 22
Number series E-1101 — E-1122

Phosphates are the most important traffic on the ONCFM network, accounting for 75% of all freight tonne-km in 1978. To handle this tonnage, and to increase the capacity of the electric locomotive fleet, the administration ordered from Hitachi the 22 heavy duty six-axle 3 kV dc machines which now form class E-1100. Placed in service in 1977, these are the first main line dc electric locomotives supplied to an African railway by a Japanese manufacturer.

Design of the electrical equipment includes fine vernier control between main resistance notches to prevent power surges and hence avoid wheel-slip. Traction motors are nose-suspended, and with relatively low gearing the class has considerable haulage power. Electric rheostatic braking is provided. Secondary suspension is of the coil spring type, and bogie design is conceived to ensure optimum adhesion.

Livery is the striking white, red, mauve and grey adopted as standard for all modern ONCFM locomotives.

ONCFM class E-1100 no E-1104 at Fez in April 1979
(Marcel Vleugels)

Netherlands

NS class 1100

Operating system Netherlands Railways (NS)
Year introduced 1950
Axle arrangement Bo+Bo
Gauge 1435 mm *(4 ft 8½ in)*
Power supply system 1.5 kV dc
One-hour output 2030 kW *(2720 hp, 2760 ch)*
Continuous output 1900 kW *(2545 hp, 2580 ch)*
Maximum speed 135 km/h *(84 mph)*
Maximum tractive effort 152 kN *(34 200 lbs)*
Continuous tractive effort 92 kN *(20 700 lbs)* at
  70 km/h *(43½ mph)*
Weight in working order 80 tonnes *(79 tons)*
Length over buffers 12 984 mm *(42 ft 7⅛ in)* (see
  text)
Bogie wheelbase 2950 mm *(9 ft 8⅛ in)*
Wheel diameter 1250 mm *(4 ft 1¼ in)*
Traction motors Four dc series-wound Alsthom type
  TA 628A, fully suspended with Alsthom flexible drive
Control Rheostatic
Electric brake None
Builder
  mechanical parts Alsthom
  electrical equipment Alsthom
Number built 60
Number series 1101—1160

**Top right: Blue liveried no 1152 at
Roosendaal in January 1979** *(Yves
Steenebruggen)*

**Bottom left: A programme to refurbish and
modernise the 1100s was undertaken by NS
in 1978. Work includes provision of
protective noses of the French pattern.
Modified no 1141 was photographed at
Heerlen in March 1979** *(Antoon Hermans)*

**Bottom right: Parent design for the 1100
series was the French National Railways
(SNCF) class BB-8100, 171 of which were
constructed between 1949 and 1955. No
BB-8250 heads a heavy block tank train near
Marseilles in September 1976** *(Yves
Steenebruggen)*

**Below: Moroccan Railways (ONCFM)
operate a 3 kV version of the French and
Dutch designs as class E-700. No E-705 is
seen near Casablanca in April 1979** *(Marcel
Vleugels)*

Maids-of-all-work on the NS 1·5 kV dc system are the class 1100 machines supplied by the French builder Alsthom between 1950 and 1956, and based on the French National Railways (SNCF) class BB-8100, of which 171 are in service. Drawgear and buffers are mounted on the bogies, which are coupled. The four traction motors are 750 V machines similar to those of the SNCF CC-7100 series. Motor groupings are series and series-parallel with four and three field-weakening steps respectively to give nine economic running notches. A significant difference between the NS locomotives and their French counterparts is the adoption of spring-borne traction motors to allow the top speed to be increased from the 105 km/h (65 mph) of the BB-8100 to 135 km/h (84 mph).

The 1100s have undergone several livery changes during their useful careers. Nos 1101-1150 were originally finished in turquoise before Berlin blue was adopted as standard in 1954. The last ten received this from new, and earlier units were similarly treated after overhaul. Since 1971, many of the class have been painted in the present warm yellow and grey.

In 1978, NS embarked on a programme of refurbishment of the entire class intended to prolong their service lives at least until 1985. Principal modifications carried out at the Tilburg workshops include the provision of roller bearings, suspension improvements and the addition to the cab of a nose similar to that of contemporary French designs. This increases by 500 mm (1 ft 7¾ in) the overall length, and is intended to offer better protection for the crew in event of an accident. No 1129 was the first example to be treated and the work was scheduled to be completed by 1981.

In addition to the SNCF class BB-8100 referred to above, Alsthom have also supplied an 88 tonne 3 kV dc version with regenerative braking to Moroccan Railways (ONCFM class E-700).

Netherlands

NS class 1200

Operating system Netherlands Railways (NS)
Year introduced 1951
Axle arrangement Co-Co
Gauge 1435 mm *(4 ft 8½ in)*
Power supply system 1 5 kV dc
One-hour output 2360 kW *(3165 hp, 3210 ch)*
Continuous output 2210 kW *(2960 hp, 3000 ch)*
Maximum speed 135 km/h *(84 mph)*
Maximum tractive effort 194 kN *(43 500 lbs)*
Continuous tractive effort 165 kN *(37 200 lbs)* at
60 km/h *(37 mph)*
Weight in working order 108 tonnes *(106.5 tons)*
Length over buffers 18 085 mm *(59 ft 4 in)*
Bogie wheelbase 2438+2286=4724 mm
(15 ft 6 in)
Wheel diameter 1100 mm *(3 ft 7¼ in)*
Traction motors Four dc series-wound type TM 94,
nose-suspended, axle-hung
Control Rheostatic
Electric brake None
Builder
  mechanical parts Werkspoor (under Baldwin
  licence)
  electrical equipment Heemaf (under Westinghouse
  licence)
Number built 25
Number series 1201 — 1225

Although most of the locomotives supplied to NS for its major post-war electrification schemes were of French origin, the 25 class 1200 units were licence-built in the Netherlands to the designs of two American companies, Baldwin Locomotive Works and Westinghouse. Construction of the bogies, which have roller bearing axle-boxes, was carried out at Baldwin's Philadelphia plant, and Westinghouse provided certain items of electrical equipment. Assembly of the locomotives was undertaken by Werkspoor in Amsterdam between 1951 and 1953, with the remaining electrical apparatus coming from Heemaf. Design speed of the 1200 series is 150 km/h (93 mph) but they are restricted to 135 km/h on the NS network. Since their introduction these impressive machines have established a long record of performance and reliability, and in 1979 NS began a programme of modernisation at its Tilburg works which assures the future of the class until the 1990s.

Livery details are as for the 1100 series (see previous entry) except that no 1215 was finished in a mahogany colour scheme for a brief period before receiving standard Berlin blue.

NS class 1200 no 1207 at Maastricht in June 1976
(Marcel Vleugels)

Netherlands

NS class 1500

Operating system Netherlands Railways (NS)
Year introduced Built 1954, first entered NS service 1970
Axle arrangement Co-Co
Gauge 1435 mm *(4 ft 8½ in)*
Power supply system 1.5 kV dc
One-hour output 2185 kW *(2930 hp, 2970 ch)*
Continuous output 1932 kW *(2590 hp, 2625 ch)*
Maximum speed 135 km/h *(84 mph)*
Maximum tractive effort 198 kN *(44 600 lbs)*
Continuous tractive effort 89 kN *(20 000 lbs)* at 78 km/h *(48 mph)*
Weight in working order 97 tonnes *(95.5 tons)*
Length over buffers 18 102 mm *(59 ft 4⅝ in)*
Bogie wheelbase 2438 + 2331 = 4769 mm *(15 ft 7¾ in)*
Wheel diameter 1092 mm *(3 ft 7 in)*
Traction motors Six dc series-wound Metropolitan-Vickers type MV 146, nose-suspended, axle-hung
Control Rheostatic
Electric brake None
Builder
  mechanical parts British Railways (Gorton Works)
  electrical equipment Metropolitan-Vickers
Number built 7 (of which 6 entered NS service)
Number series 1501 — 1506

NS class 1500 no 1501 (formerly BR no E27003 *Diana*) piloting a class 1100 included as reserve power during a test run at Rotterdam on 6 May 1970, two days before being handed over for duty *(L Albers/NS)*

The NS class 1500 locomotives started their working lives as British Railways class EM2 on the 1·5 kV dc Manchester-Sheffield line, where they handled passenger traffic from their construction in 1954 until 1968, by which time passenger services had declined. After withdrawal, the class was stored at Bury until purchased in 1969 by NS to ease a severe motive power shortage. All seven locomotives were shipped from Harwich to Zeebrugge in September of that year.

After arrival in the Netherlands, the locomotives were tested before six were selected for the extensive modifications needed to suit NS operating conditions. The work was carried out in NS workshops, and, as well as major electrical overhaul, included substitution of air, rather than vacuum-braking, fitting of single-arm pantographs and the provision of electric train heating facilities. Driver's cabs were modernised and standard NS vigilance equipment fitted. The first refurbished unit, no 1501, entered service in May 1970 and all six were operational by June of the following year, principally handling passenger duties which included certain prestigious TEE traffic. By the beginning of 1980, increased NS traffic had reversed an earlier decision to phase out these locomotives by 1981/2 and their future appears secure until the mid-1980s.

During the latter part of their BR careers, these locomotives bore the names of Greek gods, and these are recorded below, together with their final BR numbers:

1501	E27003 *Diana*	1505	E27001 *Ariadne*
1502	E27000 *Electra*	1506	E27002 *Aurora*
1503	E27004 *Juno*	—	E27005 *Minerva* (this unit
1504	E27006 *Pandora*		cannibalised for spares and subsequently sold for scrap)

New Zealand

NZR class Ea

Operating system New Zealand Railways (NZR)
Year produced 1968
Axle arrangement Bo-Bo
Gauge 1067 mm *(3 ft 6 in)*
Power supply system 1.5 kV dc
One-hour output 960 kW *(1285 hp, 1305 ch)*
Continuous output 800 kW *(1070 hp, 1085 ch)*
Maximum speed 72 km/h *(45 mph)*
Maximum tractive effort 103 kN *(23 000 lbs)*
Continuous tractive effort 101 kN *(22 700 lbs)* at
  33 km/h *(20½ mph)*
Weight in working order 55 tonnes *(54 tons)*
Length over buffers 11 582 mm *(38 ft 0 in)*
Bogie wheelbase 2400 mm *(7 ft 10½ in)*
Wheel diameter 1016 mm *(3 ft 4 in)*
Traction motors Four dc series-wound, nose-
  suspended, axle-hung
Control Rheostatic
Electric brake Rheostatic
Builder
  mechanical parts Tokyo Shibaura Electric Co.
    (Toshiba)
  electrical equipment Tokyo Shibaura Electric Co.
    (Toshiba)
Number built 5
Number series 1 — 5

Ordered in 1966, the five NZR class Ea locomotives were specially designed by the Japanese company Toshiba to handle freight traffic over the difficult 13 km (8 mile) Otira-Arthur's Pass line in New Zealand's South Island. This short electrified section, which was opened in 1923, forms the central part of the Christchurch-Greymouth route through the Southern Alps, and includes continuous 3% (1 in 33) gradients through the 8553 m (5¼ mile) Otira Tunnel, rising to a summit of 737 m (2417 ft) at Arthur's Pass.

The line was electrified from the start using the present 1·5 kV dc overhead system. Until the arrival in April 1968 of the Ea series, motive power was provided by a class of five 508 kW (680 hp) Bo+Bo machines built in 1922 by English Electric and designated class Eo. With nearly double the power of the Eo, three Ea units in multiple are able to maintain a speed of 32 km/h (20 mph) on a 3% gradient with a trailing load of 508 tonnes (500 tons), compared with 381 tonnes (375 tons) at 27 km/h (17 mph) for three of the earlier machines.

As two or three Ea locomotives are normally used in multiple, a driver's cab is provided at one end only, with gangway access to allow the crew to pass through coupled units. Resistance control is used, with motor groupings of series and series-parallel and no field weakening. Electric rheostatic braking is sufficiently powerful to hold the maximum load for three locomotives of 610 tonnes (600 tons) at 32-40 km/h (20-25 mph) on a downward 3% grades.

**NZR class Ea locomotives nos 4 (leading)
and 1 heading an enthusiasts' special at
Arthur's Pass** *(Roy Sinclair)*

New Zealand

NZR class Ew

Operating system New Zealand Railways (NZR)
Year introduced 1952
Axle arrangement Bo-Bo-Bo
Gauge 1067 mm *(3 ft 6 in)*
Power supply system 1.5 kV dc
One-hour output 1340 kW *(1800 hp, 1820 ch)*
Continuous output 1120 kW *(1500 hp, 1521 ch)*
Maximum speed 95 km/h *(60 mph)*
Maximum tractive effort 187 kN *(42 000 lbs)*
Continuous tractive effort 104 kN *(23 400 lbs)* at
44.5 km/h *(28 mph)*
Weight in working order 76 tonnes *(75 tons)*
Length over buffers 18 900 mm *(62 ft 0 in)*
Bogie wheelbase 2600 mm *(8 ft 6⅜ in)*
Wheel diameter 927 mm *(3 ft 0½ in)*
Traction motors Six dc series-wound, nose-
suspended, axle-hung
Control Rheostatic
Electric brake None
Builder
  mechanical parts Robert Stephenson & Hawthorns
  electrical equipment English Electric
Number built 7
Number series 1800—1806

The seven 1340 kW British built Ew units are the most powerful electric locomotives to operate on NZR's modest 1·5 kV dc network and employ the unusual configuration of an articulated two-section body carried on three two-axle bogies. This arrangement has been little used outside Italy, but was found to combine high power with a sufficiently flexible wheelbase for the NZR 1067 mm (3 ft 6 in) gauge system.

The seven members of the class were delivered between March and November 1952, and were originally intended for both passenger and freight work within the limits of the Wellington area electrification, duties they shared with the Ed series. From 1952 to 1967 they handled traffic on the most southerly 42 km (26 miles) of the North Island Main trunk line between the traction exchange point of Paekakariki and Wellington. Since 1967, lowering of the trackbed in certain tunnels on this section of line has permitted through running into Wellington with diesel power, and the Ew units are now mainly employed on heavy peak-hour suburban passenger duties out of Wellington, a task to which they have reportedly adapted well.

NZR class Ew no 1806 at Wellington in 1970
(NZR)

Norway

NSB class El.13

Operating system Norwegian State Railways (NSB)
Year introduced 1957
Axle arrangement Bo-Bo
Gauge 1435 mm *(4 ft 8½ in)*
Power supply system 15 kV ac 16⅔ Hz
One-hour output 2650 kW *(3550 hp, 3600 ch)*
Maximum speed 100 km/h *(62 mph)* or 115 km/h *(71 mph)*
Maximum tractive effort 187 kN *(41 900 lbs)*
One-hour tractive effort 128 kN *(28 700 lbs)* at 69 km/h *(43 mph)*
Weight in working order 72 tonnes *(71 tons)*
Length over buffers 15 000 mm *(49 ft 2½ in)*
Bogie wheelbase 3230 mm *(10 ft 7⅞ in)*
Wheel diameter 1350 mm *(4 ft 5⅛ in)*
Traction motors Four single-phase commutator, fully suspended with Brown Boveri spring drive
Control h.t. tap-changer
Electric brake None
Builder
  mechanical parts A/S Thunes Mekaniske Vaerksted
  electrical equipment A/S Norsk Elektrisk & Brown Boveri
Number built 37
Number series 13.2121 — 13.2144 and 13.2151 — 13.2163

Maids-of-all-work on NSB's 15 kV ac lines are the 2650 kW E1.13 units built in Norway by Thune and NEBB. These 72 tonne locomotives first appeared in 1957 as a substantially more powerful development of the E1.11 series, which they closely resemble. Contemporary German and Swiss practice is reflected in both electrical and mechanical design, with high-tension control, BBC spring drive and SLM pattern bogies. Driving wheels of later machines are of the disc rather than spoked pattern. Certain members of the class with rebuilt traction motors are permitted to run at the increased maximum speed of 115 km/h (71 mph).

Deliveries of the 37-strong series were made in small batches over the ten year period up to 1966, as NSB electrification progressed. By the beginning of 1980, when 2440 route-km (1515 miles) of the 4241 km (2634 mile) system were under the wires, the versatile E1.13s were to be found on most parts of the network handling a wide variety of traffic.

NSB class El.13 no 13.2162 at Stavanger in May 1976.
Note snowplough and windscreen grilles to offer protection against falling rocks on mountain lines
(Svein Sando/NSB)

Norway

NSB class El.14

Operating system Norwegian State Railways (NSB)
Year introduced 1968
Axle arrangement Co-Co
Gauge 1435 mm *(4 ft 8½ in)*
Power supply system 15 kV ac 16⅔ Hz
One-hour output 5075 kW *(6805 hp, 6900 ch)*
Maximum speed 120 km/h *(75 mph)*
Maximum tractive effort 344 kN *(77 200 lbs)*
One-hour tractive effort 213 kN *(47 800 lbs)* at
76 km/h *(47 mph)*
Weight in working order 105 tonnes *(103.5 tons)*
Length over buffers 17 740 mm *(58 ft 2⅜ in)*
Bogie wheelbase 1850+1850=3700 mm
(12 ft 1⅝ in)
Wheel diameter 1270 mm *(4 ft 2 in)*
Traction motors Six single-phase commutator, frame-suspended with Brown Boveri spring drive
Control h.t.tap-changer
Electric brake Rheostatic
Builder
  mechanical parts A/S Thunes Mekaniske Vaerksted
  electrical equipment A/S Norsk Elektrisk & Brown Boveri
Number built 31
Number series 14.2164—14.2190, 14.2197—
14.2200

Like the El.16 described in the following entry, the El.14 was designed originally for operation on mountain lines, notably the spectacular Oslo-Bergen route which was electrified throughout in 1964. Traffic requirements on this line demanded a design capable of taking 700 tonne trailing loads up continuous grades of 2·5% (1 in 40) at a minimum speed of 50 km/h (31 mph). Construction of the class was carried out at the Oslo factory of Thune, with deliveries extending from 1968 to 1973.

Used as a powerful all-purpose machine, the El.14 has a relatively light axle-load of 17·5 tonnes. Bogies are licence-built to Swiss (SLM) designs based on those of the Swiss Federal Railways (SBB) class Ae 6/6. To provide a flexible wheelbase for the abundant curves on the NSB network, each wheelset has lateral sideplay of 10 and 3 mm in either direction for centre and outer axles respectively. The locomotives are equipped with electric rheostatic braking for which resistances are mounted beneath a prominent roof cowling. Small snowploughs are provided, as well as grilles over the cab windows to serve as protection against the rock-falls which are an operating hazard of Norwegian mountain routes.

The livery of these units is the standard NSB deep red relieved with yellow flashes.

NSB class El.14 no 14.2174 at Marienborg in May 1972
(Frank Stenvall)

NSB class El.16

Operating system Norwegian State Railways (NSB)
Year introduced 1977
Axle arranncement Bo-Bo
Gauge 1435 mm *(4 ft 8½ in)*
Power supply system 15 kV ac 16⅔ Hz
Continuous output 4440 kW *(5950 hp, 6035 ch)*
Maximum speed 140 km/h *(87 mph)*
Maximum tractive effort 328 kN *(73 700 lbs)*
Continuous tractive effort 201 kN *(45 200 lbs)* at 78 km/h *(48 mph)*
Weight in working order 80 tonnes *(79 tons)*
Length over buffers 15 520 mm *(50 ft 11 in)*
Bogie wheelbase 2700 mm *(8 ft 10¼ in)*
Wheel diameter 1300 mm *(4 ft 3⅛ in)*
Traction motors Four separately-excited ripple current ASEA type LJH108, fully suspended with hollow shaft drive
Control Thyristor
Electric brake Rheostatic
Builder
 mechanical parts A/S Strommens Vaerksted, A/S Thunes Mekaniske Vaerksted
 electrical equipment ASEA
Number built 10 + 4 ordered 1980
Number series 16.2201 — 16.2210 (+ 4 on order)

Introduction of the thyristor-controlled El.16 series followed trials on the Oslo-Bergen line in February 1976 with Swedish State Railways (SJ) class Rc4 no 1137. Although generally similar to the Swedish Rc family, the Norwegian units have been specially adapted for operation in the harsh physical and climatic conditions which prevail on the Bergen line. As well as extremely low winter temperatures, these include long continuous gradients of 2·0 to 2·5% (1 in 50 to 1 in 40) rising to a summit of 1301 m (4267 ft).

Body construction was carried out in Norway by Strømmens Vaerksted and incorporates specially strengthened front ends. The distinctive nose profile is intended both to keep the cab windows clear of snow and to withstand the impact of hanging ice in the Bergen line's 200 or so tunnels and snowsheds. The use of toughened windscreen glass obviates the need for the protective grilles fitted to other NSB motive power as a precaution against falling rocks.

The thyristor equipment of the parent Rc4 design is retained, but with a continuous rating of 4440 kW, the El.16 is rather more powerful. Optimum use of adhesive power is made possible by the employment of Pressductor wheel-slip control equipment, which monitors the behaviour of each axle individually and automatically reduces current to the traction motor of any slipping axle. Unlike SJ units, the El.16 has rheostatic braking.

Originally only six locomotives were ordered from ASEA. These were joined in 1980 by four more to form the present class and in the same year a further four were ordered by NSB.

NSB class El.16 no 16.2201 at the head of the daytime Oslo-Bergen express on 17 January 1978. This was the first occasion one of these locomotives had taken sole charge of a scheduled passenger train *(ASEA)*

Pakistan

PR class BCU-30

Operating system Pakistan Railways (PR)
Year introduced 1968
Axle arrangement Bo-Bo
Gauge 1676 mm *(5 ft 6 in)*
Power supply system 25 kV ac 50 Hz
One-hour output 2725 kW *(3650 hp, 3700 ch)*
Continuous output 2360 kW *(3160 hp, 3205 ch)*
Maximum speed 120 km/h *(75 mph)*
Maximum tractive effort 249 kN *(56 000 lbs)*
Continuous tractive effort 125 kN *(28 200 lbs)* at
  68 km/h *(42 mph)*
Weight in working order 81 tonnes *(80 tons)*
Length over buffers 16 510 mm *(54 ft 2 in)*
Bogie wheelbase 2743 mm *(9 ft 0 in)*
Wheel diameter 1092 mm *(3 ft 7 in)*
Traction motors Four dc series-wound, nose-
  suspended, axle-hung with resilient drives
Control Thyristor
Electric brake None
Builder
  mechanical parts Metropolitan-Cammell, English
    Electric (on behalf of British Rail Traction Group)
  electrical equipment AEI, English Electric (on
    behalf of British Rail Traction Group)
Number built 29
Number series 7001 — 7029

Electrification of the 287 km (178 mile) Lahore-Khanewal line of the former Pakistan Western Railway* followed a feasibility study completed in 1965 by the United Kingdom Railway Advisory Service (UKRAS). The system adopted was 25 kV ac 50 Hz and motive power for the scheme came in the shape of these 29 locomotives supplied by AEI and English Electric, acting as the British Rail Traction Group. Assembly of the body and underframe was carried out at the Washwood Heath (Birmingham) works of Metropolitan-Cammell and bogies were built at Vulcan Foundry.

A significant feature of the design is the application of thyristors to control rectified voltage to the traction motors. As well as being the first British built locomotives so equipped, the BCU-30 series also represented the world's first export order for machines of this type. Special design consideration was given to the climatic conditions under which the class would operate. These include ambient temperatures of up to 48°C (118°F) and a relative humidity factor of 100%. Wind-blown sand is a further seasonal hazard. Other features of the design include automatic wheel-slip correction, a driver operated weight-transfer compensation device and multiple-unit control facilities. Provision was made for the installation of rheostatic braking in readiness for the once projected Lahore-Rawalpindi electrification. Although delivery of the 29 locomotives was completed in 1969, it was not until the following year that the Lahore-Khanewal scheme was energised throughout.

*After a period of administrative upheaval following the establishment of East Pakistan as the independent state of Bangladesh in 1970, the Pakistan Western Railway formally became Pakistan Railways in May 1974.

PR class BCU-30 no 7019, photographed shortly after delivery, and lettered for the Pakistan Western Railway *(GEC Traction)*

Poland

PKP class EU07

Operating system Polish State Railways (PKP)
Year introduced 1963
Axle arrangement Bo-Bo
Gauge 1435 mm *(4 ft 8½ in)*
Power supply system 3 kV dc
One-hour output 2080 kW *(2790 hp, 2830 ch)*
Continuous output 2000 kW *(2680 hp, 2720 ch)*
Maximum speed 125 km/h *(78 mph)*
Maximum tractive effort 260 kN *(58 500 lbs)*
Continuous tractive effort 141 kN *(31 700 lbs)* at
  49 km/h *(30 mph)*
Weight in working order 80 tonnes *(79 tons)*
Length over buffers 15 915 mm *(52 ft 2½ in)*
Bogie wheelbase 3048 mm *(10 ft 0 in)*
Wheel diameter 1250 mm *(4 ft 1¼ in)*
Traction motors Four dc series-wound type EE541/A,
  spring-borne with Alsthom-type quill drive
Control Rheostatic
Electric brake None
Builder
  mechanical parts Pafawag (Państwowa Fabryka
    Wagonów)
  electrical equipment Dolmel
Number built 243
Number series EU07-001 — EU07- 243

These 80 tonne mixed-traffic units are the Polish licence-built version of the British designed class EU06, 20 of which were constructed in 1961/2 by AEI, English Electric and Vulcan Foundry. Principally employed on passenger duties, the class is found throughout the PKP electrified network.

The design follows conventional modern dc practice, but particular attention has been paid to the specification of the electrical equipment to provide a satisfactory level of reliability during Poland's severe winters. Body and cab construction also incorporate features to protect equipment and crew from adverse climatic conditions. Traction motors are 1·5 kV machines permanently connected in pairs in series, and speed is controlled by motor grouping and field-weakening. Provision is made for two locomotives to operate in multiple.

In 1973, the Pafawag works at Wroclaw introduced an express passenger version, class EP08, of which examples with top speeds of 140 and 160 km/h (87 and 100 mph) are in PKP service. These locomotives are distinguishable by their livery of orange and green. A further derivative of the design appeared in 1977 in the shape of the ET41 twin-unit Bo-Bo + Bo-Bo of 4160 kW (5580 hp) for heavy mineral traffic. At least 100 of these have been delivered by the Cegielski works at Poznán, with construction of a further 300 planned during the period 1980-5.

PKP class EU07 no EU07-143 at Lublin *(John Chalcraft)*

Construction under licence in Poland of the EU07 followed delivery in 1961/2 of 20 similar EU06 units built in the United Kingdom. One of these, no EU06-10, is seen here shortly after entering service *(GEC Traction)*

No EP08-003 is one of 15 units based on the EU07 but with increased maximum speed for express passenger work *(E Barnes)*

The twin-unit ET41 was developed from the EU07 to handle important PKP mineral traffic and has a top speed of 100 km/h. No ET41-059-A/-B was photographed in May 1979 at Lublin *(Gottfried Schilke)*

Poland

PKP class ET22

Operating system Polish State Railways (PKP)
Year introduced 1971
Axel arrangement Co-Co
Gauge 1435 mm *(4 ft 8½ in)*
Power supply system 3 kV dc
One-hour output 3120 kW *(4180 hp, 4240 ch)*
Continuous output 3000 kW *(4020 hp, 4080 ch)*
Maximum speed 125 km/h *(78 mph)*
Maximum tractive effort 344 kN *(77 200 lbs)*
Continuous tractive effort 212 kN *(47 600 lbs)* at 50 km/h *(31 mph)*
Weight in working order 120 tonnes *(118 tons)*
Length over buffers 19 240 mm *(63 ft 1½ in)*
Bogie wheelbase 1900 + 1900 = 3800 mm *(12 ft 5⅝ in)*
Wheel diameter 1250 mm *(4 ft 1¼ in)*
Traction motors Six dc series-wound, spring-borne with flexible quill drive
Control Rheostatic
Electric brake None
Builder
  mechanical parts Pafawag (Panstwowa Fabryka Wagonów)
  electrical equipment Dolmel
Number built Reported to be 550 (see text)
Number series ET22-001 — ET22-550

Series construction of the domestically built ET22 series began in 1971, when it replaced the 2405 kW (3225 hp) ET21 on the production lines at Pafawag's Wrocław works as type 201E. Although classified as a freight locomotive by PKP and principally used as such, the specification is appropriate for a mixed-traffic unit. With a top speed of 120 km/h (75 mph) and spring-borne traction motors, the ET22 is also useful motive power for heavier passenger traffic and is accordingly equipped for electric train heating. Some later examples are reported to have multiple-unit control equipment and Soviet-type automatic couplers for working coal traffic between Silesia and Gdańsk.

The class was known to be still in production in 1980, by which time 550 were reported to have been built. Two prototypes of a more powerful version of the class numbered ET22-701 and -702 have also been supplied to PKP. These units too have automatic couplers. A single prototype of a 160 km/h express version of the ET22 appeared in 1974, bearing the number EP23-001. The design has also formed the basis of Poland's first export order for main line electric locomotives. In 1973, a fleet of 23 similar machines was supplied to Morocco to form ONCFM class E-1000 (see p 85).

PKP class ET22 no ET22-010 at Dęblin *(John Chalcraft)*

Poland

PKP class ET40

Operating system Polish State Railways (PKP)
Year introduced 1975
Axle arrangement Bo-Bo+Bo-Bo
Gauge 1435 mm *(4 ft 8½ in)*
Power supply system 3 kV dc
Continuous output 4080 kW *(5465 hp, 5545 ch)*
Maximum speed 100 km/h *(62 mph)*
Maximum tractive effort 490 kN *(110 200 lbs)*
Continuous tractive effort 309 kN *(69 400 lbs)* at 46 km/h *(29 mph)*
Weight in working order 164 tonnes *(162 tons)*
Length over buffers 34 420 mm *(112 ft 11⅛ in)*
Wheel diameter 1250 mm *(4 ft 1⅛ in)*
Traction motors Eight dc series-wound, nose-suspended, axle-hung
Control Rheostatic
Electric brake Rheostatic
Builder
  mechanical parts Škoda
  electrical equipment Škoda
Number built 60
Number series ET40-01-A/ET40-01-B— ET40-60-A/ET40-60-B

This series of Czechoslovak built machines was the first of three twin-unit designs delivered to PKP during the late 1970s for the haulage of heavy mineral traffic. Intended primarily for operation on the Katowice-Gdańsk-Gdynia coal railway, the class was developed from the Czechoslovak State Railways (ČSD) class E469 mixed-traffic series which dates from 1960. Each of the two body sections is provided with one cab only and cannot be operated independently. Conventional resistance control is employed and the locomotives are equipped with rheostatic braking. Livery is the standard PKP two-tone green.

Manufacturer's designation for the class is type 77E.

PKP class ET40 no ET40-03-A and -B. Despite being purely a freight design, a connecting cable for train heating is visible *(Škoda)*

CP class 0 272551

Operating system Portuguese Railways (CP)
Year introduced 1963
Axle arrangement Bo-Bo
Gauge 1665 mm *(5 ft 9 9/16 in)*
Power supply system 25 kV ac 50 Hz
One-hour output 2176 kW *(2915 hp, 2960 ch)*
Continuous output 2044 kW *(2740 hp, 2780 ch)*
Maximum speed 120 km/h *(75 mph)*
Maximum tractive effort 199 kN *(44 600 lbs)*
Continuous tractive effort 119 kN *(26 700 lbs)* at 62 km/h *(39 mph)*
Weight in working order 70.5 tonnes *(69.5 tons)*
Length over buffers 15 380 mm *(50 ft 5½ in)*
Bogie wheelbase 3200 mm *(10 ft 6 in)*
Wheel diameter 1300 mm *(4 ft 3⅛ in)*
Traction motors Four dc series-wound type TAO 645, frame-suspended with Alsthom flexible drive
Control h.t. tap-changer
Electric brake None
Builder
  mechanical parts SOREFAME (for 50 Hz Group)
  electrical equipment ACEC, AEG-Telefunken, Alsthom, Brown Boveri, Oerlikon, MTE, Siemens (for 50 Hz Group)
Number built 20
Number series 0 272551 — 0 272570

Introduced in 1963 for the Lisbon-Oporto main line electrification, these locomotives were the second series supplied to CP to the designs of the European 50 Hz Group. Performance characteristics equal those of the 15 class 0 272501 units delivered in 1956, and the specifications of the electrical equipment are similar, with high-tension control and water cooled ignitron rectifiers. Electrical components were supplied by various members of the 50 Hz Group. The Henschel designed bogies of the earlier series are retained, but body construction is of stainless steel, forming a self-supporting structure. Assembly of this was undertaken in Portugal by SOREFAME under licence from the American company Budd. As well as offering a weight saving of some 3 tonnes over the earlier units, this unusual and characteristically styled construction was intended to harmonise with contemporary stainless steel coaching stock also built by SOREFAME.

The external appearance of these locomotives has changed little since delivery, although they now bear prominent orange and white diagonal warning stripes (see photo) and the modern "CP" logotype has replaced the original stainless steel characters which formerly embellished the bodysides and cab fronts. Although CP has adopted a rather intricate computerised numbering system, the locomotives still bear their original numbers, 2551-2570 on the front of the cab.

CP class 0 272551 no 0 272556 at Lisbon Campolido in May 1977 *(Marcel Vleugels)*

Portugal

CP class 0 382601

Operating system Portuguese Railways (CP)
Year introduced 1974
Axle arrangement B-B
Gauge 1665 mm *(5 ft 5 9/16 in)*
Power supply system 25 kV ac 50 Hz
One-hour output 2930 kW *(3925 hp, 3980 ch)*
Continuous output 2880 kW *(3860 hp, 3915 ch)*
Maximum speed 160/100 km/h *(100/62 mph)*
Maximum tractive effort (low gear) 314 kN *(71 500 lbs)*; (high gear) 208 kN *(46 800 lbs)*
Continuous tractive effort (low gear) 187 kN *(42 000 lbs)* at 55 km/h *(34 mph)*; (high gear) 116.5 kN *(26 200 lbs)* at 89 km/h *(55 mph)*
Weight in working order 78 tonnes *(77 tons)*
Length over buffers 17 480 mm *(57 ft 4¼ in)*
Bogie wheelbase 2200 mm *(7 ft 2⅝ in)*
Wheel diameter 1140 mm *(3 ft 8⅞ in)*
Traction motors Two ripple current type TAB 660, frame-suspended with Alsthom flexible drive
Control h.t. tap-changer
Electric brake None
Builder
  mechanical parts Alsthom (for 50 Hz Group)
  electrical equipment ACEC, AEG-Telefunken, Alsthom, Brown Boveri, MTE, Siemens (for 50 Hz Group)
Number built 12
Number series 0 382601 — 0 382612

Like their predecessors described in the previous entry, the multi-purpose 0 382601 series was supplied to CP by the 50 Hz Group, with the French company MTE acting as project manager. An original order for five units was later increased to twelve to form the present class. Design of these silicon rectifier machines follows closely that of the 15 class E40 locomotives supplied by the Group in 1971 to Turkish State Railways (TCDD—see p 132), and these in turn were derived from the French National Railways (SNCF) class BB-17000 (see p 48). The single-motor bogies were specially developed for the Portuguese broad gauge, and incorporate alternative gear ratios of 100 or 160 km/h (62 or 100 mph) according to traffic requirements. In fact CP line speeds were restricted to 100 km/h until 1979, when locomotives of this class took charge of limited express services running between Lisbon and Oporto at up to 140 km/h (87 mph).

Of obvious French origin, body styling is based on that of the SNCF BB-15000 series (see p 45) with the distinctive raking of the cab windows and a nose designed to protect crew and locomotive equipment in event of an impact. On a system with numerous level crossings, this provision may be regarded as a considerable advantage. Colour scheme is the standard CP orange relieved by mahogany cab window surrounds and roof. Diagonal white warning flashes are applied to the nose.

CP class 0 382601 no 0 382607 at Lisbon's Santa Apolonia station in May 1975 *(Peter J Howard)*

Romania

CFR classes 40, 41 and 42

Operating system Romanian State Railways (CFR)
Year introduced 1965
Axle arrangement Co-Co
Gauge 1435 mm *(4 ft 8½ in)*
Power supply system 25 kV ac 50 Hz
One-hour output 5400 kW *(7240 hp, 7340 ch)*
Continuous output 5100 kW *(6835 hp, 6930 ch)*
Maximum speed (class 40) 120 km/h *(75 mph)*;
(class 41) 160 km/h *(100 mph)*
Maximum tractive effort (class 40) 412 kN
(92 600 lbs); (class 41) 304 kN *(68 400 lbs)*
Continuous tractive effort (class 40) 260 kN
(58 400 lbs) at 69.5 km/h *(43 mph)*; (class 41)
195 kN *(43 900 lbs)* at 92.5 km/h *(57 mph)*
Weight in working order 120 or 126 tonnes *(118 or
124 tons)*
Length over buffers 19 800 mm *(64 ft 11½ in)*
Bogie wheelbase 2250 + 2100 = 4350 mm
(14 ft 3¼ in)
Wheel diameter 1250 mm *(4 ft 1¼ in)*
Traction motors Six dc series-wound type LJE 108,
fully suspended with ASEA hollow-shaft drive
Control h.t. tap-changer
Electric brake Rheostatic
Builder
 mechanical parts (40-0001 — 0010) Swedloc AB
 (consortium of ASJ, Motala-Verkstad and NOHAB);
 (remainder) Electroputere, under ASEA licence
 electrical equipment (40-0001 — 0030) ASEA;
 (remainder) Electroputere, under ASEA licence
Number built Not known (see text)
Number series 40-0001 — 40-0??? (note class 41
and 42 locomotives are integrated in this number
series)

Principal motive power for both heavy passenger and freight work on the Romanian electrified network is provided by the Swedish designed class 40/41/42 silicon rectifier units. This highly successful series was developed by ASEA as a "stretched" six-axle version of the Swedish State Railways (SJ) Rbl prototypes from the same builder. The CFR order, which included an agreement to build under licence, followed comparative trials in Romania with Czechoslovak, East German, French and Swedish locomotives during 1963 when test runs were conducted over a specially electrified section of the steeply graded Predeal Pass route between Braşov and Sinaia.

The first ten units were constructed by the Swedloc consortium in Sweden and delivered to Romania in 1965/6. One of this batch, originally numbered 060-EB-001, was supplied with thyristor control equipment and regenerative braking, but has since been converted to conform with the rest of the class. In 1967, the first Romanian built locomotive was completed at the Craiova works of Electroputere. By mid-1980 the fleet was around 440-strong and included versions with differing gear ratios. Class 40 (formerly class 060-EA) is geared for a maximum of 120 km/h (75 mph), while class 41 (ex-060-EA1) has a top speed of 160 km/h (100 mph). This latter series, some of which are equipped with single-arm pantographs, is distinguishable by a waist-level band of red rather than the blue of the class 40. Certain class 40 units are ballasted to increase their adhesive weight from 120 to 126 tonnes. A third version of this type, designated class 42 (ex-060-EA2), has also been reported but details have not emerged from Romania.

The design has been exported by Electroputere, mainly to Yugoslavia (JŽ class 461). A reciprocal agreement exists between the two countries whereby CFR receives four-axle electric locomotives (also of Swedish design—see p 154) from Yugoslav industry. A small number are reported to have been sent to China, and in Norway six broadly similar machines (NSB class El.15) operate on the 15 kV ac Narvik-Kiruna iron ore line.

**One of the first Romanian built machines, class 40 no 40-0013
(ex-060-EA-013), at Sinaia in August 1977**
(Pascal Pontremoli)

Class 41 no 41-0251, bearing its original number 060-EA1-251, at Oradea in 1976. Note the single-arm pantographs. CFR enginemen have observed the custom of equipping their cab interior with curtains and a pot plant! *(Günter Haslbeck)*

Left: Electroputere has supplied locomotives of similar design to Yugoslav Railways. JŽ class 461 no 461-015 stands at Stalać in August 1976 *(Günter Haslbeck)*

South Africa

SAR classes 1E and 1ES

Operating system South African Railways (SAR)
Year introduced 1925
Axle arrangement Bo+Bo
Gauge 1065 mm *(3 ft 6 in)*
Power supply system 3 kV dc
One-hour output 896 kW *(1200 hp, 1215 ch)*
Continuous output 808 kW *(1085 hp, 1100 ch)*
Maximum speed (class 1E) 72 km/h *(45 mph)*;
(class 1ES) 40 km/h *(25 mph)*
Maximum tractive effort 176 kN *(39 600 lbs)*
Continuous tractive effort 73 kN *(16 400 lbs)* at
39 km/h *(24 mph)*
Weight in working order 68 tonnes *(67 tons)*
Length over coupler centres 13 310 mm
(43 ft 8 in)
Bogie wheelbase 2819 mm *(9 ft 3 in)*
Wheel diameter 1219 mm *(4 ft 0 in)*
Traction motors Four dc series-wound Metropolitan-
Vickers type 182R, nose-suspended, axle-hung
Control Rheostatic
Electric brake Regenerative
Builder
  mechanical parts (E1-E78 and E139-E160) —
  SLM; (E79-E95 and E98-E122) — Metropolitan-
  Vickers; (E161-E180) — Werkspoor; (E181-E190)
  — Robert Stephenson & Hawthorns
  electrical equipment Metropolitan-Vickers
Number built 172
Number series E1-E95, E98-E122, E139-E190

Although in dwindling numbers, examples of SAR's first electric locomotive design, the successful 1E series, remained in service as this book was prepared for press. Earliest members of the class were put to work in 1925 between Ladysmith and Estcourt as part of SAR's pioneer 3 kV dc electrification of the steeply graded Pietermaritzburg-Glencoe section of the Natal main line. For this scheme Metropolitan-Vickers designed and supplied the initial series of 78 units (nos E1-78), followed in 1927 by a further 17 (nos E79-95) to handle increased traffic.

These locomotives are of the articulated bogie type, so that no traction loads are transmitted to the body. Electro-pneumatic control is employed and the four traction motors are so connected that two are always in series. Pairs of motors can be grouped in series or parallel, and one stage of field-weakening is available in the latter. Regenerative braking can be applied in either grouping. Multiple-unit control provision allows up to three locomotives to handle heavier trains.

By 1938 a further 67 units had entered service following extensions to the Natal electrification. Numbered E98-122 and E139-180, these machines differ in the layout of internal and roof-mounted equipment, and have an improved cab design. The last ten locomotives of the class, nos E181-190, were shipped from England in 1945 in "knocked-down" form owing to wartime transport problems and assembled in SAR workshops.

The principal derived design is the electrically similar centre-cab ES series, used exclusively for shunting. In 1964 two 1E units, nos E114 and E146, were converted to class ES and renumbered E525 and E526. Many of the 1E series have also been modified as shunters by suppression of the parallel motor grouping. Re-designated class 1ES, 39 examples had been so treated by mid-1979, leaving some 40 class 1E machines handling lighter duties in Natal and the Western Transvaal.

Two SAR class 1E units, coupled in multiple and led by no E107, at Durban with a local train to Port Shepstone in August 1975 *(Marc Dahlström)*

South Africa

SAR classes 5E and 5E1

Operating system South African Railways (SAR)
Year introduced (5E) 1955; (5E1) 1959
Axle arrangement Bo-Bo
Gauge 1065 mm *(3 ft 6 in)*
Power supply system 3 kV dc
One-hour output (5E) 1508 kW *(2020 hp, 2050 ch)*;
(5E1) 1940 kW *(2600 hp, 2635 ch)*
Continuous output (5E) 1300 kW *(1740 hp,*
1765 ch); (5E1) 1456 kW *(1950 hp, 1980 ch)*
Maximum speed 97 km/h *(60 mph)*
Maximum tractive effort (5E) 200 kN *(45 000 lbs)*;
(5E1) 250 kN *(56 200 lbs)*
Continuous tractive effort (5E) 104 kN
(23 400 lbs) at 44 km/h *(27 mph)*; (5E1) 122 kN
(27 400 lbs) at 43 km/h *(27 mph)*
Weight in working order 86.4 tonnes *(85 tons)*
Length over coupler centres 15 494 mm
(50 ft 10 in)
Bogie wheelbase 3430 mm *(11 ft 3 in)*
Wheel diameter 1219 mm *(4 ft 0 in)*
Traction motors Four dc series-wound type EE529
(5E) or MV281, AEI281AZX/281AX/281BX (5E1),
nose-suspended, axle-hung
Control Rheostatic
Electric brake Regenerative
Builder
 mechanical parts (5E) Vulcan Foundry;
 (5E1) E364-E498: Vulcan Foundry, E591-E1145:
 Union Carriage and Wagon Co.
 electrical equipment (5E) English Electric;
 (5E1) E364-E498: AEI, E591-E1145: AEI/English
 Electric
Number built (5E) 160; (5E1) 690
Number series (5E) E259-E363, E536-E590; (5E1)
E364-E498, E591-E1145

In the early 1950s, SAR concluded that operating requirements on its expanding 3 kV dc network would be best met by a four-axle design capable of multiple-unit operation and incorporating as much power as gauge limitations and electric traction techniques would permit. The resulting 5E series foreshadowed the large and important family of Bo-Bo locomotives which now form the major part of the SAR 3 kV dc fleet.

Contracts for the supply of the 160 class 5E machines were placed with the English Electric Company. The locomotives were constructed at Vulcan Foundry, Newton-le-Willows, and deliveries extended from 1955 to 1959. The later 5E1 series incorporates bogies of improved design and has an increased output made possible by advances in traction motor manufacturing techniques. After construction of 135 units (nos E364-498) in England, production switched to South Africa where the Union Carriage and Wagon Company fulfilled all subsequent orders. The first domestically built locomotive appeared in 1963 and by 1969 555 had been supplied by this manufacturer.

Both the 5E and the 5E1 have regenerative braking, and as many as five or even six units are coupled in multiple on the heaviest trains. The 5Es are based in Eastern Transvaal, while the numerous 5E1 series serve the Cape Western, Orange Free State, Natal and Western Transvaal districts.

SAR class 5E1 no E780 leads another member of the same class at Bethlehem in August 1975 *(Marc Dahlström)*

South Africa

SAR classes 6E and 6E1

Operating system South African Railways (SAR)
Year introduced 6E — 1970; 6E1 — 1969
Axle arrangement Bo-Bo
Gauge 1065 mm *(3 ft 6 in)*
Power supply system 3 kV dc
One-hour output 2492 kW *(3340 hp, 3385 ch)*
Continuous output 2252 kW *(3020 hp, 3060 ch)*
Maximum speed 113 km/h *(70 mph)*
Maximum tractive effort 311 kN *(70 000 lbs)*
Continuous tractive effort 193 kN *(43 400 lbs)* at
41 km/h *(25½ mph)*
Weight in working order 88.9 tonnes *(87.5 tons)*
Length over coupler centres 15 494 mm
(50 ft 10 in)
Bogie wheelbase 3430 mm *(11 ft 3 in)*
Wheel diameter 1219 mm *(4 ft 0 in)*
Traction motors Four dc series-wound AEI type
283AZ, nose-suspended, axle-hung
Control Rheostatic
Electric brake Regenerative
Builder
  mechanical parts Union Carriage and Wagon Co.
  electrical equipment AEI (South Africa), English
  Electric (South Africa), GEC, GEC Engineering
  (South Africa)
Number built (class 6E) 80; (class 6E1) 859
including units on order in August 1980
Number series (class 6E) E1146—E1225; (class
6E1) E1226—E1599, E1601—E2085

The significantly improved performance of the 6E and 6E1 series over the earlier 5E/5E1 is due largely to developments in traction motor design and insulating techniques, enabling the continuous rating to be raised from 1456 to 2252 kW. The extra power both increases the top speed to 113 km/h and gives greater haulage capacity. To ensure optimum use of tractive effort both classes are equipped with electronic wheel-slip detection and control, and a vernier device to prevent power surges between main resistance notches. Principal differences between the two sub-series are in bogie design and in the form of mass-transfer control adopted to prevent unloading of the leading axles during starting. The 6E has an air bellows device between bogies and locomotive frames, while the 6E1 has prominent low-level traction rods to transmit haulage and braking forces from the bogies to the body. Both classes are equipped to provide train air and vacuum braking and can operate in multiple with classes 5E and 5E1.

Late in 1978, class 6E1 no E1525, suitably re-geared and fitted with an aerodynamic "bullet" nose, attained a speed of 245 km/h (152·2 mph) between Midway and Westonaria, near Johannesburg. The run was part of a programme of trials to investigate the stability of the Scheffel cross-anchor rolling stock bogie, and established both SAR and world narrow-gauge speed records.

To assess the potential of the basic design for development as an ac machine, 6E1 no E1600 was converted in 1979 to a 25 kV ac 50 Hz prototype, using thyristor control equipment supplied by the 50 Hz Group. Traction motors of the main series are retained, and the locomotive is both lighter (85·5 tonnes) and slightly more powerful.

Although most of the class are finished in standard maroon and yellow, certain 6E1s are painted blue and yellow for use on SAR's prestigious Cape Town-Johannesburg and Pretoria *Blue Train*.

Deliveries of the 6E1 series had passed the 700 mark by 1980, when new orders were announced which will eventually bring the total number to 859. Together with the 80 6E locomotives this will represent the largest construction outside the USSR of a unified electric locomotive design, a title held at the time this book was compiled by the German Federal (DB) 139/140 series (see p 59).

Left: No E1224 is an example of the numerically smaller 6E series, which differs from the 6E1 in the form of mass transfer control adopted *(SAR)*

Below: Two SAR class 6E1 locomotives at the head of the celebrated *Blue Train* at Denver in August 1975 *(Marc Dahlström)*

South Africa

SAR class 7E

Operating system South African Railways (SAR)
Year introduced 1978
Axle arrangement Co-Co
Gauge 1065 mm *(3 ft 6 in)*
Power supply system 25 kV ac 50 Hz
One-hour output 3240 kW *(4340 hp, 4400 ch)*
Continuous output 3000 kW *(4020 hp, 4075 ch)*
Maximum speed 100 km/h *(62 mph)*
Maximum tractive effort 450 kN *(101 200 lbs)*
Continuous tractive effort 300 kN *(67 400 lbs)* at 35 km/h *(22 mph)*
Weight in working order 123.5 tonnes *(122 tons)*
Length over coupler centres 18 465 mm *(60 ft 7 in)*
Bogie wheelbase 2200 + 2200 = 4400 mm *(14 ft 5¼ in)*
Wheel diameter 1220 mm *(4 ft 0 in)*
Traction motors Six separately-excited pulsating current type MG680, nose-suspended, axle-hung
Control Thyristor
Electric brake Rheostatic
Builder
  mechanical parts Union Carriage and Wagon Co.
  electrical equipment 50 Hz Group
Number built 100 + 25 ordered 1980
Number series E7001 — E7100, E7101 — E7125

SAR's first ac locomotive, class 7E no E7001 (SAR)

Capacity limitations imposed by the 3 kV dc power supply system led SAR in the mid-1970s to adopt 25 kV ac at industrial frequency for future major electrification schemes. The first application of this policy was the 420 km (261 mile) line connecting the Transvaal coalfields with the deep water port of Richards Bay, where traffic requirements called for bulk loads of export coal of up to 160 wagons grossing 8640 tonnes (8500 tons). Limited electric haulage started in June 1978 when the first thyristor-controlled class 7E freight locomotives entered service.

With no domestic experience in the construction of motive power for 25 kV, SAR commissioned the European 50 Hz Group to oversee the execution of their initial order for 100 units and to supply principal electrical equipment. Contract details provided for the manufacture in South Africa of all mechanical components and certain items of electrical apparatus, including BBC designed transformers for ten machines. Project managers for the order were Siemens and assembly of the locomotives was carried out at the Nigel works of Union Carriage and Wagon. Delivery of the first 100 units was completed in little over a year. The 7E has a continuous rating of 3000 kW (4020 hp) at 35 km/h (22 mph) and is equipped for multiple-unit working. Rheostatic braking is fitted and the locomotive can provide both air and vacuum train braking. Bogies have cast-steel monobloc frames and secondary suspension is of the coil spring type. Prominent inclined traction rods, similar to those of the 6E1 series, transmit haulage and braking forces from bogies to the body.

Late in 1979, deliveries of 50 generally similar units designated 7E1 started from Dorman Long on behalf of the Japanese consortium Nissho Iwai, which includes Hitachi. A further 25 class 7E locomotives were ordered from the 50 Hz Group during the same year.

South Africa

SAR class 9E

Operating system South African Railways (SAR)
Year introduced 1978
Axle arrangement Co-Co
Gauge 1065 mm *(3 ft 6 in)*
Power supply system 50 kV ac 50 Hz
One-hour output 4068 kW *(5450 hp, 5525 ch)*
Continuous output 3780 kW *(5065 hp, 5135 ch)*
Maximum speed 90 km/h *(56 mph)*
Maximum tractive effort 538 kN *(121 000 lbs)*
Continuous tractive effort 383 kN *(86 100 lbs)* at
34.5 km/h *(21½ mph)*
Weight in working order 168 tonnes *(165.5 tons)*
Length over coupler centres 21 132 mm
(69 ft 4 in)
Bogie wheelbase 1970+1970=3940 mm
(12 ft 11⅛ in)
Wheel diameter 1220 mm *(4 ft 0 in)*
Traction motors Six separately-excited pulsating
current GEC type G415AZ, axle-suspended
Control Thyristor
Electric brake Rheostatic
Builder
  mechanical parts Union Carriage and Wagon Co.
  electrical equipment GEC Traction
Number built 25 (plus 6 ordered in 1980 for delivery
by 1982)
Number series E9001 — E9025 (+ ?E9026—
E9031)

SAR class 9E no E9002 *(SAR)*

The 864 km (537 mile) Sishen-Saldanha Bay iron ore railway is the world's first common-user line to employ a 50 kV ac 50 Hz power supply. Energised throughout in 1978, construction was undertaken by the South African Iron and Steel Industrial Corporation (ISCOR). On 1 April 1977, before electric operations began, ownership of the line was transferred to SAR following demands for access to its facilities from independent mining companies.

The 25 thyristor-controlled class 9E units which now operate the line were designed in the United Kingdom by GEC Traction, and are the world's most powerful 1065 mm gauge locomotives. Three of these machines in multiple are used to haul 202 loaded four-axle wagons grossing 20 200 tonnes (19 900 tons), and within their continuous rating can tackle the maximum gradient facing loaded trains of 0.4% (1 in 250). On downhill runs, the rheostatic braking of three coupled units can hold a full train at 55 km/h (34 mph) on a 0.6% (1 in 167) gradient. These operations are undertaken in harsh conditions which include frequent electrical and dust storms as well as a salt-laden atmosphere as the line approaches the Atlantic coast.

Construction of the class was carried out in South Africa by Union Carriage and Wagon. Each locomotive has a full-width cab specially designed for tropical working conditions. At no 2 end the roof is lowered for nearly half the body length to give clearance for the roof-mounted 50 kV equipment. Gangway access is provided to allow passage between coupled locomotives. The advanced power control equipment developed by GEC Traction permits an operating voltage range from 25 to 55 kV. Traction motors are separately-excited and derived from those of the SAR 6E1 series. All 25 units are equipped with train and locomotive air brakes, but six can also provide vacuum braking for SAR stock so fitted. Although designed for a maximum speed of 90 km/h (56 mph), in service the class is restricted to 72 km/h (45 mph). A unique feature of the 9E is the provision of a motor-scooter to enable a crew member to inspect his 2.3 km (2516 yd) train. This machine is housed in a cabinet mounted beneath the body.

During 1980 an order for a further six units was placed with GEC Traction.

Spain

RENFE classes 269 and 269-500

Operating system Spanish National Railways (RENFE)
Year introduced 1973
Axle arrangement B-B
Gauge 1676 mm *(5 ft 6 in)*
Power supply system 3 kV dc
One-hour output 3240 kW *(4340 hp, 4400 ch)*
Continuous output 3100 kW *(4155 hp, 4210 ch)*
Maximum speed (class 269) 140/80 km/h *(87/50 mph)*; (class 269-500) 160/90 km/h *(100/56 mph)*
Continuous tractive effort (class 269 — high gear) 163 kN *(36 600 lbs)* at 66.3 km/h *(41 mph)*; (low gear) 263 kN *(59 100 lbs)* at 40.3 km/h *(25 mph)*; (class 269-500 — high gear) 143 kN *(32 200 lbs)* at 75.2 km/h *(47 mph)*; (low gear) 231 kN *(52 000 lbs)* at 45.7 km/h *(28 mph)*
Weight in working order 88 tonnes *(87 tons)*
Length over buffers 17 270 mm *(56 ft 8 in)*
Bogie wheelbase 2280 mm *(7 ft 5¾ in)*
Wheel diameter 1250 mm *(4 ft 1¼ in)*
Traction motors Two dc series-wound tandem type, fully suspended with WN cardan drive
Control Rheostatic
Electric brake Rheostatic
Builder
  mechanical parts CAF, MACOSA (under Mitsubishi licence)
  electrical equipment Westinghouse (under Mitsubishi licence)
Number built (class 269) 108; (class 269-500) 22
Number series 269-001 — 269-108, 269-501 — 269-522

The major part of the RENFE electric locomotive fleet is formed of a large family of four-axle single-motor bogie machines designed in Japan by Mitsubishi. By far the largest series is the multi-purpose class 269, which in 1979 numbered 130 units. Their introduction in 1973 followed the successful performance of the generally similar class 279 (16 units) and 289 (40 units) built in 1967 and 1969 respectively for dual-voltage (3 kV/1·5 kV dc) operation.

As with these earlier classes, construction of the 269 series was carried out in Spain by CAF and Westinghouse under Mitsubishi licence. The single-motor bogies are provided with two gear ratios, and traction motors are of the tandem type, with two armatures mounted on a single shaft. Final drive from the gearbox is of the cardan shaft type with WN flexible couplings. Like the two preceding Japanese designs, the 269 has rheostatic brakes, and notching in both braking and motoring is automatic. Multiple-unit control equipment is fitted, but can only be used with locomotives of the same class. Solid-state detection and control of wheel-slip is employed, and the mechanical design incorporates low-level traction links to transmit tractive effort to the body and to minimise weight transfer within the bogie.

The 22-strong 269-500 series has higher gearing in both passenger and freight modes (see data) and is used mainly for express work.

To provide motive power for its continuing electrification plans, RENFE in 1979 ordered 25 more locomotives of this design with gearing of 160/100 km/h (100/62 mph), including four with full chopper control. The 21 resistance-controlled machines are to be designated class 269-200; the chopper units will become series 269-600. Also under development is a B-B-B version of the 269-600, class 251.

RENFE class 269 no 269-108 heading a train of *Talgo* stock at Madrid Atocha station in April 1979 *(Marcel Vleugels)*

Spain

RENFE classes 276 and 286

Operating system Spanish National Railways (RENFE)
Year introduced 1956 (see text)
Axle arrangement Co-Co
Gauge 1676 mm *(5 ft 6 in)*
Power supply system 3 kV dc
One-hour output 2355 kW *(3155 hp, 3200 ch)*
Continuous output 2208 kW *(2960 hp, 3000 ch)*
Maximum speed 110 km/h *(68 mph)*
Maximum tractive effort 330 kN *(74 100 lbs)*
Continuous tractive effort 162 kN *(36 400 lbs)* at 49.5 km/h *(31 mph)*
Weight in working order 120 tonnes *(118 tons)*
Length over buffers 18 830 mm *(61 ft 9⅜ in)*
Bogie wheelbase 2525+2850=5375 mm *(17 ft 7⅝ in)*
Wheel diameter 1250 mm *(4 ft 1¼ in)*
Traction motors Six dc series-wound Alsthom type TA-630A, fully suspended with Alsthom flexible drive
Control Rheostatic
electric brake Regenerative
Builder
　mechanical parts Alsthom, Babcock & Wilcox, CAF, Euskalduna, MACOSA, MTM
　electrical equipment Alsthom, GEE, Oerlikon, SICE, Westinghouse
Number built 136
Number series 276 001 — 276 100, 286 001 — 286 036

This Spanish 3 kV dc derivative of the French National Railways (SNCF) CC-7100 series (see p 38) was developed to provide principal motive power for both passenger and freight traffic over much of the 2500 route-km (1550 miles) of line electrified by RENFE between 1954 and 1958. With due provision for the broader Spanish gauge of 1676 mm (5 ft 6 in), the 276/286 series retains the mechanical features of the SNCF machines, including the oscillating pivot body mounting, but differs in other respects. The most important of these, necessitated by the higher RENFE 3 kV line voltage, is the provision of 1·5 kV traction motors. The Spanish units are also equipped with regenerative braking and further differ from their French sisters in rated output, service weight and top speed (see data).

The first 20 locomotives (nos 276-001-020) were constructed in France by Alsthom from 1952, although they did not enter service until 1956, when the first Catalan electrification was commissioned. Subsequent deliveries came from Spanish industry, building under licence from Alsthom. The last example entered service in 1965. Originally the class was numbered in the 7600 and 8600 series.

Three members of the class, nos 276-030, 276-062 and 276-066, have modified buffers and drawgear, train air braking, locomotive-to-train telephone and single-arm pantographs. These units are intended for haulage of *Talgo* express services and are finished in a livery of red and two shades of grey, rather than the standard grey and green of the remainder of the class.

RENFE class 276 no 276-066, photographed at Madrid Atocha depot in April 1979, is one of three units specially modified for *Talgo* haulage *(Marcel Vleugels)*

Work stained no 7660 (new no 276-060), also seen at Madrid's Atocha depot, bears the standard livery for the class of grey and green *(Marcel Vleugels)*

Spain

RENFE class 277

Operating system Spanish National Railways (RENFE)
Year introduced 1952
Axle arrangement Co-Co
Gauge 1676 mm *(5 ft 6 in)*
Power supply system 3 kV dc
One-hour output 2685 kW *(3600 hp, 3650 ch)*
Continuous output 2208 kW *(2960 hp, 3000 ch)*
Maximum speed 110 km/h *(68 mph)*
Maximum tractive effort 307 kN *(69 000 lbs)*
Continuous tractive effort 136 kN *(30 500 lbs)* at 58 km/h *(36 mph)*
Weight in working order 120 tonnes *(118 tons)*
Length over buffers 20 657 mm *(67 ft 9¼ in)*
Wheel diameter 1220 mm *(4 ft 0 in)*
Traction motors Six dc series-wound, nose-suspended, axle-hung
Control Rheostatic
Electric brake Regenerative
Builder
  mechanical parts Vulcan Foundry
  electrical equipment English Electric
Number built 75
Number series 277 001 — 277 075

The impressive RENFE 277 series was built by English Electric and Vulcan Foundry from 1952 for passenger and freight service on lines in northern Spain then being electrified. These included the León-Ponferrada line and the steeply graded León-Oviedo route, which crosses the Cantabrian mountains through the Pajares Pass. The design is a development of a series of 15 2240 kW (3000 hp) Co-Co machines supplied to Brazil in 1950 for operation on the 3 kV dc Santos-Jundiai line and now included in Brazilian Federal stock as RFFSA class 1000. Speed is regulated conventionally by means of resistances, motor groupings, and field weakening, and provision is made for multiple-unit control. Regenerative braking is fitted. Bogies of the first 20 examples have Timken roller-bearing axle-boxes.

Deliveries of the class of 75 units continued until 1959. Original number series was 7701-7775.

In 1954/5, seven locomotives of generally similar design but for 1·5 kV dc operation were supplied by English Electric/Vulcan to the Central system of Indian Government Railways. These machines are now designated Indian Railways (IR) class WCM1.

No 277-022 bearing its original number 7722 at Valladolid in October 1966 *(Brian Garvin)*

Sweden

SJ class Da

Operating system Swedish State Railways (SJ)
Year introduced 1952
Axle arrangement 1-C-1
Gauge 1435 mm *(4 ft 8½ in)*
Power supply system 15 kV ac 16⅔ Hz
One-hour output 1840 kW *(2465 hp, 2500 ch)*
Continuous output 1780 kW *(2385 hp, 2420 ch)*
Maximum speed 100 km/h *(62 mph)*
Maximum tractive effort 177 kN *(39 700 lbs)*
Continuous tractive effort 80 kN *(18 100 lbs)* at 79.5 km/h *(49 mph)*
Weight in working order 75 tonnes *(74 tons)* total ; 51 tonnes *(50 tons)* adhesive
Length over buffers 13 000 mm *(42 ft 7¾ in)*
Rigid wheelbase 2000+3400=5400 mm *(17 ft 8⅝ in)*
Wheel diameter (driving wheels) 1530 mm *(5 ft 0¼ in)* or 1486 mm *(4 ft 10½ in)* ; (carrying wheels) 980 mm *(3 ft 2⅝ in)*
Traction motors Two single-phase commutator type KJC 137, frame-mounted with jackshaft/side-rod drive
Control l.t. tap-changer
Electric brake None
Builder
mechanical parts ASJ, Motala Verkstad, NOHAB
electrical equipment ASEA
Number built 93
Number series 790-823, 883-941

Construction of rod-driven main line electric locomotives ended later in Sweden than elsewhere and the SJ fleet is still characterized by machines of this type. Built between 1952 and 1957, the comparatively modern class Da represents the final development of the wooden-bodied 1-C-1 Dg and Ds series of 1925. Progressive traction motor improvements enabled the installed power to be raised from the 1220 kW (1635 hp) of these original designs to 1840 kW (2465 hp) for the Da. The number of running notches was also increased from 16 to 27 and multiple-unit control facilities fitted.

Mechanical design follows the pattern of the 1925 locomotives in which two traction motors are mounted in the main frames and geared to a common final jackshaft powering all three driven axles by means of coupling rods. Pony trucks perform guiding and carrying functions. Various class members have been equipped with SAB resilient wheels of 1486 mm diameter, and some have special cab insulation for service in northern Sweden.

Duties of the class mostly cover freight and secondary passenger work in the central and southern parts of the country, although some are allocated to Kiruna for operation over the *Riksgränsbanan* iron ore line into Norway.

Class Da no 799 *(SJ)*

Sweden

SJ class Dm3

Operating system Swedish State Railways (SJ)
Year introduced 1960
Axle arrangement 1-D+D+D-1
Gauge 1435 mm *(4 ft 8½ in)*
Power supply system 15 kV ac 16⅔ Hz
One-hour output
   ("900" Series) 6150 kW *(8240 hp, 8360 ch)*;
   ("1200" Series) 7200 kW *(9650 hp, 9785 ch)*
Continuous output ("900" Series) 5340 kW
   (7155 hp, 7255 ch); ("1200" Series) 6420 kW
   (8605 hp, 8725 ch)
Maximum speed 75 km/h *(47 mph)*
Maximum tractive effort ("900" Series) 780 kN
   (176 000 lbs); ("1200" Series) 932 kN *(210 000
   lbs)*
Continuous tractive effort ("900" Series) 427 kN
   (95 900 lbs) at 51.8 km/h *(32 mph)*; ("1200"
   Series) 427 kN *(95 900 lbs)* at 59 km/h *(37 mph)*
Weight in working order ("900" Series) 265
   tonnes *(261 tons)* total, 235 tonnes *(231 tons)*
   adhesive; ("1200" Series) 270 tonnes *(266 tons)*
   total, 240 tonnes *(236 tons)* adhesive
Length over buffers 35 250 mm *(115 ft 7¾ in)*
Rigid wheelbase 2000+3400+2000=7400 mm
   (24 ft 3⅜ in)
Wheel diameter (driving) 1530 mm *(5 ft 0¼ in)*;
   (carrying) 980 mm *(3 ft 2⅝ in)*
Traction motors Six single-phase commutator ASEA
   type KJD137, frame-mounted with jackshaft/side-rod
   drive
Control l.t. tap-changer
Electric brake Rheostatic on "1200" Series only
Builder
   mechanical parts ASJ, Motala Verkstad, NOHAB
   electrical equipment ASEA
Number built 19
Number series (class Dm outer units) 976, 978, 979,
   981, 982, 984, 1201-1230, 1246, 1248; (class Dm3
   centre units) 977, 980, 983, 1231-1245, 1247

With examples built as late as 1970, the triple-unit Dm3 was the final SJ side-rod design, and is used exclusively for iron ore haulage on the *Riksgränsbanan* which links the mines of Kiruna with the Norwegian ice-free port of Narvik. This line lies within the Arctic circle and operating conditions are arduous, with loaded westbound trains of 5200 tonnes facing continuous gradients of 1% (1 in 100).

In strict SJ parlance, the Dm3 is a cabless central power unit marshalled between the two halves of a Dm series twin locomotive to form a very powerful three-section machine. Two traction motors are mounted in each body section and power is transmitted to the coupled wheels by jackshaft drive. No pantograph is fitted to the centre section; current collection is effected by one of the outer units.

The first three Dm3 centre units were built in 1960 and when combined with a 900 series Dm locomotive give a continuous output of 5340 kW (7155 hp). Further Dm3 construction followed between 1967 and 1970 with deliveries of 16 units intended for operation with Dm locomotives placed in service several years earlier. These later 1200 series machines are equipped with rheostatic braking and with an increased combined continuous rating of 6420 kW (8605 hp), rank amongst the most powerful locomotives in the world.

Modifications to various members of the class include the provision of SAB resilient wheels and the fitting of Soviet-type SA3 automatic centre-couplers to permit heavier train loads than traditional drawgear.

As the accompanying table shows, each of the three locomotive sections bears a different number.

SJ Dm+Dm3+Dm combination led by no 1205 at Kiruna in September 1974 *(Lars Olov Karlsson)*

Sweden

SJ class Ra

Operating system Swedish State Railways (SJ)
Year introduced 1955
Axle arrangement Bo-Bo
Gauge 1435 mm *(4 ft 8½ in)*
Power supply system 15 kV ac 16⅔ Hz
One-hour output 2650 kW *(3550 hp, 3600 ch)*
Continuous output 2520 kW *(3375 hp, 3425 ch)*
Maximum speed 150 km/h *(93 mph)*
Maximum tractive effort *(846 & 847)* 147 kN
(33 100 lbs); *(987-994)* 177 kN *(39 700 lbs)*
Continuous tractive effort *(987-994 only)* 89 kN
(20 100 lbs) at 104.5 km/h *(65 mph)*
Weight in working order *(846 & 847)* 62 tonnes
(61 tons); *(987-994)* 64 2 tonnes *(63 tons)*
Length over buffers 15 100 mm *(49 ft 6½ in)*
Bogie wheelbase 2900 mm *(9 ft 6⅛ in)*
Wheel diameter 1300 mm *(4 ft 3⅛ in)*
Traction motors Six single-phase commutator ASEA
type KJB 97, fully suspended with ASEA hollow-axle
drive
Control l.t. tap-changer
Electric brake None
Builder
 mechanical parts ASEA, ASJ, Motala Verkstad,
 NOHAB
 electrical equipment ASEA
Number built 10
Number series 846 & 847, 987-994. The locomotives
also bear the numbers "Rapid 1-10."

Designed for fast light passenger services, the remarkable Ra units were Sweden's first modern express locomotives. When introduced in 1955, they incorporated the world's highest power-to-weight ratio both for locomotive (23·4 kg/kW) and traction motor (3·65 kg/kW). They were also the fastest motive power yet to appear on a Swedish railway (although the scope for speeds in the order of 150 km/h was very limited) and this title was retained until the arrival in 1970 of the 160 km/h Rc3 series.

The first two units, nos 846 and 847, were built as prototypes by NOHAB, with electrical equipment by ASEA. Special design consideration was given to keeping the axle-loading to a minimum, resulting in a service weight of only 62 tonnes. Because of their limited application in traffic, no further construction took place until 1961, when the remaining eight locomotives were delivered to handle fast inter-city services. These later units show a slight weight increase which improves their tractive capabilities. Further construction was effectively halted by ASEA's pioneering developments in semi-conductor and thyristor technology.

Livery of the class is orange and white, and the locomotives bear a supplementary number series "Rapid 1-10" in view of the nature of their work. Present duties cover passenger traffic on a number of lines from Stockholm and the entire class is based at Stockholm's Hagalund depot.

SJ *Rapid 4,* **alias no 988, at Stockholm C in October 1973**
(Lars Olov Karlsson)

Sweden

SJ classes Rc1, Rc2, Rc3 and Rc4

Operating system Swedish State Railways (SJ)
Year introduced Rc1—1967; Rc2—1969; Rc3—1970; Rc4—1975
Axle arrangement Bo-Bo
Gauge 1435 mm *(4 ft 8½ in)*
Power supply system 15 kV ac 16⅔ Hz
One-hour output 3600 kW *4825 hp, 4890 ch)*
Continuous output 3400 kW *(4555 hp, 4620 ch)*
Maximum speed (Rc1, Rc2 & Rc4) 135 km/h *(84 mph);* (Rc3) 160 km/h *(100 mph)*
Maximum tractive effort (Rc1) 275 kN *(61 800 lbs);* (Rc2) 280 kN *(63 000 lbs);* (Rc3) 235 kN *(52 900 lbs);* (Rc4) 290 kN *(65 200 lbs)*
Continuous tractive effort (Rc1, Rc2, Rc4) 154 kN *(34 600 lb)s* at 78.8 km/h *(49 mph);* (Rc3) 142 kN *(32 000 lbs)* at 91.8 km/h *(57 mph)*
Weight in working order Rc1 — 76 tonnes *(75 tons);* Rc2 & Rc3 — 77 tonnes *(76 tons);* Rc4 — 78 tonnes *(77 tons)*
Length over buffers Rc1 — 15 470 mm *(50 ft 9 in);* Rc2-Rc4 — 15 520 mm *(50 ft 11 in)*
Bogie wheelbase 2700 mm *(8 ft 10¼ in)*
Wheel diameter 1300 mm *(4 ft 3⅛ in)*
Traction motors Four ripple-current ASEA type LJH108, fully suspended with ASEA hollow-shaft drive
Control Thyristor
Electric brake None
Builder
 mechanical parts ASJ, KVAB, Motala Verkstad, NOHAB
 electrical equipment ASEA
Number built Rc1 — 20; Rc2 — 100; Rc3 — 10; Rc4 — 110 + 40 for delivery from late 1981
Number series (Rc1) 1007-1026; (Rc2) 1027-1056, 1067-1136; (Rc3) 1057-1066; (Rc4) 1137-1200, 1251-1256, 1263-1302 + 40 units for delivery from late 1981

The largest and most important part of the SJ electric locomotive fleet is formed by the highly successful Rc family, with 280 examples in service or on order in mid-1980. Intended as a high powered, low maintenance mixed-traffic unit, the Rc1 was the world's first thyristor-controlled locomotive design to enter series production. Construction of the 20-strong class in 1967-68 followed the experimental installation of ASEA thyristor equipment in Rb1 prototype no 1001 in 1965.

The Rc2 and Rc3 series of 1969 and 1970 respectively are improved versions of the Rc1 with oil-cooled thyristor convertors and harmonic filters. They differ from each other only in gear ratio. In 1975 the Rc4 appeared, with refinements to the design of the power control equipment and the provision of ASEA Pressductor wheel-slip protection to improve further adhesion characteristics. Later machines of this series incorporate a static convertor for power supply to auxiliaries. An option on 30 examples of the further improved Rc5 being developed by ASEA was announced by SJ in 1979.
Derivatives of the basic Rc design are:

– SJ class Rm, a series of six units (SJ nos 1257-62) delivered in 1977 for iron ore haulage in northern Sweden. Based on the Rc4, special features include rheostatic braking, modified bogies, ballasting to give a 23 tonne axle-load, SA3 automatic couplers and extra heating facilities to protect equipment and crew from Arctic conditions. The class was designed for operation with up to three units coupled in multiple. Maximum speed is 100 km/h (62 mph). Depressed iron ore traffic later resulted in the provision of conventional drawgear and buffers in place of SA3 couplers so that the Rm series could be used as general purpose freight units.

– Austrian Federal Railways (ÖBB) class 1043: ten locomotives (ÖBB nos 1043.01-10) supplied by ASEA in 1971/2 (4 units) and 1973 (6 units) following trials in Austria with Rc2 no 1049. These locomotives are generally similar to the Rc2, but are fitted with single-arm pantographs. Seven units have rheostatic brakes.

– Norwegian State Railways (NSB) class El.16 (see p 94).

– National Railroad Passenger Corporation (AMTRAK) class AEM7 (see p 148) developed after successful trials in the USA in 1976/7 with Rc4 no 1166, which bears plates commemorating its visit.

No 1137, the first Rc4 *(SJ)*

Rc3 no 1064 is one of a sub-series of ten locomotives geared for 160 km/h running (ASEA)

Class Rm was derived from the Rc4 design for iron ore haulage in northern Sweden. No 1257 is seen new in February 1977 (SJ)

Between 1971 and 1973 Swedish industry delivered to Austrian Federal Railways (ÖBB) ten thyristor units based on the Rc2. Similarity to the parent design is visible in this photograph of ÖBB no 1043.03 at Salzburg early in 1976 (Herbert Korntheuer)

Switzerland

BLS class Ae4/4

Operating system Berne-Loetschberg-Simplon
 Railway (BLS)
Year introduced 1944
Axle arrangement Bo-Bo
Gauge 1435 mm *(4 ft 8½ in)*
Power supply system 15 kV ac 16⅔ Hz
One-hour output 2945 kW *(3945 hp, 4000 ch)*
Continuous output 2520 kW *(3380 hp, 3425 ch)*
Maximum speed 125 km/h *(78 mph)*
Maximum tractive effort 236 kN *(52 900 lbs)*
Continuous tractive effort 155 kN *(34 800 lbs)* at
 75 km/h *(47 mph)*
Weight in working order 80 tonnes *(79 tons)*
Length over buffers 15 600 mm *(51 ft 2⅛ in)*
Bogie wheelbase 3250 mm *(10 ft 8 in)*
Wheel diameter 1250 mm *(4 ft 1¼ in)*
Traction motors Four single-phase commutator
 Brown Boveri type ELM 983s, fully suspended with
 Brown Boveri flexible disc drive
Control h.t. tap-changer
Electric brake Rheostatic
Builder
 mechanical parts SLM
 electrical equipment Brown Boveri
Number built 8 (of which 4 converted to class Ae 8/8)
Number series 251, 252, 257, 258

Ae4/4 no 257 at Brig in September 1978
heading a Lötschberg Tunnel push-pull
car-carrying train *(Yves Steenebruggen)*

Generally regarded as the forerunner of the modern electric locomotive, the BLS Ae4/4 was the first high powered all-adhesion non-articulated design, and profoundly influenced the development of this form of traction both within Switzerland and abroad. A significant feature of the Ae4/4 was that for the first time in a bogie locomotive an output of 1000 metric hp per axle was installed, and that this was achieved within a 20 tonne axle-load limit. To help meet this latter requirement the all-welded body makes extensive use of light alloys. Other special features include a device for equalizing axle loads on starting, rheostatic braking, and anti-slip brake and automatic regulation of brake-shoe pressure to stop skidding.

Several modifications have been made to the Ae4/4s since their construction. In 1957-8, the rheostatic braking capacity of nos 251-256 was increased, necessitating removal of one pantograph to provide extra room for roof-mounted resistances. Nos 257 and 258 incorporated this feature when new. Tap-changer equipment of improved design was fitted in 1967-8, when the class was also modified for multiple-unit and push-pull working.

The eight Ae4/4s built by SLM and Brown Boveri between 1944 and 1955 were joined in 1959 by the first of three examples of a twin-unit version of the class, designated Ae8/8. The usefulness of these "double" locomotives on the exacting Lötschberg route prompted BLS to form two more similar units by converting four of the Ae4/4 series. Accordingly, in 1966 nos 253-256 became class Ae8/8 nos 274 and 275.

Present livery of the four remaining Ae4/4s is chocolate brown.

A 6475 kW twin-unit version of the Ae4/4,
designated class Ae8/8, appeared in 1959.
The first example, no 271, is illustrated here
(BLS)

Switzerland

BLS class Ae6/8

Operating system Berne-Loetschberg-Simplon Railway (BLS)
Year introduced 1926
Axle arrangement 1-Co+Co-1
Gauge 1435 mm *(4 ft 8½ in)*
Power supply system 15 kV ac 16⅔ Hz
One-hour output 4415 kW *(5915 hp, 6000 ch)*
Maximum speed 100 km/h *(62 mph)*
Maximum tractive effort 353 kN *(79 400 lbs)*
One-hour tractive effort 245 kN *(55 100 lbs)* at 65 km/h *(40 mph)*
Weight in working order 140 tonnes *(138 tons)* total, 120 tonnes *(118 tons)* adhesive
Length over buffers 20 260 mm *(66 ft 5⅝ in)*
Bogie wheelbase 2200+1900=4100 mm *(13 ft 5⅜ in)*
Wheel diameter (driving) 1350 mm *(4 ft 5⅛ in)*; (carrying) 950 mm *(3 ft 1⅜ in)*
Traction motors Twelve single-phase commutator, fully suspended with Sécheron spring drive
Control l.t.switchgear
Electric brake Rheostatic
Builder
  mechanical parts (201-204) Breda; (205-208) SLM
  electrical equipment Sécheron
Number built 8
Number series 201-208

Principal motive power on the independent BLS system before the introduction of the Ae4/4 was provided by the 140 tonne Ae6/8 series. Originally designated Be6/8, these locomotives were the first BLS main line units with individual axle drive and were constructed to haul 550 tonne loads at 50 km/h (31 mph) over the continuous 2·7% (1 in 37) gradients of the Lötschberg line.

The locomotive body is carried on an articulated underframe and each driven axle is powered by two traction motors. The first four units (nos 201-204), delivered in 1926 (2) and 1931 (2), had an original hourly rating of 3310 kW (4435 hp) and a top speed of 75 km/h (47 mph). In 1939 this was uprated to 3885 kW (5205 hp) and the locomotives re-geared for 90 km/h (56 mph). In the same year the first of a further batch of four (nos 205-208) appeared with performance characteristics similar to those of nos 201-204 in their modified form. These later machines were provided with more commodious cabs, and the first four were similarly equipped during the mid-1950s. At the same time all eight locomotives were provided with improved rheostatic braking, resulting in the removal of one pantograph to provide room for roof-mounted resistances.

A further remarkable modification took place between 1961 and 1964, when the provision of new transformer and tap-changer equipment allowed the hourly rating to be raised further to 4415 kW (5915 hp) and the top speed to 100 km/h (62 mph). Now retained as powerful reserve locomotives, these impressive machines are also used as centre units marshalled into the heaviest BLS freight trains.

BLS class Ae6/8 no 204. Note the roof-mounted braking resistances *(BLS)*

Switzerland

BLS class Re4/4

Operating system Berne-Loetschberg-Simplon Railway (BLS)
Year introduced 1964
Axle arrangement Bo-Bo
Gauge 1435 mm *(4 ft 8½ in)*
Power supply system 15 kV ac 16⅔ Hz
One-hour output 4945 kW *(6630 hp, 6720 ch)*
Maximum speed 140 km/h *(87 mph)*
Maximum tractive effort 314 kN *(70 500 lbs)*
One-hour tractive effort 231 kN *(52 000 lbs)* at 78 km/h *(48 mph)*
Weight in working order 80 tonnes *(79 tons)*
Length over buffers (161-173) 15 100 mm *(49 ft 6½ in)*; (174-189) 15 470 mm *(50 ft 9 in)*
Bogie wheelbase 2800 mm *(9 ft 2¼ in)*
Wheel diameter 1250 mm *(4 ft 1¼ in)*
Traction motors Four dc series-wound BBC type GRLM 763, fully suspended with BBC spring drive
Control h.t. tap-changer
Electric brake Rheostatic
Builder
  mechanical parts SLM
  electrical equipment BBC
Number built 29 + 6 ordered 1980
Number series 161-189, 190-195

GBS no 178, one of four Re4/4s lettered for constituent companies of the BLS group, at Brig in September 1978 *(Yves Steenebruggen)*

In selecting a powerful new locomotive for demanding mountain work, the BLS administration in 1964 departed from established Swiss practice, eschewing ac motors in favour of a rectifier machine with dc traction motors. This design, later classified Re4/4, proved successful and led to subsequent orders to bring the total number to 29—over half the BLS locomotive fleet. With an hourly rating of 4945 kW, the Re4/4 is more powerful than its predecessor, the Ae4/4 (see p 116), and with a design speed of 140 km/h is the fastest motive power operated by BLS. Performance includes the capability of taking a trailing load of 630 tonnes up 2·7% (1 in 37) gradients at 80 km/h. To ensure optimum adhesion, special design features include a low level traction system and automatic compensation of weight transfer from the leading axle. Provision is made for push-pull and multiple-unit operation, enabling the Re4/4s to handle the full range of BLS traffic.

The first five units, delivered 1964-67, were until 1969 designated class Ae4/4 and numbered 261-265. Nos 166-173 entered service in 1970 and were followed by a further 16 between 1972 and 1975. This final series incorporates detail improvements, mainly to the control equipment. Provision is also made for the eventual adoption of automatic couplers, producing a slight increase in length. Four of these later machines are normally operated by railways within the BLS group and are lettered accordingly. These are nos 177 of the Spiez-Erlenbach-Zweisimmen-Bahn (SEZ), 178 of the Gürbetal-Bern-Schwarzenburg-Bahn (GBS) and 179 and 180 of the Bern-Neuenburg-Bahn (BN).

In 1968, no 161 was fitted experimentally with thyristor control equipment and underwent trials on Austrian and German Federal systems as well as in Switzerland.

Orders were placed in 1980 for a further six Re4/4s, to be numbered 190-195, for delivery by 1982.

Switzerland

RhB class Ge4/4 II

Operating system Rhaetian Railways (RhB)
Year introduced 1973
Axle arrangement Bo-Bo
Gauge 1000 mm *(3 ft 3⅜ in)*
Power supply system 11 kV ac 16⅔ Hz
One-hour output 1690 kW *(2270 hp, 2300 ch)*
Continuous output 1520 kW *(2035 hp, 2065 ch)*
Maximum speed 90 km/h *(56 mph)*
Maximum tractive effort 179 kN *(40 200 lbs)*
Continuous tractive effort 102 kN *(22 800 lbs)*
at 53 km/h *(33 mph)*
Weight in working order 50 tonnes *(49¼ tons)*
Length over buffers 12 960 mm *(42 ft 6¼ in)*
Bogie wheelbase 2300 mm *(7 ft 6½ in)*
Wheel diameter 1070 mm *(3 ft 6⅛ in)*
Traction motors Four pulsating current series-wound
  BBC type 6 FHO 4338, fully suspended with BBC
  spring drive
Control Thyristor
Electric brake Rheostatic
Builder
  mechanical parts SLM
  electrical equipment BB
Number built 10
Number series 611-620

These ten 1690 kW Ge4/4 II units were ordered in 1970 for service throughout the RhB 11 kV ac 16⅔ Hz metre-gauge network, and at the time of writing remain Switzerland's only series-built thyristor-controlled locomotives. Their electrical design draws on experience gained with Berne-Lötschberg-Simplon Re4/4 thyristor prototype no 161, also equipped by BBC. Mechanical construction is based on the Swiss Federal (SBB) Re4/4 II (see p 128) and incorporates compensated body suspension and electro-pneumatically equalized axle-loading to give optimum adhesion. Multiple-unit control equipment is fitted, and the locomotives are provided with rheostatic braking capable of absorbing 520 kW.

Haulage characteristics of these compact machines are impressive. The Ge4/4 II can take 265 tonnes up a 3·5% (1 in 28) gradient compared with the 270 tonnes for the more powerful 65 tonne Ge6/6 II Bo-Bo-Bo units. They are also the fastest locomotives in the RhB fleet, with a top speed of 90 km/h (56 mph) which proves useful on flatter stretches of line.

Livery is green and black with a silver roof, and all ten units bear the names of locations served by the RhB.

RhB class Ge4/4 II no 616 *Filisur (SLM)*

Switzerland

RhB class Ge6/6 1

Operating system Rhaetian Railways (RhB)
Year introduced 1921
Axle arrangement C-C
Gauge 1000 mm *(3 ft 3⅜ in)*
Power supply system 11 kV ac 16⅔ Hz
One-hour output 840 kW *(1125 hp, 1140 ch)*
Maximum speed 55 km/h *(34 mph)*
Maximum tractive effort 176 kN *(39 600 lbs)*
Weight in working order 66 tonnes *(65 tons)*
Length over buffers 13 300 mm *(43 ft 7⅝ in)*
Bogie wheelbase 2000+1275=3275 mm
 (10 ft 9 in)
Wheel diameter 1070 mm *(3 ft 6⅛ in)*
Traction motors Two single-phase commutator
 Brown Boveri type ELM 86/12, frame-suspended with
 jackshaft/side-rod drive
Control l.t. switchgear
Electric brake Rheostatic
Builder
 mechanical parts SLM
 electrical equipment Brown Boveri, Oerlikon
Number built 15
Number series 401-415

Fifteen examples of this "Baby Crocodile" design were constructed by SLM and Brown Boveri between 1921 and 1929, and in 1980 all but one survived in light service as reserve power on the RhB single-phase network. Developed as a scaled-down metre-gauge version of the Swiss Federal Railways' (SBB) Ce6/8 II (see p 124), the Ge6/6 I comprises a central machinery compartment mounted on two three-axle bogies which are pivotted beneath each cab. The nose housing is mounted on the bogie, articulating the body to provide a sufficiently flexible wheelbase for sharp curves and also to avoid clearance difficulties. One traction motor powers each bogie and transmission is by means of jackshafts and coupling rods.

With a one-hour rating of 840 kW, the Ge6/6 I was at the time of its introduction the world's most powerful metre-gauge locomotive, and performance capabilities include hauling a 150 tonne load at 32 km/h (20 mph) up a gradient of 4·5% (1 in 22).

In 1926, SLM and Brown Boveri delivered to Swiss Federal Railways three generally similar units (SBB class De6/6) for operation on the standard-gauge Seetal line.

The RhB units have retained their original chocolate brown livery.

RhB class Ge6/6 I no 407 at St Moritz in July 1978 *(Brian Garvin)*

Switzerland

RhB class Gem4/4

Operating system Rhaetian Railways (RhB)
Year introduced 1968
Axle arrangement Bo-Bo
Gauge 1000 mm *(3 ft 3⅜ in)*
Power supply system 1 kV dc
One-hour output (electric operation) 675 kW *(900 hp, 915 ch)*; (diesel operation) 765 kW *(1025 hp, 1040 ch)*
Continuous output (electric operation) 540 kW *(720 hp, 730 ch)*; (diesel operation) 750 kW *(1005 hp, 1020 ch)*
Maximum speed 65 km/h *(40 mph)*
Maximum tractive effort (electric or diesel operation) 175 kN *(39 200 lbs)*
One-hour tractive effort (electric operation) 107 kN *(24 000 lbs)* at 23 kmh *(14 mph)*; (diesel operation) 98 kN *(22 000 lbs)* at 28 km/h *(17½ mph)*
Weight in working order 50 tonnes *(49¼ tons)*
Length over buffers 13 540 mm *(44 ft 5 in)*
Bogie wheelbase 2200 mm *(7 ft 2⅝ in)*
Wheel diameter 920 mm *(3 ft 0¼ in)*
Diesel engines two Cummins VT12-825B1 12-cylinder "vee" of 485 kW *(650 hp)* gross at 2000 rpm
Traction motors Four dc series-wound Brown Boveri type EMR 475, nose-suspended, axle-hung
Control Rheostatic
Electric brake (electric operation) regenerative; (diesel operation) rheostatic
Builder
  mechanical parts SLM, SWS
  electrical equipment Brown Boveri, Oerlikon, Sécheron
Number built 2
Number series 801 & 802

The Gem4/4 electro-diesel locomotives were introduced in 1968 primarily for electric operation on the metre-gauge Bernina line, but also to provide reserve power capable of operation on all parts of the RhB system.

Linking St Moritz with Tirano via the 2257 m (7403 ft) Bernina Pass, the 61 km (38 mile) Bernina line is one of the steepest adhesion-worked lines in Europe, with a ruling gradient of 7% (1 in 14) for 27 km (17 miles). Electric traction, using a 1 kV dc overhead power supply, has been used since the opening of the line in 1910. When operating electrically on the Bernina line one Gem4/4 is permitted a maximum load of 70 tonnes, while two in multiple may be loaded to 130 tonnes. Operation in multiple is also possible with the line's principal motive power, the Abe4/4 emus nos 41-49. Regenerative braking is available when running electrically. Away from the 1 kV catenary, power comes from two diesel/generator sets developing a gross 970 kW (1300 hp). The multiple-unit facility is retained and dynamic braking is provided.

Parent depot for both locomotives is Poschiavo. As well as reinforcing Bernina line emu traffic, they are also used for snow clearance. As diesel units they are specially employed to handle extra winter traffic between Landquart, Chur and Arosa.

Two examples of a rack-and-adhesion diesel-only design bearing some similarities to the RhB units are in service with the Furka-Oberalp-Bahn (FO class HGm4/4).

RhB class Gem4/4 no 801 at Pontresina in July 1975
(Yves Steenebruggen)

Switzerland

SBB class Ae4/7

Operating system Swiss Federal Railways (SBB/CFF/FFS)
Year introduced 1927
Axle arrangement 2-Do-1
Gauge 1435 mm *(4 ft 8½ in)*
Power supply system 15 kV ac 16⅔ Hz
One-hour output 2295 kW *(3075 hp, 3120 ch)*
Maximum speed 100 km/h *(62 mph)*
Maximum tractive effort 196 kN *(44 100 lbs)*
One-hour tractive effort 127 kN *(28 700 lbs)* at 65 km/h *(40 mph)*
Weight in working order (10901-72, 11003-27) 118 tonnes *(116 tons)* total, 77 tonnes *(76 tons)* adhesive; (10973-11002) 123 tonnes *(121 tons)* total, 79 tonnes *(78 tons)* adhesive
Length over buffers (10901-72, 11003-27) 16 760 mm *(54 ft 11⅞ in)*; (10973-11002) 17 100 mm *(56 ft 1¼ in)*
Rigid wheelbase 1950+1950+1960=5860 mm *(19 ft 2¾ in)*
Wheel diameter (driving) 1610 mm *(5 ft 3⅜ in)*; (carrying) 950 mm *(3 ft 1⅜ in)*
Traction motors Four single-phase commutator, frame-mounted with Brown Boveri Büchli flexible drive
Control l.t. switchgear
Electric brake Regenerative on nos. 10973-11002 only
Builder
  mechanical parts SLM
  electrical equipment Brown Boveri, Oerlikon, Sécheron
Number built 127
Number series 10901-11027

Dating from 1927, the Ae4/7 provides striking evidence of the longevity of the electric locomotive. With the exception of nos 10906 and 10965, withdrawn following accident damage, the entire class remained in service at the beginning of 1980 and although planned retirement was due to begin during the following year, SBB traction requirements foresee their survival until the 21st century.

The design of the Ae4/7 was derived from the earlier Ae3/6 I 2-Co-1 series and represents the second phase of Swiss electric locomotive development in the adoption of individual axle drive rather than coupled side-rod transmission. The four body-mounted traction motors transmit torque by means of Büchli drives, whereby the motor output pinions engage gearwheels mounted outside each driving wheel to which they are flexibly coupled to permit wheelset movement. This apparatus virtually obscures the driving wheels when the locomotive is viewed from the transmission side.

Of the 127 units built by SLM between 1927 and 1934, 97 were originally delivered as 2-Co-Al machines with the outer pair of carrying axles forming a so-called *Java* axle with the adjacent driving axle. This arrangement was intended to improve behaviour at speed on curving track, but was later abandoned in favour of the present 2-Do-1 configuration with a conventional Bissel axle.

Main variants within the class are:
- nos 10973-11002, which have regenerative braking originally provided for Gotthard line service, and at 123 tonnes are five tonnes heavier than the rest of the class.
- nos 10931-10951 and 11009-11017 which are equipped for the control of two units in multiple.

Since 1964 113 examples have been electrically and mechanically modernised, and today the class can be found on all but the heaviest and fastest SBB traffic.

SBB class Ae4/7 no 10998, seen from the transmission side, at Solothurn in August 1978 *(Günther Barths)*

Switzerland

SBB class Ae6/6

Operating system Swiss Federal Railways
(SBB/CFF/FFS)
Year introduced 1952
Axle arrangement Co-Co
Gauge 1435 mm *(4 ft 8½ in)*
Power supply system 15 kV ac 16⅔ Hz
One-hour output 4290 kW *(5750 hp, 5830 ch)*
Continuous output 3972 kW *(5320 hp, 5395 ch)*
Maximum speed 125 km/h *(78 mph)*
Maximum tractive effort (11401 & 2) 324 kN
(72 800 lbs); (remainder) 393 kN *(88 200 lbs)*
One-hour tractive effort (11401 & 2) 208 kN
(46 800 lbs) at 74 km/h *(46 mph)*; (remainder)
221 kN *(49 600 lbs)* at 70 km/h *(43½ mph)*
Weight in working order (11401 & 2) 124 tonnes
(122 tons); (remainder) 120 tonnes *(118 tons)*
Length over buffers 18 400 mm *(60 ft 4⅜ in)*
Bogie wheelbase 2150+2150=4300 mm
(14 ft 1¼ in)
Wheel diameter 1260 mm *(4 ft 1⅝ in)*
Traction motors Six single-phase commutator type
GLM 982 St/10 WB 900, fully suspended with BBC
spring drive
Control h.t. tap-changer
Electric brake Regenerative
Builder
 mechanical parts SLM
 electrical equipment Brown Boveri, Oerlikon
Number built 120
Number series 11401-11520

Experience gained with the BLS Ae4/4 and SBB Re4/4 I four-axle all-adhesion designs was soon applied to meeting the severe motive power demands imposed by the Gotthard and Simplon mountain routes into Italy. Traffic conditions on these lines called for more installed power than the 2945 kW (3945 hp) of the Ae4/4, leading to the development by SLM, Brown Boveri and Oerlikon of the six-axle Ae6/6.

The first two examples, nos 11401 and 11402, were delivered as prototypes in 1952 and 1953, and with an hourly rating of 4290 kW (5750 hp) proved capable of maintaining a speed of 75 km/h (47 mph) with 600 tonne passenger trains on gradients of 2·6% (1 in 39). By employing modern construction techniques, including an all-welded body, the designers of the Ae6/6 achieved an axle-load of 20·6 tonnes and this was further reduced in the main series to 20 tonnes. Bogie design, which was based on that of the Re4/4 I, was modified for production locomotives, construction of which extended from 1955 to 1966. The first 25 units, nos 11401-11425, are embellished with chrome "whiskers" on the cab front with one band extending along the locomotive sides at waist level. This series is named after the Swiss cantons while the remainder of the class bears the names of towns and traffic centres served by SBB. In each case the appropriate coat of arms is displayed on the body side and all units bear the cross of Helvetia on the cab front.

Ever increasing traffic demands over the Gotthard and Simplon routes has led to the migration of some Ae6/6s to heavy freight work on the more level lines of the Swiss Plateau, leaving mountain duties to the more modern Re4/4 II, Re4/4 III and Re6/6 locomotives.

No 11424 *Neuchâtel* at
Göschenen in September 1978
(Yves Steenebruggen)

**From no 11426, Ae6/6s are devoid of
the chrome nose
and bodyside styling of
the first batch. No 11427** *Stadt Bern* **is seen
at Gortnellen in September 1978**
(Yves Steenebruggen)

Switzerland

SBB class Ce6/8 II

Operating system Swiss Federal Railways (SBB/CFF/FFS)
Year introduced 1920
Axle arrangement 1-C+C-1
Gauge 1435 mm *(4 ft 8½ in)*
Power supply system 15 kV ac 16⅔ Hz
One-hour output 1650 kW *(2210 hp, 2240 ch)*
Maximum speed 65 km/h *(40 mph)*
Maximum tractive effort 255 kN *(57 300 lbs)*
Continuous tractive effort 165 kN *(37 000 lbs)* at 36 km/h *(22 mph)*
Weight in working order 128 tonnes *(126 tons)* total, 104 tonnes *(102½ tons)* adhesive
Length over buffers 19 460 mm *(63 ft 10⅛ in)*
Bogie rigid wheelbase 3000+1700=4700 mm *(15 ft 5 in)*
Wheel diameter (driving) 1350 mm *(4 ft 5⅛ in)*; (carrying) 950 mm *(3 ft 1⅜ in)*
Traction motors Four single-phase commutator, bogie-mounted with jackshaft/side-rod drive
Control l.t. switchgear
Electric brake Originally regenerative, but no longer used
Builder
  mechanical parts SLM
  electrical equipment Oerlikon
Number built 33, of which 12 converted for heavy shunting
Number series 14251-14283. The 12 units converted for heavy shunting were 14267, 14269, 14274-14283

Locomotives of the classic Swiss "Crocodile" articulated type were built in two versions during the 1920s for freight haulage over mountain routes, notably the Gotthard line, and although the few survivors have been relegated to shunting duties, the class is featured as an illustration of first generation Swiss electric locomotive practice.

The Ce6/8 II series dates from 1920 and originally totalled 33 units numbered 14251-14283. Between 1942 and 1947, thirteen were subjected to traction motor modifications which increased their hourly rating to 2680 kW (3590 hp) and top speed to 75 km/h (47 mph). Reclassified Be6/8 II, these locomotives became nos 13251-13259, 13261 and 13263-13265. From 1965, a further twelve units were converted for heavy yard shunting. Regenerative braking equipment was taken out of use and visual modifications included the removal of one pantograph and the provision of shielded retreats for yard staff at each end of the locomotive. Nine examples survived in this form in 1980. In addition, one Be6/8 II unit has reverted to its original number 14253 and is retained as an operational museum locomotive at Erstfeld, on the Gotthard line.

The more powerful Be6/8 III of 1810 kW (2425 hp) appeared in 1926 and 18 examples (nos 13301-13318) were built). Nos 13302 and 13305 are preserved. In Austria, machines of similar concept were introduced in 1923 and 1926 (ÖBB classes 1089 and 1189 respectively).

SBB class Ce6/8 II no 14280 at Basle in July 1977 *(Brian Garvin)*

Switzerland

SBB class Ee3/3 IV

Operating system Swiss Federal Railways (SBB/CFF/FFS)
Year introduced 1962
Axle arrangement C
Gauge 1435 mm *(4 ft 8½ in)*
Power supply system *(four-current)* 15 kV ac 16⅔ Hz; 25 kV ac 50 Hz; 1.5 kV dc; 3 kV dc
One-hour output 390 kW *(522 hp, 529 ch)*
Maximum speed 60 km/h *(37 mph)*
Maximum tractive effort 118 kN *(26 500 lbs)*
One-hour tractive effort 59 kN *(13 200 lbs)* at at 24 km/h *(15 mph)*
Weight in working order 48 tonnes *(47 tons)*
Length over buffers 10 020 mm *(32 ft 10½ in)*
Rigid wheelbase 4000 mm *(13 ft 1½ in)*
Wheel diameter 1040 mm *(3 ft 5 in)*
Traction motors Two dc series-wound, axle-suspended with side-rod drive
Control Rheostatic
Electric brake Rheostatic
Builder
 mechanical parts SLM
 electrical equipment Sécheron
Number built 10
Number series 16551 — 16560

While most electrified railway systems use diesel traction for shunting duties, thereby avoiding the high cost of electrifying yards and sidings, SBB has progressively developed electric locomotive designs specifically for work of this kind. The Ee3/3 IV is a modern example of Swiss practice in this field, and includes the added feature of being able to operate under four different power supply systems. This is intended to simplify the handling of exchange traffic at points where the Swiss 15 kV ac low frequency catenary meets French (25 kV ac 50 Hz and 1·5 kV dc) or Italian (3 kV dc) systems.

In ac operation the Ee3/3 IV is a rectifier machine, with a fixed-ratio transformer output converted to dc and controlled by resistances. Rheostatic control is also employed when the locomotive is working from dc, with the two traction motors connected in series for 3 kV and parallel for 1·5 kV. Design of the underframes, transmission and running gear is derived from the earlier class Em3/3 diesel-electric shunter. Livery is the standard brown applied to all SBB shunting locomotives.

Locations at which these locomotives operate and respective voltages, other than the SBB 15 kV include:-

Basle, Vallorbe	SNCF 25 kV ac 50 Hz
Geneva	SNCF 1·5 kV dc
Chiasso	FS 3 kV dc

SBB class Ee3/3 IV no 16556 at Geneva in August 1978 *(Günther Barths)*

Switzerland

SBB class HGe4/4

Operating system Swiss Federal Railways (SBB/CFF/FFS)
Year introduced 1954
Axle arrangement Bo-Bo
Gauge 1000 mm *(3 ft 3⅜ in)*
Power supply system 15 kV ac 16⅔ Hz
One-hour output 1605 kW *(2150 hp, 2180 ch)*
Maximum speed (adhesion) 50 km/h *(31 mph)*; (rack) 33 km/h *(21 mph)*
Maximum tractive effort (rack) 275 kN *(6 800 lb)*
One-hour tractive effort (rack or adhesion) 186 kN *(41 900 lbs)* at 31 km/h *(19 mph)*
Weight in working order 54 tonnes *(53 tons)*
Length over coupler centres 13 200 mm *(43 ft 3¾ in)*
Bogie wheelbase 3150 mm *(10 ft 4 in)*
Wheel diameter 1028 mm *(3 ft 4½ in)*
Traction motors Four single-phase commutator, axle-suspended and with sprung rack wheels
Control h.t. tap-changer
Electric brake Rheostatic
Builder
  mechanical parts SLM
  electrical equipment Oerlikon
Number built 2
Number series 1991 and 1992

The Swiss Federal Railways' only narrow-gauge line, and also the only one employing rack operation, is the 74 km (46 mile) metre-gauge Brünig route which links Lucerne and Interlaken via the 1035 m (3396 ft) summit of the Brünig Pass. The line was opened in June 1888 with steam traction and employs the Riggenbach ladder rack system with four rack sections totalling 9 km (5·6 miles). Maximum gradient is 12% (1 in 8½).

Electrification using the standard Swiss 15 kV single-phase system took place in 1941-42, when a series of 16 rack-equipped motor luggage vans (class Deh4/6) was supplied by SLM, Brown Boveri, Oerlikon and Sécheron. These were joined in 1954 by the two 1605 kW class HGe4/4 locomotives, specially designed for rack operation on the steepest sections of the line, between Meiringen and Giswil. Although limited to 33 km/h in rack operation, it is sufficient measure of the hauling power of the HGe4/4 units to record that the starting tractive effort of 275 kN in this mode exceeds that of the 4650 kW (Re4/4 II).

Appropriately the locomotives bear the names and coats of arms of the two principal locations they serve. No 1991 is named *Meiringen*, no 1992 *Giswil*.

SBB class HGe4/4 no 1992 *Giswil* **at Meiringen in July 1977** *(Brian Garvin)*

Switzerland

SBB class Re4/4 I

Operating system Swiss Federal Railways
 (SBB/CFF/FFS)
Year introduced 1946
Axle arrangement Bo-Bo
Gauge 1435 mm *(4 ft 8½ in)*
Power supply system 15kV ac 16⅔ Hz
One-hour output (10001-26) 1825 kW *(2445 hp,*
 2480 ch); (10027-50) 1855 kW *(2485 hp, 2520 ch)*
Continuous output (10001-26) 1680 kW *(2250 hp,*
 2285 ch); (10027-50) 1760 kW *(2360 hp, 2390 ch)*
Maximum speed 125 km/h *(78 mph)*
Maximum tractive effort 137 kN *(30 900 lbs)*
One-hour tractive effort (10001-26) 79kN
 (17 800 lbs) at 83 km/h *(51½ mph)*; (10027-50
 80 kN *(18 100 lbs)* at 83 km/h *(51½ mph)*
Weight in working order 57 tonnes *(56 tons)*
Length over buffers (10001-26) 14 700 mm *(48 ft*
 2¾ in); (10027-50) 14 900 mm *(48 ft 10⅝ in)*
Bogie wheelbase 3000 mm *(9 ft 10¼ in)*
Wheel diameter 1040 mm *(3 ft 5 in)*
Traction motors Four single-phase commutator type
 8 w 600 (10001-26 or 10 w 700 (10027-50), fully
 suspended with BBC spring drive
Control l.t. tap-changer
Electric brake Regenerative on 10001-26 only
Builder
 mechanical parts SLM
 electrical equipment Brown Boveri, Oerlikon,
 Sécheron
Number built 50
Number series 10001—10050

In contrast with the high powered BLS Ae4/4 series intended for mountain work, the Swiss Federal Railways' first modern all-adhesion design was the Re4/4 I, a light, free-running machine of modest power developed for rapid inter-city services on easily graded routes. The appearance of the class coincided with the introduction of new lightweight all-steel stock which could be operated in a push-pull configuration, and the use of modern improved constructional and electrical techniques offered a weight saving of 36 tonnes against the earlier Ae3/6 I previously employed for lighter duties.

The class is divided into two series. The first 26 are equipped with multiple-unit control equipment for push-pull operation and have regenerative braking. Their appearance is characterized by the addition of frontal access doors, originally intended to allow staff to pass through the locomotive when operating in the push-pull mode. This feature is absent on the later series, nos 10027-10050, built in 1950/1. These slightly more powerful machines are also devoid of the multiple-unit control and electric braking of their predecessors. Four locomotives, nos 10033, 10034, 10046 and 10050 bear red and cream Trans-Europe Express (TEE) livery in place of the usual green. The first two of these are equipped with one DB/ÖBB type pantograph to facilitate through running between Zurich and Lindau on *TEE* services.

Until the late 1960s, the class was numbered 401-450.

SBB class Re4/4 I (first series) no 10012 at Göschenen in September 1978 *(Yves Steenebruggen)*

Re4/4 Is of the second series are slightly more powerful than nos 10001-10026 and lack frontal connecting doors. No 10050, one of four finished in *TEE* livery, was photographed at Basle in August 1973 *(ILA Günther Barths)*

127

Switzerland

SBB class Re4/4 II

Operating system Swiss Federal Railways (SBB/CFF/FFS)

Year introduced 1964

Axle arrangement Bo-Bo

Gauge 1435 mm *(4 ft 8½ in)*

Power supply system 15 kV ac 16⅔ Hz

One-hour output (11101-06) 4010 kW *(5375 hp, 5450 ch)*; (remainder) 4650 kW *(6230 hp, 6320 ch)*

Maximum speed 140 km/h *(87 mph)*

Maximum tractive effort 255 kN *(57 400 lbs)*

One-hour tractive effort (11101-06) 144 kN *(32 400 lbs)* at 100 km/h *(62 mph)*; (remainder) 167 kN *(37 600 lbs)* at 100 km/h *(62 mph)*

Weight in working order (11101-06) 79 tonnes *(78 tons)*; (remainder) 80 tonnes *(79 tons)*

Length over buffers (11101-06) 14 800 mm *(48 ft 6⅝ in)*; (11107-11155) 14 900 mm *(48 ft 10⅝ in)*; (11156-11304) 15 410 mm *(50 ft 6¾ in)* (see text)

Bogie wheelbase 2800 mm *(9 ft 2¼ in)*

Wheel diameter 1260 mm *(4 ft 1⅝ in)*

Traction motors Four single-phase commutator, fully-suspended with Brown Boveri spring drive

Control h.t. tap-changer

Electric brake Regenerative

Builder
  mechanical parts SLM
  electrical equipment Brown Boveri, Oerlikon, Sécheron

Number built 204 + 45 on order for delivery 1981/2

Number series 11101-11304 + 45 units on order, to be numbered 11305-11349

Class Re4/4 II no 11265 at Brig in August 1978
(Günther Barths)

SBB's largest class, the highly successful Re4/4 II, was developed as a standard design capable of meeting a wide variety of motive power demands. These range from express work on Switzerland's more level routes, where good acceleration and high top speed are required, to heavy freight duties on mountain lines with two locomotives operating in multiple.

Six 4010 kW prototype units entered service in 1964. Originally numbered 11201-6, these became nos 11101-6 in 1967, when deliveries of the first production batch of 49 started. By 1975 SLM had constructed 204 at their Winterthur works, and in 1979 an order was placed for a further 45 to handle planned expansion in 1982 of SBB's internal passenger services. In 1971, 20 generally similar class Re4/4 III units entered service. Intended for service on mountain routes, these machines are geared for a top speed of 125 km/h (77 mph). Three Swiss private railways also operate versions of the Re4/4 II. The Süd-Ost-Bahn (SOB) introduced its solitary class Re4/4 III no 41 in 1967, the Emmental-Burgdorf-Thun (EBT) line acquired class Re4/4 nos 111 and 112 in 1969 and in the same year class Re4/4 II no 21 was delivered to the Mittel-Thurgau-Bahn (MThB).

Main variants within the SBB series are:
- nos 11103/06/08/09/12/13/33 and 11141 which are finished in "Swiss Express" red and light grey livery and fitted with automatic couplers for service with SBB Mk III stock.
- nos 11158-61 and 11249-53 which bear the Trans-Europe Express (TEE) red and cream livery.
- nos 11107-09 and from 11156, which are equipped with single-arm pantographs.
- nos 11196-201 on which one of the two pantographs is of the DB/ÖBB type (design of SBB pantographs differs owing to finer clearance tolerances), enabling these units to penetrate German Federal and Austrian Federal networks. In addition certain locomotives have been adapted or constructed to accept automatic couplers at a later date, increasing their overall length to 15510 mm (50 ft 18⅝ in).

No 11103, seen here at Zurich in August 1978, is one of eight Re4/4 II units fitted with automatic couplers and finished in light grey and red *Swiss-Express* livery for service with Mk III stock (*ILA Günther Barths*)

Nine of the Re4/4 II series bear the *TEE* red and cream colour scheme, including no 11159, photographed at Airolo in September 1978 (*Yves Steenebruggen*)

The twenty examples of the generally similar Re4/4 III series have a lower gear ratio to give a top speed of 125 km/h. No 11352 leads another member of the class on a heavy Gotthard line freight at Göschenen in September 1978 (*Yves Steenebruggen*)

Switzerland

SBB class Re6/6

Operating system Swiss Federal Railways (SBB/CFF/FFS)
Year introduced 1972
Axle arrangement Bo-Bo-Bo
Gauge 1435 mm *(4 ft 8½ in)*
Power supply system 15 kV ac 16⅔ Hz
One-hour output 7800 kW *(10455 hp, 10 600 ch)*
Continuous output 7240 kW *(9700 hp, 9835 ch)*
Maximum speed 140 km/h *(87 mph)*
Maximum tractive effort 395 kN *(88 700 lbs)*
One-hour tractive effort 267 kN *(60 000 lbs)* at 106 km/h *(66 mph)*
Weight in working order 120 tonnes *(118 tons)*
Length over buffers 19 310 mm *(63 ft 4¼ in)*
Bogie wheelbase (11601 & 02) 2800 mm *(9 ft 2¼ in)*; (remainder) 2900 mm *(9 ft 6⅛ in)*
Wheel diameter 1260 mm *(4 ft 1⅝ in)*
Traction motors Six single-phase commutator, fully suspended with BBC spring drive
Control h.t. tap-changer
Electric brake Regenerative
Builder
  mechanical parts SLM
  electrical equipment Brown Boveri
Number built 89, + 35 for delivery from 1981
Number series 11601 — 11689, 11690 — 11724 (to be delivered from 1981)

With a one-hour rating of 7800 kW, the Re6/6 is the world's most powerful single-unit electric locomotive and shows a remarkable 82% increase in power-to-weight ratio over the Ae6/6 introduced just 20 years earlier. The class was developed to increase capacity and speeds over the Gotthard and Simplon mountain routes and at the same time to reduce expensive double-heading with less powerful Re4/4 II and Re4/4 III units. The Bo-Bo-Bo axle configuration incorporates several features intended to permit higher speeds on curving mountain routes and to reduce rail wear. Transverse couplings between bogies reduce dynamic guiding forces, and low level traction devices give high adhesion factors. All bogies have some degree of sideplay—the centre one as much as 127 mm (5 in) in each direction. Each axle has 10 mm (0·4 in) lateral movement within the bogie. The Re6/6 can take 800 tonnes over the Gotthard line at 80 km/h (50 mph) and can also sprint at its maximum of 140 km/h (87 mph) over the straighter stretches of track away from the Alps.

Of the four prototypes which appeared in 1972, the first two, nos 11601 and 11602, were built with articulated bodies, a technique which has found much favour in neighbouring Italy and in Switzerland on the metre-gauge Rhaetian Railways (RhB). The third and fourth machines have rigid bodies and this arrangement was adopted for the rest of the class. As a further experiment, no 11604 was delivered with secondary air suspension in place of the conventional helical springs of the rest of the class.

SBB has continued the pleasing practice of naming mountain locomotives and all Re6/6s bear names and crests of important traffic centres. No 11613 *Rapperswil* enjoys the distinction of being the 5000th motive power unit constructed by SLM. By June 1980 81 of the initial production run of 85 units had entered service. During the same year SBB announced a new order for 35 more for delivery from 1981.

The first two of the four prototype Re6/6s feature a twin-section body, as seen in this view of no 11602 *Morges* at Zurich Hbf in July 1975 *(Yves Steenebruggen)*

Re6/6 no 11611 *Rüti ZH (SLM)*

Taiwan

TRA classes E200 and E300

Operating system Taiwan Railway Administration (TRA)
Year introduced 1977
Axle arrangement Co-Co
Gauge 1067 mm *(3 ft 6 in)*
Power supply system 25 kV ac 60 Hz
One-hour output 2880 kW *(3860 hp, 3915 ch)*
Continuous output 2800 kW *(3750 hp, 3805 ch)*
Maximum speed 110 km/h *(68 mph)*
Maximum tractive effort 267 kN *(60 000 lbs)*
Continuous tractive effort 197 kN *(44 300 lbs)*
Weight in working order 96 tonnes *(94½ tons)*
Length over coupler centres 16 460 mm *(54 ft 0 in)*
Wheel diameter 914 mm *(3 ft 0 in)*
Traction motors Six dc series-wound General Electric type GE-761, nose-suspended, axle-hung
Control Thyristor
Electric brake None
Builder
  mechanical parts General Electric
  electrical equipment General Electric
Number built 86 (84 in service—see text)
Number series E201—E235, E301—E349

Full electric working on TRA's busy 1067 mm (3 ft 6 in) West Trunk main line was formally inaugurated on 1 July 1979, when the final section of the 456 km (283 mile) route between Kee-lung and Kaohsiung was energised. The single-phase 25 kV ac 60 Hz system is employed, and principal motive power in an all-thyristor fleet is provided by 84* series E200 and E300 mixed traffic units built at General Electric's Erie (Pennsylvania) plant in 1977-79. Designated GE model E42C, the two classes form one of the largest US export orders for electric locomotives, and differ only in the installation in the 35 E200 units of a 350 kW (470 hp) motor/alternator set providing a 440 V ac 60 Hz supply for train auxiliaries. Machines of the E300 series are ballasted to compensate for the absence of this equipment.

The locomotives employ thyristor control, with automatic regulation of tractive effort and of wheel-slip. Up to three units may be operated in multiple, and driver vigilance and deadman equipment is fitted, foreshadowing possible one-man operation. To withstand harsh atmospheric conditions on coastal sections of the West Trunk line, corrosion-proof Corten steel is used in construction of the locomotive structure. Body design incorporates large removeable side panels allowing routine access to equipment. Livery is orange and grey.

The E42Cs share West Trunk duties with a series of 20 2100 kW (2815 hp) Bo-Bo units (TRA class E100) and 13 five-car emus, both supplied by the British company GEC Traction.

*GE's original contract was for 74 locomotives and included the 35 E200 units. This was followed by a later order for 12 E300 machines including replacements for two of the original order lost at sea in a violent storm during shipment to Taiwan.

TRA class E300 no E326 at Taipei with the *Kuan Kuang Hao* express from Kaohsiung in February 1978. First vehicle of the train is a generator van *(William D Middleton)*

Turkey

TCDD class E 40

Operating system Turkish State Railways (TCDD)
Year introduced 1971
Axle arrangement B-B
Gauge 1435 mm *(4 ft 8½ in)*
Power supply system 25 kV ac 50 Hz
One-hour output 2920 kW *(3915 hp, 3970 ch)*
Continuous output 2860 kW *(3820 hp, 3885 ch)*
Maximum speed 130/90 km/h *(80/56 mph)*
Maximum tractive effort (low gear) 309 kN
(69 450 lbs); (high gear) 215 kN *(48 200 lbs)*
Continuous tractive effort (low gear) 209 kN
(47 000 lbs) at 49 km/h *(30½ mph)*; (high gear)
145 kN *(32 600 lbs)* at 71 km/h *(44 mph)*
Weight in working order 77 tonnes *(76 tons)*
Length over buffers 14 995 mm *(49 ft 2⅜ in)*
Bogie wheelbase 1608 mm *(5 ft 3¼ in)*
Wheel diameter 1100 mm *(3 ft 7¼ in)*
Traction motors Two dc series-wound Alsthom type
TAB 660 B, fully suspended with Alsthom "dancing
ring" transmission
Control h.t. tap-changer
Electric brake Rheostatic
Builder
  mechanical parts (E 40 001 — 008) Alsthom, MTE
  (for 50 Hz Group); (E 40 009 — 015) Eskişehir
  Locomotive Works
  electrical equipment Alsthom, Schneider (for
  50 Hz Group)
Number built 15
Number series E 40 001 — E 40 015

The TCDD E 40 silicon rectifier units were introduced in 1971 for use on the first stage of the Ankara single-phase electrification, from Sincan to Kayaş. They are also now employed on suburban services from Istanbul's Hydarpasa station. Design of the locomotives, which were supplied by the 50 Hz Group, follows closely that of the French National Railways (SNCF) class BB-17000 (see p 48). In common with the SNCF machines, the E 40 has single-motor bogies with alternative gear ratios. To suit TCDD operating conditions, the maximum speed in high gear is 130 km/h (80 mph) compared with the 150 km/h (93 mph) of the BB-17000. The E 40 further differs from the BB-17000 in having rheostatic braking. Multiple-unit control facilities are provided and the locomotives are frequently used in a push-pull formation with purpose-built coaching stock from TCDD's Adapazari plant. Livery is dark and light blue with white lettering.

Construction of the first eight units was carried out in France, while nos E 40 009-E 40 015 were assembled in Turkey at the Eskişehir locomotive works using components supplied by the 50 Hz Group.

**TCDD class E 40 no E 40 002 at Ankara in May 1974
with a local train to Kayaş** *(Benno Bickel)*

USSR

SZD classes ChS2 and ChS2 T

Operating system Soviet Railways (SZD)
Year introduced 1958
Axle arrangement Co-Co
Gauge 1524 mm *(5 ft 0 in)*
Power supply system 3 kV dc
Continuous output 3708 kW *(4970 hp, 5040 ch)*
Maximum speed 160 km/h *(100 mph)*
Maximum tractive effort 314 kN *(70 500 lbs)*
Continuous tractive effort 141 kN *(37 700 lbs)* at
93 km/h *(58 mph)*
Weight in working order (ChS2) 123 tonnes
(121 tons); (ChS2T) 126 tonnes *(124 tons)*
Length over coupler centres 18 920 mm
(62 ft 0⁷⁄₈ in)
Bogie wheelbase 4600 mm *(15 ft 1⅛ in)*
Wheel diameter 1250 mm *(4 ft 1¼ in)*
Traction motors Six dc series-wound, fully
suspended with Škoda flexible drive
Control Rheostatic
Electric brake (ChS2) none; (ChS2T) rheostatic
Builder
  mechanical parts Škoda
  electrical equipment Škoda
Number built 944 (of which approximately 300 are
class ChS2)
Number series ChS2-001 — ChS2T-944

Since 1958, no less than 944 of these 3 kV dc express units have been supplied to SZD by the Czechoslovak builder Škoda, forming the world's most numerous export electric locomotive design. Developed to meet exacting haulage requirements and harsh climatic conditions, the ChS2 entered series production in 1962. This followed a trial period with two prototypes (nos ChS2-001 and -002) completed four years earlier. Some 300 had been built at Plzeň by 1964 when production switched to the ChS2 T. Designated Škoda type 53E, this version differs from the earlier series, mainly in the provision of rheostatic braking and is based on a prototype delivered to SZD in 1963. Construction of the class ended in 1972 in favour of a more powerful (4800 kW) design which resembles the ChS4 T (see following entry) and is also rather confusingly designated class ChS2 T by SZD.

The class sees passenger service over most parts of the SZD 3 kV dc network, but has been especially associated with the Moscow-Leningrad route, where its 160 km/h (100 mph) capability enabled start-to-stop average speeds to be raised to 130 km/h (80 mph).

SZD class ChS2 no ChS2-003 *(Škoda)*

SZD class ChS4 T

Operating system Soviet Railways (SZD)
Year introduced (prototype) 1971; (main series) 1973
Axle arrangement Co-Co
Gauge 1524 mm *(5 ft 0 in)*
Power supply system 25 kV ac 50 Hz
Continuous output 4920 kW *(6590 hp, 6685 ch)*
Maximum speed 160 km/h *(100 mph)*
Maximum tractive effort 304 kN *(68 350 lbs)*
Continuous tractive effort 165 kN *(37 000 lbs)* at 109 km/h *(68 mph)*
Weight in working order 126 tonnes *(124 tons)*
Length over coupler centres 19 980 mm *(65 ft 6⅝ in)*
Bogie wheelbase 2300 + 2300 = 4600 mm *(15 ft 1⅛ in)*
Wheel diameter 1250 mm *(4 ft 1¼ in)*
Traction motors Six dc series-wound, fully suspended with Škoda flexible drive
Control h.t. tap-changer
Electric brake Rheostatic
Builder
  mechanical parts Škoda
  electrical equipment Škoda
Number built unconfirmed, but thought to be around 100 by 1980
Number series Not known

With the Soviet electric traction industry largely committed to the construction of freight units, all SZD express passenger locomotives for both dc and ac operation have been supplied by Škoda in Czechoslovakia, where various designs have been developed specifically to suit Soviet operating requirements.

Production of the silicon rectifier ChS4 T series began in 1973 following trials with a prototype built two years earlier. The design is an improved version of the glass-fibre-bodied ChS4 series, of which 229 examples were built between 1965 and 1972, and differs principally in the installation of very powerful (5000 kW continuous) rheostatic braking, and thyristor rectifiers to provide a dc power supply for auxiliary services.

Škoda reverted to metal body construction for the ChS4 T, and the locomotives have a massive appearance which makes full use of the generous Soviet loading gauge; height with pantographs lowered is 5195 mm (17 ft 0½ in). Designed to operate under severe climatic conditions including temperatures as low as −50°C (−122°F), the ChS4 T is capable of maintaining on level track the rated maximum of 160 km/h (100 mph) with a trailing load of 1000 tonnes. A 3 kV dc version of similar appearance (SZD class ChS2 T) has been built by Škoda since 1972.

ChS4 T-245 photographed new at Škoda's Plzeň works *(Škoda)*

SZD class ChS200

Operating system Soviet Railways (SZD)
Year introduced 1975
Axle arrangement Bo-Bo+Bo-Bo
Gauge 1524 mm *(5 ft 0 in)*
Power supply system 3 kV dc
One-hour output 8400 kW *(11 260 hp, 11 410 ch)*
Continuous output 8000 kW *(10 720 hp, 10 870 ch)*
Maximum speed 200 km/h *(125 mph)* or 160 km/h
(100 mph)
Maximum tractive effort 451 kN *(101 400 lbs)*
Continuous tractive effort
204 kN *(45 900 lbs)* at 138 km/h *(86 mph)*
(tractive effort figures apply to 200 km/h version)
Weight in working order 157 tonnes *(154½ tons)*
Length over coupler centres 33 080 mm
(108 ft 6⅜ in)
Bogie wheelbase 3200 mm *(10 ft 6 in)*
Wheel diameter 1250 mm *(4 ft 1¼ in)*
Traction motors Eight dc series-wound Škoda type
AL 4741 FIT, fully suspended with Škoda cardan shaft
drive
Control Rheostatic
Electric brake Rheostatic
Builder
  mechanical parts Škoda
  electrical equipment Škoda
Number built 2 prototypes, 20 production machines
Number series ChS200-001 — ChS200-022

With a continuous rating of 8000 kW (10 720 hp), the Czechoslovak built twin-unit ChS200 is claimed to be the world's most powerful electric locomotive presently in service. The design was developed from the Czechoslovak State Railways (ČSD) ES499.0 series (see p 32) for high speed express work on selected SZD lines energised at 3 kV ac. Two prototypes numbered ChS200-001 and -002 were delivered by Škoda in 1975 and subjected to exhaustive trials both in Czechoslovakia and the USSR. Series deliveries commenced in 1979 of an initial batch of 20 locomotives for service on the Moscow-Leningrad route. Ten of these machines are geared for 200 km/h (125 mph) running; the remainder are restricted to 160 km/h (100 mph).

Locomotive running speed is automatically controlled and maintained at values preset by the driver, regardless of load or line conditions. Rheostatic braking operates independently of the overhead supply with a continuous capacity of 7200 kW (9650 hp) and is blended automatically with locomotive air braking. Transition from running to braking to maintain preset speed is also automatic.

Cabs are heat and sound insulated and air conditioned to provide a constant internal temperature within an external range of −50° to +40°C (−122° to 104°F). The front ends of the production machines differ slightly from those of the prototype in having a less angular treatment to increase their aerodynamic properties. Electric train heating facilities are provided. In 1980, development by Škoda of a thyristor-controlled 25 kV ac version designated type 81E was at an advanced stage, with a prototype expected to appear in 1981.

**ChS200 prototype no ChS200-001 at
Scherbinka in July 1977**

USSR

SZD class VL8

Operating system Soviet Railways (SZD)
Year introduced 1953
Axle arrangement Bo+Bo+Bo+Bo
Gauge 1524 mm *(5 ft 0 in)*
Power supply system 3 kV dc
One-hour output 4200 kW *(5630 hp, 5710 ch)*
Continuous output 4095 kW *(5490 hp, 5865 ch)*
Maximum speed 100 km/h *(62 mph)*
One-hour tractive effort 346 kN *(77 800 lbs)* at 42.6 km/h *(26½ mph)*
Continuous tractive effort 297 kN *(66 800 lbs)* at 44.3 km/h *(27½ mph)*
Weight in working order 184 tonnes *(181 tons)*
Length over coupler centres 27 520 mm *(90 ft 3½ in)*
Bogie wheelbase 3200 mm *(10 ft 6 in)*
Wheel diameter 1200 mm *(3 ft 11¼ in)*
Traction motors Eight dc series-wound, nose-suspended, axle-hung
Control Rheostatic
Electric brake Regenerative
Builder
  mechanical parts (VL8-001 — 200 and certain units numbered from VL8 — 1201) Novocherkassk Works; (remainder) Tbilisi Works. Bodies and bogies for later Tbilisi built units supplied by Voroshilovgrad Works
  electrical equipment Novocherkassk Works; Tbilisi Works
Number built Not revealed officially, but thought to be around 1500
Number series Not known

SZD's twin-unit VL8 heavy freight design was developed during the early 1950s to increase capacity on 3 kV dc lines, including sections of the Trans-Siberian railway. The class also sees limited use in passenger service.

The two permanently coupled body sections of the locomotive are each carried on two two-axle bogies. These are articulated and traction loads are not transmitted to the body. Traction motors are 1·5 kV machines with groupings of series, series-parallel and parallel. Four field-weakening steps in each give 15 running notches. Regenerative braking operates in the 100-12 km/h (62-7½ mph) speed range.

A prototype locomotive, no N8-001* was built in 1953 at the Novocherkassk Works, and series deliveries from this plant started two years later. In 1958, the design entered production at the then newly completed Tbilisi factory in Georgia, no N8-201* being the first locomotive built there. Construction at Novocherkassk ended in 1964 but continued until 1967 at Tbilisi, where the design was succeeded by the VL10 (see following entry). Bogies and bodies for Tbilisi built units delivered in 1966/7 were fabricated at the Voroshilovgrad "October Revolution" diesel locomotive works and supplied to Tbilisi for fitting out. At least 1500 examples are known to have been built at the two plants.

As originally designed, the VL8s proved heavy on track wear and consequently from 1962 were restricted to 80 km/h (50 mph). Suspension improvements carried out experimentally in 1973 to no VL8-321 have since been applied to the entire class, allowing restoration of the 100 km/h speed limit.

To examine the potential of a 6 kV dc power supply system, the Tbilisi Works in 1966 built an electronically controlled prototype based on the mechanical design of the VL8. Numbered VL8 V-001, the locomotive was tested extensively at both 3 kV and 6 kV, and was the world's first to operate at the latter voltage.

A development of the VL8 is the mixed-traffic six-axle VL23, which although mechanically different, retains many electrical features of the earlier design, including traction motors.

*The original N8 class designation was changed in 1963 to VL8 to incorporate the initials of Vladimir Lenin, founder of Soviet communism, who is regarded as a pioneering figure in Soviet railway electrification.

SZD class VL8 no VL8-963 at Lvov in 1972

SZD classes VL10 and VL10u

Operating system Soviet Railways (SZD)
Year introduced 1961
Axle arrangement Bo-Bo + Bo-Bo
Gauge 1524 mm *(5 ft 0 in)*
Power supply system 3 kV dc
One-hour output 5200 kW *(6970 hp, 7065 ch)*
or 5700 kW *(7640 hp, 7745 ch)* (see text)
Maximum speed 100 km/h *(62 mph)* or 110 km/h
(68 mph)
One-hour tractive effort 384 kN *(86 400 lbs)* at
47.3 km/h *(29½ mph)* (applies to 5200 kW version)
Weight in working order (VL10) 184 tonnes
(181 tons); (VL10u) 200 tonnes *(197 tons)*
Length over coupler centres 30 440 mm
(99 ft 10½ in)
Bogie wheelbase 3000 mm *(9 ft 10⅛ in)*
Wheel diameter 1250 mm *(4 ft 1¼ in)*
Traction motors Eight dc series-wound, nose-
suspended, axle-hung
Control Rheostatic
Electric brake Regenerative
Builder
 mechanical parts (VL10-—500, 1501—?)
 Tbilisi Works; (VL10-501—?) Novocherkassk
 Works
 electrical equipment Tbilisi Works; Novocherkassk
 Works
Number built Not known
Number series Not known

Successor to the VL8 (see previous entry) as standard heavy freight motive power on Soviet 3 kV dc lines was the VL10. Two prototypes numbered T8-001 and -002 (later VL10-001 and -002) were constructed at Tbilisi in 1961 and 1962 respectively. Further small batches, probably not numbering more than 30 units in all, were built at the same works up to 1967, with bodies supplied by Voroshilovgrad and bogies from Novocherkassk. Series production commenced in 1968 at Tbilisi, and during the following year at Novocherkassk. The latter plant is reported to have manufactured all bodies and bogies.

With an hourly rating for most of the class of 5200 kW, the VL10 is nearly 25% more powerful than its predecessor and has superior tractive effort characteristics, especially at higher speeds. Later locomotives employ traction motors of improved design, yielding a total output of 5700 kW and an increased top speed of 110 km/h. Service weight of the VL10 is 184 tonnes, but in 1974 no VL10-1110 was experimentally ballasted to 200 tonnes to give a 25 tonne axle-load. Further units were subsequently treated similarly, and this modified design entered production as the VL10 u. An experimental VL10 T version with automatically controlled electric braking has also been reported.

First examples of a development of the class designated VL11 were built at Tbilisi in 1977 for trial purposes. This design, to be built in two- and three-unit versions, is rated at 5360 kW (7180 hp) hourly for an eight-axle locomotive and is expected to succeed the VL10 as the standard dc freight unit. However, the extensive testing which must precede introduction of any new Soviet design implies that the VL10 remained in production in 1980.

SZD class VL10 nos VL10-170 and -174 in a formidable 10 400 kW (13 935 hp) combination at Kashuri in 1969

USSR

SLD class VL22 m

Operating system Soviet Railways (SZD)
Year introduced (prototype) 1941; (series production) 1946
Axle arrangement Co+Co
Gauge 1524 mm *(5 ft 0 in)*
Power supply system 3 kV dc
One-hour output 2400 kW *(3215 hp, 3260 ch)*
Continuous output 1835 kW *(2460 hp, 2495 ch)*
Maximum speed 80 or 100 km/h *(50 or 62 mph)* depending on gear ratio
One-hour tractive effort (low gear ratio) 213 kN *47 800 lbs)* at 40 km/h *(24½ mph)*; (high gear ratio) 176 kN *(39 500 lbs)* at 48 km/h *(30 mph)*
Continuous tractive effort (low gear ratio) 151kN *(33 900 lbs)* at 44 km/h *(27 mph)*; (high gear ratio) 125 kN *(28 000 lbs)* at 53 km/h *(33 mph)*
Weight in working order 132 tonnes *(130 tons)*
Length over coupler centres 16 390 mm *(53 ft 9¼ in)*
Wheel diameter 1200 mm *(3 ft 11¼ in)*
Traction motors Six dc series-wound, nose-suspended, axle-hung
Control Rheostatic
Electric brake Regenerative on some units only
Builder
  mechanical parts Kolomna Locomotive Works; Novocherkassk Works
  electrical equipment Dynamo Works, Moscow; Novocherkassk Works
Number built Not revealed officially, but thought to be around 2000
Number series Not known

The origins of this large class can be traced to a series of eight class S Co+Co machines supplied by General Electric in 1932 for operation on the Suram Pass section of the Trans-Caucasus line. A small number of similar locomotives, class Ss, was constructed in the USSR during the early 1930s and in a modified form this design was adopted as a standard all-purpose unit in preference to the VL19 of purely Soviet origin. Re-classified VL22, the first of this new series appeared in 1938 and was equipped with six 340 kW (455 hp) nose-suspended motors developed by the Dynamo Works in Moscow.

In 1941, no VL22-178 was experimentally fitted with 400 kW (536 hp) traction motors to form the prototype of the present VL22 m series. Mass production began in 1946, at first at the Kolomna Locomotive Works but from 1947 at Novocherkassk. The first series-built machine was no VL22 m-184. Production ended in 1958 after some 2000 examples had been constructed, including variants with differing gear ratios giving top speeds of 80 or 100 km/h to suit various traffic requirements. All members of the class are equipped for multiple-unit operation, and some have regenerative braking. The external appearance of the VL22 m is characterised by hand-railed platforms forward of each cab giving access to the locomotive via central front doors. It is likely that the original VL22 series was later re-motored and absorbed into the main class.

These locomotives remain in secondary service in many parts of SZD's 3 kV dc network, including the Yaroslavl division of the Moscow Railway and the Zakavkazskaja Railway in the Caucasus.

SZD class VL22 m no VL22 m-1892

SZD classes VL60, VL60 K, VL60 P and VL60 R

Operating system Soviet Railways (SZD)
Year introduced (VL60) 1957; (VL60P) 1961;
(VL60K & VL60R) 1962
Axle arrangement Co-Co
Gauge 1524 mm (5 ft 0 in)
Power supply system 25 kV ac 50 Hz
One-hour output 4140 kW (5550 hp, 5625 ch)
or 4650 kW (6230 hp, 6320 ch)
Maximum speed (VL60P) 110 km/h (68 mph);
(remainder) 100 km/h (62 mph)
One-hour tractive effort (VL60P) 223 kN
(50 000 lbs) at 73 km/h (45½ mph); (remainder)
312 kN (70 100 lbs) at 52 km/h (32 mph) or 314 kN
(70 550 lbs) at 52 km/h (32 mph)
Weight in working order (VL60P) 129 tonnes
(127 tons); (remainder) 138 tonnes (136 tons)
Length over coupler centres 20 800 mm
(68 ft 3 in)
Bogie wheelbase 2300 + 2300 = 4600 mm
(15 ft 1⅛ in)
Wheel diameter 1250 mm (4 ft 1¼ in)
Traction motors Six dc series-wound, nose-
suspended, axle-hung
Control l.t. tap-changer
Electric brake (VL60, VL60K & VL60P) none;
(VL60R) regenerative
Builder
mechanical parts Novocherkassk Works
electrical equipment Novocherkassk Works
Number built Not revealed officially, but thought to be
around 2500
Number series Not known

The VL60 was the first Soviet series-built ac design and with its descendants remains the world's most numerous type of electric locomotive. Prototypes numbered N60-001 and -002 (later re-classified VL60) were constructed in 1957 and 1958 at Novocherkassk. Originally designed for 20 kV operation, these were mercury arc rectifier machines with a service weight of 141·3 tonnes and a top speed of 110 km/h, although each locomotive was fitted with differing gear ratios. Subsequently the maximum speed was reduced to 100 km/h and a weight saving of two tonnes was effected by the use of welded steel rather than cast bogies. SZD's urgent need for motive power for newly electrified 25 kV ac lines resulted in series production in 1959, before all design problems had been solved, and various modifications to equipment were made in the light of service experience as construction progressed. These included traction motor improvements which raised the hourly output of later machines to 4650 kW and gave increased haulage capabilities. Deliveries continued until 1965, by which time at least 1800 examples had been built.

First silicon rectifier locomotives based on the VL60 design appeared in 1961. Numbered N62-001 and -002, these units had high-tension control. They were joined in 1962 by nos VL60 K-001 and -002, with control on the low-tension side, to form the basis of the silicon rectifier VL60 K series which in 1965 succeeded the VL60 as standard construction at Novocherkassk. Production ended in 1967. The VL60 R sub-series is equipped with regenerative braking and was built at Novocherkassk from 1964 to 1966 following the introduction in 1962 of two prototypes, nos VL60 R-001 and -002.

SZD fared no better with mercury arc rectifiers than any other railway, and from 1975 undertook a programme of re-equipment of earlier units with silicon semi-conductor rectifiers. Modified locomotives have been accordingly re-classified VL60 K or VL60 KR.

The locomotives detailed above are regarded as mixed-traffic machines but are mainly used for freight work. A VL60 P version specifically for passenger service appeared in prototype form in 1961 and was series-built in small numbers at Novocherkassk from 1962 to 1965. Making the structure lighter, including the use of aluminium, yields a service weight of 129 tonnes and top speed is 110 km/h. Later examples of this series are equipped to provide electric train heating.

The variants of the class are numbered in a common series, and are distinguishable by the suffix to the class designation. Numbers built of each type are unknown, but total construction is thought to be in the region of 2500 units.

SZD class VL60 K no VL60 K-317 (SZD)

SZD classes VL80 K, VL80 T and VL80 R

Operating system Soviet Railways (SZD)
Year introduced (VL80K) 1963; (VL80T) 1967;
(VL80R) 1967
Axle arrangement Bo-Bo–Bo-Bo
Gauge 1524 mm *(5 ft 0in)*
Power supply system 25 kV ac 50 Hz
One-hour output 6520 kW *(8735 hp, 8860 ch)*
Continuous output 6260 kW *(8390 hp, 8505 ch)*
Maximum speed 110 km/h *(68 mph)*
Maximum tractive effort 443 kN *(99 500 lbs)* at
52 km/h *(32 mph)*
Continuous tractive effort 401 kN *(90 200 lbs)* at
54 km/h *(33 mph)*
Weight in working order (VL80K & VL80T)
184 tonnes *(181 tons)*, (VL80R) 192 tonnes
(189 tons)
Length over coupler centres 32 840 mm
(107 ft 9 in)
Bogie wheelbase 3000 mm *(9 ft 10⅛ in)*
Wheel diameter 1250 mm *(4 ft 1¼ in)*
Traction motors Eight dc series-wound, nose-
suspended axle-hung
Control (VL80K & VL80T) l.t. tap-changer; (VL80R)
thyristor
Electric brake (VL80K) none; (VL80T) rheostatic;
(VL80R) regenerative
Builder
 mechanical parts Novocherkassk Works
 electrical equipment Novocherkassk Works
 Number built Not revealed officially, but thought to
 be in excess of 2060 units by 1980
Number series Not known

Principal motive power for the huge tonnages of freight conveyed over the extensive SZD 25 kV network (16 000 route-km—9940 miles—at the end of 1978) is provided by the important VL80 family of twin-unit rectifier locomotives. Three prototypes with high-tension control and mercury arc rectifiers were built in 1961 at Novocherkassk. Numbered N80-001, -002 and -003 and later re-designated VL80 V, these units did not prove satisfactory, and were followed in 1962 by nos N81-001 and -002 (later VL80-004 and -005) with low-tension control. Further design improvements were incorporated in subsequent locomotives which were constructed in small numbers from 1963. During the same year, no VL80 K-015 appeared with silicon rectifiers and these were adopted as standard from no VL80 K-026, delivered in 1964. Other modifications to the design were made during mass production, which extended from 1966 to 1971. Around 700 examples of this version are thought to have been delivered in this period.

The VL80 T, with rheostatic braking, appeared in 1967, when nos VL80 T-158 and -159 received this equipment. Some changes to body design were required to accommodate resistances and ventilators. Five more experimental units appeared before series production began in 1970.

Experiments with an electronically controlled version of the VL80 began in 1967, when a VL80 K was provided with thyristor control and regenerative braking. This machine became no VL80 R-300 and was followed by further trial units in 1969 and 1973. Modest series production began in 1974 and deliveries continued in 1980. Provision of regenerative braking is claimed to reduce traction power consumption by 10-12%.

**The first of the VL80 family to enter series production was the VL80 K,
equipped with silicon rectifiers. This example is no VL80 K-372** *(SZD)*

The VL80 also serves as a test-bed for development of a new generation of Soviet motive power aimed at increasing output per axle and at reducing motor maintenance. In 1967, asynchronous three-phase traction motors were fitted at Novocherkassk to no VL80 A-238. No VL80 A-751 was similarly modified in 1971, and this development continues. Other experiments have centred on the VL80 V, not to be confused with the original prototypes, with so-called thyratron commutator-less traction motors. One half of no VL80 V-216 was so equipped in 1967, and was followed by another unit numbered VL80 V-661 in 1970. Hourly output of this machine was 7480 kW (10 025 hp). Further improvements were incorporated in nos VL80 V-1129 and -1130, delivered in 1975, but this version had not entered production by 1980.

Production of the VL80 family is known to have exceeded 2060 units by 1980. SZD also operates the dual-voltage (3 kV dc/25 kV ac 50 Hz) VL82/VL82M series which dates from 1966 and is derived from the VL80.

No VL80 V-1130 is an experimental locomotive equipped with thyratron traction motors

The VL80 T sub-series, of which no VL80 T-758 is seen here, differs from the VL80 K in the provision of rheostatic brakes (*SZD*)

Thyristor-controlled class VL80 R no VL80 R-1549 photographed during the *Railway Transport 77* exhibition at Scherbinka, near Moscow, in July 1977. Later units in this series are finished in the standard green and red livery, suggesting that this example was specially turned out in red and white for exhibition purposes

United Kingdom

BR classes 73/0 and 73/1

Operating system British Rail (BR)
Year introduced (73/0) 1962; (73/1) 1965
Axle arrangement Bo-Bo
Gauge 1435 mm *(4 ft 8½ in)*
Power supply system 660-750 V dc (third rail)
One-hour output (electric operation) 1195 kW
(1600 hp, 1625 ch); (diesel operation) 450 kW
(600 hp, 610 ch)
Continuous output (electric operation) 1060 kW
(1420 hp, 1440 ch); (diesel operation) 320 kW
(430 hp, 440 ch)
Maximum speed (73/0) 130 km/h *(80 mph);* (73/1)
145 km/h *(90 mph)*
Maximum tractive effort (electric operation)
(73/0) 187 kN *(42 000 lbs),* (73/1) 178 kN
(40 000 lbs); (diesel operation) (73/0) 152 kN
(34 100 lbs), (73/1) 161 kN *(36 000 lbs)*
Continuous tractive effort (electric operation)
(73/0) 43 kN *(9600 lbs)* at 89.3 km/h *(55½ mph),*
(73/1) 35 kN *(7800 lbs)* at 109.4 km/h *(68 mph);*
(diesel operation) (73/0) 72 kN *(16 100 lbs)* at
16 km/h *(10 mph),* (73/1) 60.5 kN *(13 600 lbs)* at
18.5 km/h *(11½ mph)*
Weight in working order 77 tonnes *(76 tons)*
Length over buffers (buffers extended)
16 360 mm *(53 ft 8 in)*
Bogie wheelbase 2667 mm *(8 ft 9 in)*
Wheel diameter 1016 mm *(3 ft 4 in)*
Diesel engine English Electric type 4 SRKT
4-cylinder 4-stroke of 450 kW *(600 hp)* at 850 rpm
Main generator English Electric type EE 824/3D
(73/0) or EE 824/51D (73/1)
Traction motors Four dc series-wound English
Electric type EE 542A (73/0) or EE 546/1B (73/1),
nose-suspended, axle-hung
Control Rheostatic
Electric brake None
Builder
 mechanical parts (73/0) BR Eastleigh Works;
 (73/1) Vulcan Foundry
 Electric equipment English Electric
Number built (73/0) 6; (73/1) 43
Number series 73001—73005; 73101—73142
(two units withdrawn following accident damage)

Although widely used for underground, suburban and rapid transit systems, dc third-rail current collection systems in main line applications are relatively rare. BR's Southern Region (SR) network is a notable exception, with some 1600 route-km (1000 miles) electrified at 660 V or 750 V dc, and while emus handle most passenger traffic, SR also operates the unusual class 73/0 and 73/1 electro-diesels. These are primarily medium powered electric units provided with a 450 kW (600 hp) diesel-generator set to permit access to unelectrified yards and sidings, and to "bridge" gaps in the third rail, for example during track maintenance.

Construction of the first six units which now form class 73/0 was carried out at BR's Eastleigh works in 1962. These were originally numbered E6001-6. The numerically larger 73/1 series, formerly nos E6007-49, was built by English Electric at Vulcan Foundry between 1965 and early 1967. Gear ratio and traction motors of these units differ from those of the first six (see data), and there are other detail modifications.

Switching of motor connections takes place in both diesel and electric operation. Motor groupings are series-parallel and parallel, each with four stages of field weakening. The design of the control equipment provides for operation in multiple or in push-pull configuration with other SR diesel-electric locomotives and emu stock. Change over from electric to diesel power or vice versa can be made without stopping the locomotive and can be effected remotely. Buffers are retractable for push-pull working and the body dimensions comply with Hastings-line loading gauge requirements. Centre-couplers compatible with SR emu stock are fitted as well as conventional drawgear.

Although occasionally found in passenger service, the 73s are mainly used for freight and parcels traffic, and from time to time stray far beyond the SR electrified system on their limited diesel power.

BR class 73/0 no 73005 at BREL's Eastleigh works in July 1979 *(Ken Harris)*

United Kingdom

BR class 76

Operating system British Rail (BR)
Year Introduced 1941
Axle arrangement Bo+Bo
Gauge 1435 mm *(4 ft 8½ in)*
Power supply system 1.5 kV dc
One-hour output 1395 kW *(1868 hp, 1895 ch)*
Continuous output 1015 kW *(1360 hp, 1380 ch)*
Maximum speed 105 km/h *(65 mph)*
Maximum tractive effort 200 kN *(45 000 lbs)*
Continuous tractive effort 39 kN *(8800 lbs)* at
  90 km/h *(56 mph)*
Weight in working order 88-89 tonnes
  (87-88 tons)
Length over buffers 15 395 mm *(50 ft 6 in)*
Bogie wheelbase 3505 mm *(11 ft 6 in)*
Wheel diameter 1270 mm *(4 ft 2 in)*
Traction motors Four dc series-wound Metropolitan-
  Vickers type 186, nose-suspended, axle-hung
Control Rheostatic
Electric brake Regenerative and rheostatic
Builder
  mechanical parts BR Gorton Works
  electrical equipment Metropolitan-Vickers
Number built 58
Number series 76001 — 76054 (with gaps)

BR's class 76 1·5 kV dc locomotives were constructed for mixed-traffic operation on the Woodhead route from Manchester to Sheffield and Wath. Electrification of this line, which traditionally carried heavy mineral traffic, started before the Second World War under the auspices of the London and North Eastern Railway (LNER) but work was abandoned in 1940. Original Woodhead route traction plans provided for 88 machines of this design but this was reduced in 1949 to 58. Partial electric operations eventually began in February 1952.

A prototype locomotive, bearing the number 6701, was completed at the LNER Doncaster workshops in 1941. After trials, this machine was stored until September 1947, when it was loaned to Netherlands Railways (NS) bearing a new LNER number, 6000. The first electric locomotive to operate on NS, no 6000 ran some 500 000 km (310 000 miles) before returning to England in 1952, to become BR no 26000 (later E26000). The nickname "Tommy" affectionately bestowed on the locomotive by Dutch railwaymen was recognised officially by BR, and appropriate nameplates were worn until no E26000 was withdrawn in 1970.

The 76s are of the articulated-bogie type, with nose-suspended traction motors. These may be grouped in series or series-parallel with four weak-field steps in each. Regenerative braking was fitted from new, and rheostatic brakes were added later for use at lower speeds. Subsequent traffic changes over the Woodhead route, including the diversion of passenger services to other routes, led to the removal of train heating facilities from those units so fitted and the provision on some examples of multiple-unit control and train air brake equipment.

BR number series was originally 26000-26057 with the class designation EM1. An "E" prefix was added in the late 1960s, and for a short period the last twelve bore the names of Greek mythological characters.

By September 1980, 30 remained in stock, and BR's proposal to close the Woodhead route in 1981 had sealed the fate of these survivors. One example, restored to its original black livery and numbered 26020, is preserved at the National Railway Museum at York.

Readers are also referred to the Netherlands Railways (NS) class 1500 (see p 89), which provided express power on the Woodhead route until 1968.

BR class 76 nos 76007 and 76006 at Rotherwood in September 1978
(Ken Harris)

United Kingdom

BR class 81

Operating system British Rail (BR)
Year introduced 1959
Axle arrangement Bo-Bo
Gauge 1435 mm *(4 ft 8½ in)*
Power supply system 25 kV ac 50 Hz
Continuous output 2390 kW *(3200 hp, 3245 ch)*
Maximum speed 160 km/h *(100 mph)*
Maximum tractive effort 223 kN *(50 000 lbs)*
Continuous tractive effort 76 kN *(17 000 lbs)* at 114 km/h *(71 mph)*
Weight in working order 79.5 tonnes *(78¼ tons)*
Length over buffers 17 720 mm *(56 ft 6 in)*
Bogie wheelbase 3277 mm *(10 ft 9 in)*
Wheel diameter 1219 mm *(4 ft 0 in)*
Traction motors Four dc series-wound AEI type 189, fully suspended with Alsthom flexible drive
Control l.t. tap-changer
Electric brake None
Builder
  mechanical parts Birmingham Railway Carriage and Wagon Co.
  electrical equipment AEI (BTH)
Number built 25
Number series 81001 — 81022 (see text)

Class 81 was the first BR series-built ac locomotive to enter service and was one of five generally similar mixed-traffic designs developed by British manufacturers for the early stages of the West Coast main line electrification. Originally designated AL1, 25 units were constructed between 1959 and 1964, including two (nos E3096/7—later nos 81021/2) originally intended to have received low gear ratios for freight work. Service experience with early deliveries proved this modification unnecessary and the locomotives were supplied as standard.

Bogie design reflects French influence, especially on the adoption of Alsthom quill drive and the use of Alsthom-type pivots for body suspension. Low tension control is employed and originally the 81s were equipped with mercury arc rectifiers. Developments in semi-conductor technology resulted in the substitution of silicon rectifiers from 1970. At the same time, vacuum brakes were supplemented by train air braking, necessitating the removal of one of the two Stone-Faively pantographs to create space for roof-mounted air reservoirs. Although all five early BR ac classes were designed to the same general specification, the 40 class 85 units are especially similar to class 81, sharing many common electrical and mechanical features. The 85s differ mainly in being equipped from new with semi-conductor rectifiers and in the provision of rheostatic braking.

Twenty-two 81s remained in service in June 1980, mainly employed on freight and secondary duties throughout the West Coast electrified network.

81009 at London's Euston station in August 1978 *(Ken Harris)*

BR classes 86/0, 86/1, 86/2 and 86/3

Operating system British Rail (BR)
Year introduced 1965
Axle arrangement Bo-Bo
Gauge 1435 mm *(4 ft 8½ in)*
Power supply system 25 kV ac 50 Hz
Continuous output (86/0 & 86/3) 2685 kW *(3600 hp, 3650 ch)*; (86/1) 3730 kW *(5000 hp, 5070 ch)*; (86/2) 3015 kW *(4040 hp, 4100 ch)*
Maximum speed 160 km/h *(100 mph)* (see text)
Maximum tractive effort (86/0, 86/1 & 86/3) 258 kN *(58 000 lbs)*; (86/2) 207 kN *(46 500 lbs)*
Continuous tractive effort (86/0 & 86/3) 89 kN *(20 000 lbs)* at 108 km/h *(67 mph)*; (86/1) 95 kN *(21 300 lbs)* at 108 km/h *(67 mph)*; (86/2) 85.5 kN *(19 200 lbs)* at 125 km/h *(77½ mph)*
Weight in working order (86/0) 84 tonnes *(83 tons)*; (86/1) 87 tonnes *(86 tons)*; (86/2) 86 tonnes *(85 tons)*
Length over buffers 17 830 mm *(58 ft 6 in)*
Bogie wheelbase 3277 mm *(10 ft 9 in)*
Wheel diameter (86/0) 1143 mm *(3 ft 9 in)*; (86/1) 1150 mm *(3 ft 9¼ in)*; (86/2 & 86/3) 1155 mm *(3 ft 9½ in)*
Traction motors Four dc series-wound AEI type 282 AZ (86/0 & 86/3) or 282 BZ (86/2), nose-suspended, axle-hung. Class 86/1 has GEC type G412 AZ motors, fully suspended with hollow-shaft drive
Control h.t. tap-changer
Electric brake Rheostatic
Builder
  mechanical parts BR Doncaster Works (40 units); Vulcan Foundry (60 units)
  electrical equipment English Electric, AEI
Number built 100 (3 later modified to form class 86/1 and 58 to form class 86/2)
Number series 86001 — 86039, 86101 — 86103, 86204 — 86261. Ten units of class 86/0 are being re-classified 86/3 and renumbered 86321 — 86329

BR's second series of 100 electric locomotives for 25 kV ac operation was placed in service in 1965/6 to coincide with full electrification of the London to Birmingham, Liverpool and Manchester routes. Formerly designated AL6, the class was originally numbered E3101-E3200.

The design differs in several respects from the earlier classes AL1-AL5 (81-85), particularly in the adoption of rheostatic braking as the main locomotive service brake, the provision from new of silicon rectifiers and the use of nose-suspended traction motors. This form of transmission proved unsatisfactory in regular 160 km/h operation and necessitated subsequent modifications to many of the class to create a sufficiently large fleet of express locomotives for the full West Coast electrification to Glasgow.

The class falls into three sub-series:

- class 86/0 comprises 39 units retaining original suspension and bogies with less powerful AE1 type 282AZ traction motors. Multiple-unit control equipment has been progressively fitted to permit double-heading of heavy freight traffic in northern England and Scotland. In April 1980, BR revealed plans to equip ten class 86/0 units with SAB resilient wheels to reduce adverse effects on permanent way. The modified locomotives are designated 86/3 and it was expected that other machines in this series would be treated similarly. At the same time BR imposed a 130 km/h (80 mph) speed restriction on the 86/0 series.
- class 86/1 is formed of 3 locomotives modified in 1972 with class 87 prototype bogies, fully suspended traction motors and flexicoil secondary suspension.
- class 86/2 is fitted with SAB resilient wheels and flexicoil secondary suspension. These 58 units share front-line express duties with class 87.

A revival by BR in 1977 of the pleasing tradition of naming express locomotives has resulted in several class 86/1 and 86/2 units being so treated.

Class 86/0 no 86016 heading a northbound train of imported cars near Tring in September 1978 *(Ken Harris)*

Below: The flexicoil secondary suspension springs are clearly visible in this view of class 86/2 no 86261 at Euston in June 1979 (*Ken Harris*)

Above: The three class 86/1 units have spring-borne traction motors. No 86102 is seen arriving at London's Euston station in April 1978 (*Ken Harris*)

BR classes 87 and 87/1

Operating system British Rail (BR)
Year introduced 1973
Axle arrangement Bo-Bo
Gauge 1435 mm *(4 ft 8½ in)*
Power supply system 25 kV ac 50 Hz
Continuous output (87) 3730 kW *(5000 hp, 5070 ch)*; (87/1) 3620 kW *(4850 hp, 4920 ch)*
Maximum speed 160 km/h *(100 mph)*
Maximum tractive effort 258 kN *(58 000 lbs)*
Continuous tractive effort 95 kN *(21 300 lbs)* at 140 km/h *(87 mph)*
Weight in working order (87) 83 tonnes *(82 tons)*; (87/1) 79 tonnes *(78 tons)*
Length over buffers 17 830 mm *(58 ft 6 in)*
Bogie wheelbase 3280 mm *(10 ft 9⅛ in)*
Wheel diameter 1150 mm *(3 ft 9¼ in)*
Traction motors Four dc series-wound GEC type G412AZ (87) or G412BZ (87/1), fully suspended with hollow-shaft drive
Control (87) h.t. tap-changer; (87/1) thyristor
Electric brake Rheostatic
Builder
  mechanical parts BREL Crewe Works
  electrical equipment GEC Traction
Number built 87-35; 87/1-1
Number series 87001 — 87035, 87101

BR's most modern ac locomotives, the class 87 silicon rectifier units, were introduced in 1973 to provide the necessary extra motive power for the extension of the West Coast 25 kV electrification from Crewe to Glasgow. Although principally used for daytime express passenger work, duties of the class also include heavy freightliner traffic which often requires double-heading over steeply graded stretches of line north of Lancaster.

The design is based on that of the earlier class 86, but at 3730 kW, is considerably more powerful. Bogies are similar to those fitted experimentally to the three class 86/1 units (see previous pages), with flexicoil secondary suspension. Traction motors are fully suspended with ASEA designed hollow motor-shaft transmission. The locomotives were fitted from new with multiple-unit control equipment, and are equipped to provide train air braking only.

Principle visible features distinguishing the class 87 from earlier BR ac designs are a two- rather than three-part windscreen and the absence of frontal train identification headcode panels, which although out of use are still evident in various forms on earlier classes.

The last of the series, no 87101, was built in 1975 as a thyristor-controlled prototype with separately-excited traction motors to enable BR to explore this technique in a high powered locomotive. After an extensive and successful test programme, no 87101 was handed over for regular service in January 1977. The entire class has been named following BR's decision in 1977 to re-introduce this practice.

Class 87 nos 87016 *Sir Francis Drake* **and 87033** *Thane of Fife* **at Euston in June 1979** *(Ken Harris)*

Amtrak class AEM7

Operating system National Railroad Passenger Corporation (Amtrak)
Year introduced 1980
Axle arrangement Bo-Bo
Gauge 1435 mm *(4 ft 8½ in)*
Power supply system (three-voltage/dual frequency) 11 kV ac 25 Hz; 12.5 kV ac 60 Hz; 25 kV ac 60 Hz
Continuous output 4250 kW *(5695 hp, 5775 ch)*
Maximum speed 200 km/h *(125 mph)*
Maximum tractive effort 236 kN *(53 000 lbs)*
Weight in working order 91 tonnes *(90 tons)*
Length over coupler centres 15 590 mm *(51 ft 1¾ in)*
Bogie wheelbase 2760 mm *(9 ft 0⅝ in)*
Wheel diameter 1295 mm *(4 ft 3 in)*
Traction motors Four separately-excited ripple-current ASEA type LJH-108-1A, fully suspended with hollow-shaft drive
Control Thyristor
Electric brake Rheostatic
Builder
  mechanical parts General Motors (Electro-Motive Division), ASEA, Budd
  electrical equipment General Motors (Electro-Motive Division), ASEA
Number built 47 (including units on order in January 1981)
Number series 900-946

Amtrak class AEM7 no 900 with a test train at Wilmington, Delaware on 26 January 1980. The train includes EMD's dynamometer car coupled behind the locomotive
(William D Middleton)

Amtrak's successor to the celebrated GG1 (see p 150) for express work over former Pennsylvania and New Haven routes is the Swedish designed thyristor-controlled AEM7, the first of which appeared in January 1980. Development of the design followed extensive evaluation in Northeast Corridor service in 1976-7 with Swedish State Railways (SJ) class Rc4 no 1166 (see p 114). Modified by ASEA for 11 kV ac 25 Hz operation and numbered X995, this locomotive had been loaned to Amtrak for comparative trials with French National Railways' (SNCF) single-motor bogie unit no CC-21003 (Amtrak X996). This machine proved too sensitive to US permanent way conditions, but no X995 acquitted itself well during a test period which included a particularly severe winter.

Although based on the Rc4, design of the AEM7 differs in several respects. At 4250 kW (5695 hp), it is 25% more powerful, mainly to provide a 200 km/h (125 mph) capability. In readiness for the conversion of existing 11 kV ac 25 Hz facilities to 25 kV ac 60 Hz, the AEM7 is a dual-frequency machine equipped to operate on both systems as well as at 12·5 kV ac 60 Hz between New Haven and New Rochelle where design of local emu stock precludes the use of the higher 25 kV voltage. ASEA Pressductor wheel-slip control equipment is fitted, and rheostatic braking is blended with locomotive friction braking, which like the Rc4 is of the disc type. Power for train services such as carriage heating and air conditioning is provided by a static convertor with a rated output of 500 kW. Body design incorporates structural strengthening to meet special Amtrak requirements.

The initial order for eight units was placed in January 1978 with the Electro-Motive Division of General Motors, acting as ASEA licensee. By January 1980, 47 were on order with the possibility of this figure being increased further to 67. As this book went to press, introduction of the class was expected to lead to early withdrawal of Amtrak's remaining GG1 locomotives.

USA

Amtrak class E60CP

Operating system National Railroad Passenger Corporation (Amtrak)
Year introduced 1974
Axle arrangement Co-Co
Gauge 1435 mm *(4 ft 8½ in)*
Power supply system (three-voltage/dual-frequency) 11 kV ac 25 Hz; 12.5 kV ac 60 Hz; 25 kV ac 60 Hz
Short-time output 7310 kW *(9800 hp, 9940 ch)*
Continuous output 3805 kW *(5100 hp, 5170 ch)*
Maximum speed 195 km/h *(120 mph)* (see text)
Maximum tractive effort 334 kN *(75 000 lbs)*
Continuous tractive effort 151 kN *(34 000 lbs)*
Weight in working order
  (950-955) 176 tonnes *(173 tons)*;
  (956-975) 166 tonnes *(163½ tons)*
Length over coupler centres 21 720 mm *(71 ft 3 in)*
Bogie wheelbase 2070+2070=4140 mm *(13 ft 7 in)*
Wheel diameter 1016 mm *(3 ft 4 in)*
Traction motors Six ripple-current General Electric type 780B1, nose-suspended, axle-hung
Control Thyristor
Electric brake Rheostatic
Builder
 mechanical parts General Electric
 electrical equipment General Electric
Number built 26
Number series 950-975

The thyristor-controlled E60CP units were ordered as two batches (of 15 and 11) in 1973 by the newly formed Amtrak to replace the 40 year-old GG1s (see following entry) as principal express power on its Northeast Corridor (NEC). Constructed at GE's Erie plant, they were the first main line passenger electrics built domestically for a US railroad since the New Haven EP-5s of 1955. With an axle-load of nearly 28 tonnes for a continuous output of 3805 kW, they illustrate clearly the gulf that existed between European locomotive practice and that in North America, where manufacturers have concentrated on the production of heavy-duty diesel-electrics for freight haulage.

GE's design for Amtrak shares many features common to the 50 kV industrial E60C units supplied to the Black Mesa & Lake Powell line in 1972 (see p 151), and can operate at the standard 11 kV 25 Hz of the former Pennsylvania and New Haven networks as well as at industrial frequency (60 Hz). This foreshadows eventual adoption of the latter system on the NEC. Twenty units (nos 956-975) have a 750 kW (1005 hp) motor-alternator set to provide power for train auxiliaries; the remaining six have steam generators, although this equipment will be replaced when Amtrak retires steam-heated stock. Livery is standard "platinum mist", red and blue with black bogies and undergear.

Despite a manufacturer's design speed of 195 km/h (121 mph), tracking problems led Amtrak to restrict the class to 137 km/h (85 mph) and to retain the GG1s until suitable replacement power could be found. Eventually this took the form of the Swedish designed AEM7 featured in the preceding entry.

Amtrak class E60CP no 975 *(General Electric)*

Amtrak/NJT class GG1

Operating system National Railroad Passenger Corporation (Amtrak); New Jersey Transit (NJT)
Year introduced 1934
Axle arrangement 2-Co+Co-2
Gauge 1435 mm *(4 ft 8½ in)*
Power supply system 11 kV ac 25 Hz
One-hour output 3680 kW *(4930 hp, 5000 ch)*
Continuous output 3450 kW *(4620 hp, 4685 ch)*
Maximum speed 160 km/h *(100 mph)*
Maximum tractive effort 292 kN *(65 500 lbs)*
Weight in working order 216.5 tonnes *(213 tons)*
Length over coupler centres 24 230 mm
(79 ft 6 in)
Bogie wheelbase driving—2083+2083=4166 mm
(13 ft 8 in); carrying—2440 mm *(8 ft 0 in)*
Wheel diameter driving—1448 mm *(4 ft 9 in)*
Traction motors Six General Electric or Westinghouse double-armature single-phase commutator, fully suspended with quill drive
Control l.t. tap-changer
Electric brake None
Builder
  mechanical parts Pennsylvania Railroad (Altoona Works)
  electrical equipment General Electric, Westinghouse
Number built 139 (of which 44 remained in stock at 1 January 1980)
Number series (Amtrak units) 4890, 4895, 4896, 901, 902, 904-906, 908-917, 919-921, 924-928, 4930, 4932, 4934, 4935, 4939; (NJT units) 4872-4884

Amtrak class GG1 no 4932, photographed at Capital Beltway, Maryland, in April 1972 when still lettered for the Penn Central administration and bearing its original number 4909 *(Frank Stenvall)*

By January 1980, only 44 examples of America's most celebrated electric locomotive series, the outstanding GG1, remained in traffic. Thirty-one of these remained in Amtrak service pending deliveries of the EMD built thyristor-controlled AEM7, and 13 were retained by the New Jersey Department of Transportation for its North Jersey Coast services; the last ConRail units were retired in November 1979. Development of the GG1 followed the great Pennsylvania Railroad (PRR) 11 kV ac 25 Hz electrification schemes of the 1920s and 1930s, which included the 360 km (224 mile) New York—Washington main line. The 2-Co-2 P5a series introduced in 1932 for express work on this route had not proved entirely satisfactory, mainly due to the poor riding of the rigid driving wheelbase, and this led PRR to conduct high speed trials with borrowed New York, New Haven/Hartford Railroad class EP3a no 0354. Performance of this locomotive, which incorporated an articulated 2-Co+Co-2 axle arrangement, resulted in PRR orders for two prototypes delivered in 1934 for comparative service evaluation. Class R1 no 4800 was a 2-Do-2 design—basically a "stretched" P5a—while GG1 no 4899 (later renumbered 4800) retained the articulated configuration of the New Haven locomotive. The GG1 proved superior, entering series production in 1935. By June 1943, 139 examples had been built and the class rapidly established a record of high performance and reliability, both in difficult wartime conditions and afterwards when diminishing passenger traffic saw many of the class regeared to 145 km/h (90 mph) for freight work.

Synonymous with the GG1 is the name of Raymond Loewy, pioneer commercial and industrial designer whose wide ranging creations include the *Lucky Strike* cigarette packet! Although the basic bodyform of the GG1 was derived from later P5a units, Loewy's adoption of welded body construction and attention to styling detail transformed the rivetted clumsiness of the prototype into a classic streamlined locomotive design.

Ownership of the class passed from PRR to the newly formed Penn Central in February 1968, although by this time withdrawals had already begun. On 1 May 1971 Amtrak was formed and initially took over 30 units. Ten more units subsequently joined the Amtrak fleet including no 4935 which in 1977 was restored to original PRR Brunswick green livery by enthusiast subscription. Apart from the 13 units operated by NJT, 52 survived to be absorbed by ConRail on 1 April 1976, including prototype no 4800, now preserved. Withdrawals of Amtrak units continued during 1980.

USA

BM&LP type E60C

Operating system Black Mesa & Lake Powell Railroad (BM & LP)
Year introduced 1973
Axle arrangement Co-Co
Gauge 1435 mm *(4 ft 8½ in)*
Power supply system 50 kV ac 60 Hz
One-hour output 4180 kW *(5600 hp, 5680 ch)*
Continuous output 3805 kW *(5100 hp, 5170 ch)*
Maximum speed 116 km/h *(72 mph)*
Maximum tractive effort 561 kN *(125 000 lbs)*
Continuous tractive effort 346 kN *(77 000 lbs)* at 40 km/h *(25 mph)*
Weight in working order 193 tonnes *(190 tons)*
Length over coupler centres 19 255 m *(63 ft 2 in)*
Bogie wheelbase 2070 + 2070 = 4140 mm *(13 ft 7 in)*
Wheel diameter 1070 mm *(3 ft 6⅛ in)*
Traction motors Six ripple-current GE type GE780, nose-suspended, axle-hung
Control Thyristor
Electric brake Rheostatic
Builder
  mechanical parts General Electric
  electrical equipment General Electric
Number built 6
Number series 6000 — 6005

BM&LP class E60C no 6000 *(General Electric)*

Opened in 1973, the Black Mesa & Lake Powell Railroad (BM&LP) in northern Arizona was the world's first to employ a 50 kV power supply system in service conditions. The 124 km (77 mile) line, which is isolated from the rest of the US railway network, was purpose-built for coal haulage from open-cast coal workings at Black Mesa to the 2310 mW Navajo generating station near the Utah border. Adoption of a 50 kV line voltage has enabled the entire route to be fed by one substation located at Navajo.

Operations on the line are handled by six General Electric E60C thyristor-controlled locomotives. Delivered as two batches of three units in 1973 and 1976, these were the first series-built machines for a 50 kV line tension, and in normal operations three coupled in multiple handle bulk trainloads grossing 9200 tonnes (9040 tons). Average speed of loaded trains is 56 km/h (35 mph), and the availability of six locomotives permits six return movements daily.

The E60C is a development of the two driverless E50 units constructed in 1962 by GE for the Muskingum Electric Railroad, and incorporates low maintenance thyristor control of tractive effort, electric braking and wheel-slip. Current collection is by a single-arm pantograph. Protection is provided by a vacuum circuit-breaker, and the locomotives are designed to accommodate a voltage drop to 25 kV. The full-width body has a single cab and is built to withstand a buffing force of 450 tonnes (443 tons). Service weight is 193 tonnes (190 tons), which includes 45 tonnes (44 tons) of ballast, BM&LP train movements are controlled automatically but the leading locomotive is occupied, and the three later units include the refinements of air conditioned cabs and tinted windows.

The Amtrak series E60CP express locomotives (see p 149) also incorporate many features of the BM&LP design.

ConRail classes E44 and E44a

Operating system Consolidated Rail Corporation (ConRail)
Year introduced 1960
Axle arrangement Co-Co
Gauge 1435 mm *(4 ft 8½ in)*
Power supply system 11 kV ac 25 Hz
Continuous output (E44) 3285 kW *(4400 hp, (4460 ch)*; (E44A) *3730 kN (5000 hp, 5070 ch)*
Maximum speed (E44) 113 km/h *(70 mph)*; (E44A) 153 km/h *(95 mph)*
Maximum tractive effort (E44) 428 k N*(96 150 lbs)*; (E44A) 419 kN *(94 000 lbs)*
Weight in working order (E44) 175 tonnes *(172 tons)*; (E44A) 171 tonnes *(168 tons)*
Length over coupler centres 21 185 mm *(69 ft 6 in)*
Bogie wheelbase 1753+2210=3963 mm *(13 ft 0 in)*
Wheel diameter 1016 mm *(3 ft 4 in)*
Traction motors Six dc series-wound GE type 752E5 (E44) or 752-N2 (E44A), nose-suspended, axle-hung
Control l.t. tap-changer
Electric brake Rheostatic
Builder
  mechanical parts General Electric
  electrical equipment General Electric
Number built 66
Number series (E44) 4400—4437. 4439, 4460—65; (E44A) 4438, 4440—4459

The highly successful E44 freight units were ordered in 1959 by the Pennsylvania Railroad after independent analysis had reaffirmed the value of the company's 25 Hz electrification. Intended as replacement power for the 2-Co-2 P5a series of 1932-35, the design followed closely that of a series of 12 2460 kW (3300 hp) E33 rectifier locomotives supplied by General Electric in 1956-7 to the Virginian Railway.* North American diesel-electric practice is reflected in the "hood" type single-cab body, and the GE nose-suspended traction motors are of standard type widely used in diesel-electric applications. Most E44s were delivered with water cooled ignitron rectifiers, but the successful performance of silicon rectifiers fitted to no 4436 resulted in this equipment being incorporated in nos 4461-4465 from new, and the rest of the class was subsequently converted. From 1964, 22 units were uprated to 3730 kW (5000 hp) and re-geared (see data) to form the E44a sub-series. No 4439 of this batch has since been reinstated in the main class.

The E44s have run under three owners in their comparatively short career, reflecting the changing fortunes of US railroading. Placed in service by the Pennsylvania Railroad, the class was taken into Penn Central stock on 1 February 1968 when Pennsylvania and New York Central companies merged. On 1 April 1976, Penn Central and other bankrupt lines in the Northeast and Midwest combined under Congressional mandate to form ConRail, under whose control the locomotives now operate.

*Ten of these survive as ConRail class E33

ConRail class E44 no 4401 and E44a no 4454 *(Fred Lonnes)*

Yugoslavia

JŽ class 362

Operating system Yugoslav Railways (JŽ)
Year introduced 1960
Axle arrangement Bo-Bo-Bo
Gauge 1435 mm *(4 ft 8½ in)*
Power supply system 3 kV dc
One-hour output 3385 kW *(4535 hp, 4600 ch)*
Continuous output 2905 kW *(3895 hp, 3950 ch)*
Maximum speed 120 km/h *(75 mph)*
Maximum tractive effort 324 kN *(72 800 lbs)*
Continuous tractive effort 259 kN *(58 200 lbs)* at 45 km/h *(28 mph)*
Weight in working order 110 tonnes *(108½ tons)*
Length over buffers 18 400 mm *(60 ft 4½ in)*
Bogie wheelbase 3200 mm *(10 ft 6 in)*
Wheel diameter 1250 mm *(4 ft 1¼ in)*
Traction motors Six dc series-wound, nose-suspended, axle-hung
Control Rheostatic
Electric brake Rheostatic
Builder
  mechanical parts Ansaldo, OMFP
  electrical equipment Ansaldo, ASGEN
Number built (class 362-0) 40; (class 362-1) 10
Number series 362-001 — 362-040; 362-101 — 362-110

Territorial gains by Yugoslavia from Italy after the Second World War included 114 route-km (71 miles) of railway in the north-west of the country electrified by FS at 3 kV dc. These lines were subsequently operated by JŽ with 17 ex-FS E626-type locomotives. An expansion of this electrification took place from 1953, eventually to include the difficult Rijeka-Karlovac line with 35 km (22 miles) at a ruling gradient of 2·5% (1 in 40). Motive power for this section again came from Italy in the form of the impressive class 362 Bo-Bo-Bo units supplied from 1960 to 1968 by Ansaldo and, later, ASGEN. These locomotives, which are permitted a trailing load of 570 tonnes (560 tons) over the Rijeka-Karlovac line, are based on the Italian State Railways (FS) class E646, with a two-section body carried on three two-axle bogies. Unlike the FS design, traction motors are nose-suspended and are single-armature machines. Rheostatic braking continuously rated at 1400 kW is provided, and the control equipment is designed to avoid weight transfer during starting by keeping the motor of the forward axle of each bogie one resistance step behind the rear when connected in series. Special shunts are provided in series-parallel and parallel connections for the same purpose. A feature of the 362 series is a provision for duplicating the cooling air filters in winter to prevent the ingress of snow.

JŽ class 362 no 362 014

Yugoslavia

JŽ class 441

Operating system Yugoslav Railways (JŽ)
Year introduced 1967
Axle arrangement Bo-Bo
Gauge 1435 mm *(4 ft 8½ in)*
Power supply system 25 kV ac 50 Hz
One-hour output 4080 kW *(5465 hp, 5545 ch)*
Continuous output 3860 kW *(5175 hp, 5245 ch)*
Maximum speed 441-0 — 441-5 — 120 km/h *(75 mph)*; 441-6 — 140 km/h *(87 mph)*
Maximum tractive effort 441-0 — 441-5 — 275 kN *(61 900 lbs)*, 441-6 — 240 kN *(54 000 lbs)*
Continuous tractive effort 441-0 — 441-5 — 132 kN *(29 700 lbs)* at 103 km/h *(64 mph)*, 441-6 — 113 kN *(25 400 lbs)* at 121 km/h *(75 mph)*
Weight in working order 80 or 82* tonnes *(79 or 81* tons)* * with ballast
Length over buffers 15 470 mm *(50 ft 9 in)*
Bogie wheelbase 3100 mm *(10 ft 2 in)*
Wheel diameter 1250 mm *(4 ft 1¼ in)*
Traction motors Four ripple-current series-wound ASEA type LJE108, fully suspended with hollow-shaft drive
Control h.t. tap-changer
Electric brake 441-3 & 441-4 — rheostatic; remainder — none
Builder
  mechanical parts Simmering-Graz-Pauker (for 50 Hz-Traktion-Union); Rade Končar, Djuro Djakovič, Janko Gredelj, MIN, GUR
  electrical equipment 50 Hz-Traktion-Union (ASEA, Elin-Union, Sécheron); Rade Končar, MINEL, Energoinvest
Number built 229 (including locomotives on order 1 January 1980)
Number series See text

Yugoslav Railways' important 25 kV class 441 silicon rectifier locomotives were developed by a consortium led by the Swedish company ASEA, whose Rb1 prototypes for Swedish State Railways (SJ) the design closely follows. Construction of the first 80 units was carried out in Austria by Simmering-Graz-Pauker with electrical equipment supplied by the other three members of the 50 Hz-Traktion-Union group, ASEA, Elin-Union in Austria and the Swiss company Sécheron, who designed the rectifier equipment. Components for an additional 35 locomotives were supplied for assembly by Yugoslav industry under the auspices of Rade Končar of Zagreb, and the first of these was delivered in 1970. The original agreement signed in 1966 between 50 Hz-Traktion-Union and Rade Končar provided for a further 80 to be built under licence for JŽ. To this figure was added four machines geared for 140 km/h running, and in 1978 JŽ ordered 30 more 120 km/h units for delivery from early 1980.

The class is divided into five sub-series:
- class 441-0, which is the basic model.
- class 441-3, fitted with rheostatic brakes and multiple-unit control for service on steeply graded routes.
- class 441-4, which is similar to the 441-3 but with flange lubrication.
- class 441-5, which is as the 441-0, but with flange lubrication.
- class 441-6, geared for 140 km/h running.

Of these, the 441-0 is by far the most numerous with some 140 units in service. Only four 441-6 units have been built.

Since 1973, Rade Končar has also exported the design to Romanian State Railways (CFR) under a reciprocal agreement whereby JŽ imports Romanian built Co-Co locomotives (see p 102). CFR has in service or on order 130 locomotives of this type including eight geared for 160 km/h (100 mph) and 87 with rheostatic brakes, multiple-unit control and flange lubrication. CFR class designations are 43, 44 (mu-fitted, etc) and, probably, 45 for the 160 km/h

Class 441-0 no 441-026 at Zagreb in 1977 *(Günter Haslbeck)*

version. Special modifications to suit Romanian conditions include provision of right-hand drive.

In 1976/7, Rade Končar supplied 5 locomotives of this design to the *Nikola Tesla* generating station at Obrenovac for coal haulage on a 33 km (20½ mile) industrial line. Geared for a top speed of 120 km/h, they are to be joined by three more units in 1981.

The 441-4 sub-series is equipped with rheostatic braking, flange lubrication and multiple-unit control facilities. No 441-401 is seen new at the Graz works of SGP *(SGP)*

Yugoslav industry has supplied to Romanian State Railways (CFR) locomotives of similar design to the JŽ 441 series. CFR class 44 no 44-0035 was photographed at Bucharest Nord *(David Turnock)*

Zaïre

SNCZ class 2300

Operating system Zaïre National Railways (SNCZ)
Year introduced 1958
Axle arrangement Bo-Bo
Gauge 1067 mm *(3 ft 6 in)*
Power supply system 25 kV ac 50 Hz
Continuous output 1505 kW *(2015 hp, 2045 ch)*
Maximum speed 65 km/h *(40 mph)*
Maximum tractive effort 216 kN *(48 500 lbs)*
Continuous tractive effort 165 kN *(37 000 lbs)* at 30 km/h *(19 mph)*
Weight in working order 74 tonnes *(73 tons)*
Length over coupler centres 16 260 mm *(53 ft 4⅛ in)*
Bogie wheelbase 3000 mm *(9 ft 10⅛ in)*
Wheel diameter 1100 mm *(3 ft 7¼ in)*
Traction motors four ACEC dc series-wound, nose-suspended, axle-hung
Control h.t. tap-changer
Electric brake Rheostatic
Builder
 mechanical parts La Brugeoise et Nivelles
 electrical equipment ACEC
Number built 11
Number series 2301 — 2311

The former Kinshasa-Dilolo-Lubumbashi Railways (KDL), which merged with others in 1974 to form Zaïre National Railways (SNCZ), was the first line outside France to adopt the 25 kV ac 50 Hz power supply system when the 105 km (65 mile) Likasi-Tenke section was energised in 1952. Between then and 1970, the catenary was extended to cover the present 858 route-km (533 miles).

The Belgian built 2300 units were the first rectifier locomotives supplied to BCK, and resemble ten class 2200 machines with ac traction motors built by La Brugeoise et Nivelles and ACEC in 1956. Nos 2301-2310 were originally provided with water cooled ignitron rectifiers, but no 2311 was equipped with the silicon-diode type from new. Conversion of the first ten to dry rectifiers took place from 1964. Frequent double-heading is necessary and accordingly the locomotives are equipped for multiple-unit operation. Rheostatic braking is fitted, and locomotive auxiliaries are fed by an Arno single- to three-phase convertor.

A development of the design appeared in 1960 in the shape of the 1620 kW (2170 hp) 2400 series, 11 examples of which had entered service by 1970.

SNCZ class 2300 no 2303. The locomotive is lettered *KDL*, **originally indicative of the Kinshasa-Dilolo-Lubumbashi Railways**
(BN Constructions Ferroviaires et Métalliques)

Zaïre

SNCZ class 2600

Operating system Zaïre National Railways (SNCZ)
Year introduced 1976
Axle arrangement Bo-Bo-Bo
Gauge 1067 mm *(3 ft 6 in)*
Power supply system 25 kV ac 50 Hz
Continuous output 2400 kW *(3215 hp, 3260 ch)*
Maximum speed 75 km/h *(47 mph)*
Maximum tractive effort 282 kN *(63 400 lbs)*
Weight in working order 93 tonnes *(92 tons)*
Length over coupler centres 17 800 mm
    (58 ft 4¾ in)
Bogie wheelbase 2700 mm *(8 ft 10¼ in)*
Wheel diameter 1016 mm *(3 ft 4 in)*
Traction motors Six Hitachi pulsating-current series-
    wound, nose-suspended, axle-hung
Control Thyristor
Electric brake Rheostatic
Builder
  mechanical parts Hitachi
  electrical equipment Hitachi
Number built 10
Number series 2601 — 2610

The Hitachi built thyristor-controlled class 2600 units are the newest and most powerful electric locomotives in the SNCZ fleet. Their introduction followed the successful performance in service of 15 Bo-Bo silicon rectifier machines (SNCZ class 2500) also supplied by Hitachi between 1969 and 1972, and led to the retirement of the class 2100 ac motor locomotives which pioneered single-phase operation in Zaïre in 1952.

Features of the design reflect contemporary Japanese domestic practice, notably the adoption of a Bo-Bo-Bo axle configuration incorporating side-play in the centre bogie to provide a wheelbase of sufficient flexibility for SNCZ conditions.

Bogies are similar to those of class 2500 with secondary suspension of the flexicoil type. Traction motors are 900 V machines and their design is common to both classes, offering maintenance and training benefits. With six powered axles, installed power shows a 50% increase over the 1600 kW (2145 hp) of the 2500 series, permitting a significant reduction in double-heading.

Livery is the SNCZ standard of cream and grey separated by a narrow red band. Bogies and underframe are black.

SNCZ class 2600 no 2601 *(Hitachi)*

A well patronised Korean National Railroad passenger train, headed by a thyristor controlled WAG 1 Bo-Bo-Bo locomotive supplied by the 50 Hz Group *(William D Middleton)*

Index of Classes

Main entry references are listed in roman type, while other classes referred to in the text or illustrated as variants and derivatives of main entries are shown in italic.

Index of Classes